History of a Drowning Boy

HISTORY OF A DROWNING BOY

DENNIS NILSEN
THE AUTOBIOGRAPHY

FOREWORD BY DR MARK PETTIGREW

Red Door

Published by RedDoor
www.reddoorpress.co.uk

ISBN 978-1-913062-53-8

A CIP catalogue record for this book is available from the British Library

Cover design: Rawshock Design

Typesetting: Jen Parker, Fuzzy Flamingo
www.fuzzyflamingo.co.uk

Printed and bound in Denmark by Nørhaven

'There are no monsters in this world;
they're just people.
There are strong people and there are weak people.
I think I'm an amalgam of the two.
Judge for yourself.'

Dennis Nilsen

Contents

Foreword

In the UK, there are thought to be at least two serial killers active at any one time; in the USA the figure is estimated to be as high as fifty. Although a relatively rare phenomenon, there is a great deal of public interest in the life and crimes of serial killers. Yet, despite the inordinate amount of interest, the serial killer remains one of the least understood types of criminal; even in the academic world the simple definition of a serial killer has still not been settled.

In a saturated market of true crime novels, a large majority of which are devoted to serial killing, there are very few that include the voice of the actual killer. As such, amongst a literary sea of accounts devoted to the serial killer and his crimes, this book stands out as unique. Of course, any subjective retelling by the killer must be approached with caution; the prevalence of personality disorders, psychopathy, paranoid schizophrenia and other psychiatric and mental disorders can distort the personal account just as an attempt at self-aggrandising can misrepresent the true narrative of the crimes. Yet, the simple facts of a case can be gleaned from police records, trial testimony and crime scene evidence, whereas personal introspection offers much more of an insight into the motivation of the killer. It is such self-scrutiny that helps researchers, historians and clinicians to understand the rationale of the killer, to understand the 'why' behind the killings, the value of which outweighs any possible flaws in the killer's retelling of his crimes.

Perhaps the greatest utility of an account such as this is the insight it gives us into the normal life of a serial killer; how he is able to navigate the world without detection. Despite popular belief, serial killers are conformist most of the time. They work, they socialise, they go about daily life as the rest of us do; but how can they keep such extreme behaviour hidden from view? Harold Shipman was at large for over 20 years, able to kill approximately 250 people while still maintaining the persona of respectable local doctor. Peter Sutcliffe, the Yorkshire Ripper, attacked at least twenty women over five years without arousing the suspicions of his wife or co-workers, while Fred and Rose West murdered at least ten women and girls, including their own children, for more than fifteen years before being discovered. In this book we can learn how Dennis Nilsen murdered at least a dozen young men over five years before a chance inspection by drainage engineers led to the discovery of three dismembered corpses in his London flat. Until then, the police had no idea that a serial killer was at large in the nation's capital. Yet, it is not just a matter of maintaining a public façade, to hide from view murderous inclinations, but how the serial killer is able to maintain the duality of personas: serial killer and law-abiding citizen. For the majority of us, it is difficult to understand how a person can murder somebody in the evening then go to work the following day only to return home to dismember a corpse on the kitchen floor. Within these pages, Dennis Nilsen explains, as he understands his situation, how he is able to commit these murders without such damage to his self-perception as to render himself incapable of maintaining a semblance of normal life. In that regard, the reader may be particularly interested in two specific points: how he describes his relationship with alcohol and how he describes his victims.

Alcohol was a key feature in the life, and in the offending, of Dennis Nilsen, although he was adamant that he was not an alcoholic. Indeed, he vehemently disagreed with any suggestion that his rehabilitation plan in prison should feature any kind of work related to alcohol management. Yet, it was with the aid of music and alcohol – most often Bacardi rum – that he would slip into a fantasy world, frequently playing out in his mind the details of his interactions with dead bodies both in rehearsal and recall. Alcohol also served to embolden him in reality, in approaching men and in the moments before their murder. It was, at once, a coping mechanism and a key component in his crimes; as the reader will learn, it was only with the numbing effect of Bacardi that he could begin the grisly business of his first dismemberment. When we remember that serial killers are largely conformist outside their offending, alcohol was a means by which he was able to loosen himself from the bonds of conventionality and cross the boundary into necrophilic and murderous fantasy and behaviour.

While categorised, rudimentarily, as a necrophile, the descriptions he gives of his interactions with the bodies of the men he murdered reveal that to be a rather simplistic moniker. In fact, these memoirs reveal Dennis Nilsen not as a necrophile but a necrofetishist, someone who is aroused by contact with corpses. More than sexual contact, his words reveal the post-mortem interactions with his victims. They watched television together, bathed together and ate meals together, behaviours that mimicked what he had so much missed out on in his adult life; a fulfilling relationship, albeit on his own terms. It is in that vein that the method of victim disposal should be considered. So often in accounts of serial killers, the more lurid aspects are fixated upon with no purpose other than voyeurism of behaviour which fascinates but repulses in equal measure. Dennis Nilsen himself noted that he would have quite liked to have kept certain parts of his victims not so much as trophies but as mementoes of the relationship he shared with that person. While victims were treated with relative affection and warmth, after death, when they were used as props in a relationship fantasy until being dismembered for disposal, in retrospect, he would try to believe that he had performed an act of charity in their murder, relieving them from the suffering and misery of their lives. More broadly, when quizzed by detectives, he would note, either consciously or subconsciously, what he perceived to be the negative characteristics of his victims: those who had been in social care; those with mental health issues; self-harmed; homeless; prostitutes; those who had been in trouble with the police; drug addicts, in short, whether intentionally or not, he was denying the worth of his victims. Over sixty years ago such internalised thoughts, particularly when verbalised, were labelled as a technique of neutralisation, a part of a group of linguistic means by which an offender is able to maintain a positive self-conception and protect themselves from self-blame, or blame of others, by rationalising their actions and their crimes. Although subtle, it is such commentary, that only he could provide, which gives us an insight into how Dennis Nilsen was able to commit such crimes without arousing suspicion and without breaking under the weight of guilt for having murdered a dozen men.

As the reader will learn from these memoirs, a confluence of factors met to form Dennis Nilsen: the social and legal disapproval of his homosexuality during his early life; the long shadow cast by his grandfather and the sexual abuse he reports to have suffered as a child; the strained relationship he had with his mother; social isolation; the lack of supportive and long-lasting relationships; and alcohol abuse, they all played their part. Yet, these memoirs do not offer a neat answer as to why a boy from a fishing town in North East Scotland, a man who served in the police and in the military, became a serial killer. In all the academic and clinical research on the topic, there is no definitive answer as to why or how a person becomes one. Indeed, it is highly unlikely that any theory can or will account for all or even the majority of serial killers. Realistically, we can only identify risk factors. What this book offers, though, is an insight into how those killings are comprehended and understood by the killer in retrospect. In my own conversations with Dennis Nilsen, over several years, he did not try to excuse what he did, nor trivialise the devastating effect his actions had upon the families and loved ones of his victims. Instead, he sought to understand his actions in light of his particular circumstances. I cannot honestly say that he ever found a definitive answer as to why he became one of Britain's most infamous serial killers, but if the answer is ever to be found it will be found within these pages.

Dr Mark Pettigrew, BA (Hons); MA; PhD; FHEA

> Dr Mark Pettigrew is an award-winning researcher and criminologist. After completing his doctoral research on death row incarceration in the United States, Mark has published extensively on whole life imprisonment in England and Wales and the crimes, specifically aggravated forms of homicide, that give rise to the sentence. His current research interests include sexual paraphilias and adult homicide, homicide dynamics, and crime scene behaviours of sexually motivated killers.

Introduction

Dennis Nilsen's autobiography was written over a span of eighteen years from 1992 until he 'retired' in 2010, aged sixty-five.

Initially, he wrote four parts of autobiographical documents, which he collectively entitled *History of a Drowning Boy*. Later, he added to this and, in doing so, he revisited and rewrote about his life's events and his emotions, opinions, explanations and introspection in much more detail. In reference to those initial four parts, he later wrote, 'The typewritten manuscript was a mess, replete with typing errors, and I did not feel like spending many months crafting a finished, polished product. The time for an autobiography is near the end of one's life and not halfway through it. I decided not to re-examine the subject too seriously until I was over fifty, at least. What I had done, I did during brief periods of being locked in my cell during lunch breaks, etc.'

Eventually, his completed autobiographical documents comprised 6000 typed pages – around 3.5 million words – which he collectively titled, *Epic Nobody*. It is made up of the following:

History of a Drowning Boy	400 pages
Papers from a Prisoner	650 pages
The Human Institution	2000 pages
The Rule of Fantasy: Commentator from Prison	475 pages
Continuation Shots	475 pages
Chronicles	2000 pages

A full breakdown of chapters is shown in the Appendix.

As *History of a Drowning Boy* was the original title for his autobiography, I have retained it as the title for *this* book, which is an abridged version of the most significant excerpts from *Epic Nobody*, woven together in chronological order. Other than occasional spelling errors, grammatical changes and some sentences that have been edited for clarity, every word has been written by Dennis Nilsen. Nothing has been taken out of context, embellished, changed or sensationalised. The style of writing is sometimes inconsistent but the reader is reminded that Mr Nilsen completed this work over eighteen years and, often, on a daily basis (in diary form), so it was likely that his mood – and, therefore, his writing style – would have differed and it has been left that way.

Occasionally, the names of individuals have been changed to acknowledge that they may not have wanted to have been mentioned in Mr Nilsen's memoirs (having never been mentioned in other publications) or they may not have been available to ask their permission. It has been noted in the text where these changes have been made.

The reader is advised that this book contains references to sex, murder, dead bodies and mutilation, though nothing more than that which has been previously written in other publications about Dennis Nilsen. The narratives describing his fantasies and dreams have been redacted due to the highly explicit and often repetitive nature of the original content.

During the final eight years of his life, Mr Nilsen wrote no further autobiographical material and the content shown in this book covering that time has been taken from letters he wrote to me. Here, again, they have been reproduced in his own words.

During his thirty-five years in prison, Mr Nilsen sent and received thousands of letters and, while most of those correspondences were one-offs, many endured for several years. In this book, I have only included those correspondents who played a part in significant events in Mr Nilsen's life and I have omitted to include those who were connected to him purely through friendship (without wishing to trivialise that friendship).

However, I do believe that Mr Nilsen would have liked to have acknowledged his enduring friendship and emotional and material support with a number of individuals and, to this end, I think it is appropriate to mention the following names (listed in alphabetical (first name) order) who have not been mentioned elsewhere in this book:

Adam W, Andrea K, Angela S, Angelique W, Beverley S, Carl H, Christopher C, Daniel B, Gary R, Ian H, James S, Jane B, John R, Johnny O, Joseph D, Karen S, Maria (from Nottingham), Mark P, Matthew H, Nicky G, Norman H, Paul M, Philip H, Raj A, Rhonda B, Sarah P, Sarah (from Bury), Scott S, Steve R, Steve S, Steve T, Steven F, Terence P, Thelma C, Tina M, Tom G.

I first met Dennis Nilsen in 1992 following a year-long correspondence. Curiosity was my initial motive for contact (I had previously lived close to his flat in Melrose Avenue, North London), but we soon became friends. Over the years, he handed out to me all of his writings, notes, documents, poems, received letters, official prison papers and reports, clothing, audio cassettes, artefacts, etc., in fact, all his possessions – as they accumulated – for safe keeping.

In 2009 I was registered as his official next of kin and the following year he bequeathed the copyright of all of his writings, artworks, audio and musical recordings to me. After his death, I was shown around his prison cell, which had been left untouched, and I later took delivery of all its contents which were added to the (already substantial) archive of his belongings. I was the only civilian to attend his funeral, after which I took possession of his cremated ashes.

I have never tried to excuse, justify or explain his crimes, nor have I ever sought to financially benefit from my association with him. It has never been my intention to judge him as a person because, in doing so, I would be judging him based upon *my* life's experiences and morals, and not his. We can all judge his crimes with equal disdain but acts like those never occur without reason. To paraphrase the proverb, we never walked a mile in his shoes.

History of a Drowning Boy is the story of Dennis Nilsen's life told by Dennis Nilsen as *he* saw it. The opinions, observations and comments therein are those of Dennis Nilsen only and the reader is not expected – nor invited – to agree with them. This book is not intended to provide answers or explain his crimes but to simply lay out the facts of his life according to him.

Every publication about Dennis Nilsen has been written by persons who have imparted their own opinion based on their own point of view. But none of these, by definition, can be Dennis Nilsen's point of view. Importantly, therefore, *this* book has *not* been subjected to third-party opinion, comment, interpretation, speculation or analysis and the reader is invited to draw their own, unbiased conclusions. As Mr Nilsen, himself, once said: 'In the final analysis, it may be that a guinea pig is the best explainer of what it is like to be a guinea pig.'

The victims' remaining loved ones hold the only opinions that truly matter. The rest of us are merely detached spectators who don't feel any personal loss. Unlike them, we have never been incoherent with sleep deprivation or incapable of functioning without medication as we wrangled with our nightmares. Nor have we been deranged by dark thoughts of suicide or retribution as a result of their direct experience or the deaths of their loved ones.

Dennis Nilsen happened and his crimes can never unhappen. All we can now do is to try to decipher how they could ever have happened in the first place and to do this, honestly, we must see the view from all angles – *including* his. I am grateful to Dr Mark

INTRODUCTION

Pettigrew for his informative and insightful foreword, which provides expert context to Dennis Nilsen's story. Many may disagree with the decision to make Mr Nilsen's words public but it cannot be denied that this book provides a compelling insight into the mind of a man capable of truly terrible crimes. And if that might help prevent one future victim, then it has to be worth it.

Mark Austin, September 2020

1

Early Life | 1945

Andrew Whyte (my grandfather) married Lily Duthie and they had three children. The first, Andrew Whyte junior (my Uncle Andy), married a girl named Carrie and they conceived two children. He then went off to war as a company sergeant major (CSM) in the Gordon Highlanders who were part of the Highland Division in France in the summer of 1940. At the Fall of France, he, and what remained of the Highland Division, surrendered to the advancing German army at St Valery in Western France where they had been abandoned to their fate. Infantry weapons would be no match for viable combat against Hitler's panzer divisions and CSM Andy Whyte spent the duration as a prisoner of war (POW). Andrew and Lily Whyte's youngest child (also named Lily) was a schoolgirl when war broke out and their middle child was Elizabeth Duthie Whyte, 'Betty' – my mother.

She was a girl in her early twenties and worked at a local factory when, in May 1942, she married a Norwegian soldier, Olav Magnus Moksheim, who adopted the surname 'Nilsen' on escaping from German-occupied Norway. He was a member of the Free Norwegian forces, still loyal to the king and government in exile in England.

The firstborn of this union, Olav Magnus Nilsen junior (my brother), arrived in March 1943 and, while her husband was often away on military duties, mother and baby occupied a room at her father's house at 47 Academy Road, Fraserburgh, Aberdeenshire, in Scotland.

My grandfather, Andrew Whyte, had served on minesweepers during World War I and I've seen his medals and an old photo of him as a handsome young man, in his naval petty officer's uniform, to prove it. Now a fisherman, he was frequently away at sea and, upon his return, he slept on the settee, quickly assembled in the living room. His wife and younger daughter (my Aunty Lily) shared a bed in the other bedroom.

There seemed to be frequent rows between my grandfather and Olav senior when he was home from the army. These were probably associated with Olav's drinking; my grandfather was a fundamentalist Christian who strongly disapproved of alcohol. Circumstances of war and the cultural and psychological incompatibility of Betty and Olav, exacerbated by personal, family hostilities, doomed the match to failure and, by 1945, the marriage was effectively over.

By this time, Olav may have been seeing other women and Betty, other men, during her husband's long absences. They were both attractive enough to be able to seek out and gain extramarital partners and, for Betty, the influx of servicemen almost outnumbered the locals.

I was conceived in February 1945 and born at 4 a.m. on 23 November of that year, by which time my mother was dating other men. As she was still married at the time, Olav Magnus Nilsen's name as the 'father' was put on my birth certificate, though he had doubts about my paternity.

My sister, Sylvia, arrived in 1947 and this event provided Olav with the grounds to finally divorce my mother for her adultery (decree nisi in 1948). This done, he departed for Norway and would go on to marry another three women. When he died in 1973, he had at last worn his heart out on his fourth wife in Ghana, Africa, where he was the manager of a seafood canning factory.

After the divorce, my mother and we three children lived on in one room in our grandparents' house together with my Aunty Lily, who, in the late 1950s, would marry Robert Buchan Ritchie (Uncle Bobby), a design engineer from Sandhaven. They would go on to have three children.

Uncle Andy, having returned from the POW camp, was reunited with his wife, Carrie, and his two children and he continued to work as an engineer at the Consolidated Pneumatic Tool Company in Fraserburgh. His mother's family, as well as my mother, took – to say the least – a dim view of Carrie whom they suspected of 'carrying on' with different men while her husband was a POW. My mother recalled her disgust at Carrie when the news arrived, in 1940, that Andy had been taken prisoner. Apparently, this news was subordinated to Carrie's tears of anguish when she was told that another soldier, Jimmy Crystal, had been killed in action. The tears were thought not to be for her 'lost' husband and it was concluded that she felt more for Jimmy than she did for her own man.

It rained a lot up there in the North East of Scotland and the north wind blew in to accentuate the chill factor. It was cold in the air magnified by the cold, commanding calculation of the people. Hostility and the cold go together. The waters were grey, cold and frozen solid like the timeless rocks. The sky always seemed to be grey, changing only to stage a pattern of wild, storming clouds of battle.

The houses were prim, solid and grim with the black smoke of hell spouting from the red, clay chimney pots standing in neat rows over the grey, slate roofs. The decor of the house interior at 47 Academy Road was drab and colourless. I remember an off-white ceiling with lampshade encircling a single lightbulb and worm-like filament, an open fireplace with blazing coal fire, with metal fireguard and black, enamelled surround, a high mantlepiece, heavily curtained windows, flowered wallpaper, a polished dark wooden table, a dark sideboard with doilies and ornaments, framed, glass-

3

fronted religious texts hanging from the wall and a coloured, metal foil picture representing the Gordon Highlanders regimental badge bearing the motto, *Bydand*. There was a barometer hanging by the door, two armchairs facing each side of the fireplace, a settee against the back wall and the pungent scent of lavender and mothballs.

Inside the dark mystery of granny's bedroom, with the coloured linoleum and the small pieces of carpeting on the floor, there was also the semi-nude, bronze-coloured statue and a Singer sewing machine.

In the kitchen, we had a primitive, iron gas cooker, a wall cupboard, a rough, old kitchen sink and a leather strap on which my grandfather honed his cut-throat razor.

I remember the stairs down to street level with the small gate at the top to prevent toddlers from falling down them, and in the tiny corridor before, there was a row of coat hooks.

I remember the sound of the radio in my mother's room, her porcelain cocker spaniel, Tarzan, on the dresser. The forever-grey vistas viewed from the windows, the interminable ticking of the clock in the background and the frozen promise of a young child's dreams of happiness. This was the studio set of my background; the material bric-a-brac which formed shadows of a dark hue.

In this rough bower, I was cradled and spawned by the triple angels of ignorance, poverty and religious fundamentalism. I cried a lot with spasmodic response, and I was screamed at, probably to be quiet.

For the most part, mine was a female-dominated world; mother, grandmother and aunt. In the late forties, Sylvia was the baby, with granny spending much time looking after her. Olav was the apple of his mother's eye and I was the piggy-in-the-middle.

My grandfather, however, had taken a shine to me. He was all that I could remember of any personalised, tactile contact but this had a traumatic influence on my early development and on my future life. For years, the subject of my grandfather lay simmering, unresolved, in the veil of my subconscious. It remained a great blot, always there, and it took a long time to figure the puzzle out; to sit and think, and to try to link all those early fragments into a clearer picture.

Andrew Whyte had a fantasy life beyond the bold front of his outwardly expressed existence. In all other ways he was a good, moral man but a fantasist whose inner world seized secret libidinous expression when the pressures of his life became stressful and his will helpless to prevail and resolve them. I arrived as that object of his problems and my presence 'tempted' him as the devil tempts all men, who, in his religious mind, were all sinners. He levied and controlled his secret with the mind and body of a small, uncomprehending, male child soiled by bastardy.

I vaguely remember him as a tall, quiet, powerful figure who was forever taking me off, out of the house, to remote locations outside Fraserburgh, when he invariably took with him a vacuum flask of 'tea'. Our regular route was southwards, towards Inverallochy (his own village), along the sand dunes beside the beach of Fraserburgh Bay. We would stop where the Waters of Philorth entered the sea, short of Inverallochy itself, and we'd sit beside a deserted World War II pillbox concrete bunker with its narrow slit windows. It had been built as part of the sea defences against a possible Nazi invasion during the war, which had been over for about four and a half years by this time. In that dark and cramped interior, he would give me a drink of the 'tea' from his flask and I would feel sleepy as he pulled down my short trousers, held my penis and told me to urinate.

What began as simple fondling developed and I was held in the rough embrace of this powerful influence, which ran its strong hands over my naked skin, fondling my buttocks and the small, shrivelled pinkie between my legs. I was in a ritualistic daze of incomprehension as he held my tiny hand in his during these events. He bathed me and sometimes took me to his bed and his finger penetrated me when it pleased him; and all this to the accompaniment of his soothing, reassuring noises of fevered contentment. He was an explosion of contradictions because, in tandem with the sexual abuse and its attending physical pain, there were all the material benefits which a grandfather bestowed on a young boy: ice cream, sweets, toys, etc.

These were my only real, one-to-one contacts with someone who took a beneficial interest in me, and my conscious memory was of his strength and a feeling of comfort and security. His was the earliest embrace I could remember and it seemed correct, necessary and irreversible. He may have been a paedophile but I didn't remember him as threatening or oppressive.

By the time I had started at the infant school, on a couple of occasions, I had no control of my anus and, literally, shat my pants. I padded home feeling sore as the skitter dribbled, embarrassingly, down the leg of my short pants. My grandfather's hoarse whispers echoed in my ears, 'Be still loon [boy]…' I also found it impossible to swallow tablets, something that endured right through to my late army days. I gagged at the very prospect of swallowing them.

As my awareness increased, I was forever silent in the presence of my grandfather when we were around others not party to our secret. I was both dependent on him and fearful of him; his tactility and embrace came at a price: no sweeties for bad boys. He was both ugly and comforting in turn and there was something monstrous in his odour.

Those days were of short duration because in October 1951 he died at sea of a heart attack, aged sixty-two, when I was almost six years old. Then began my first encounter with the fact and mystery of death.

I remember being carried under my mother's arm into the room where he lay coffined and on display for all visitors. He looked asleep with his John Lennon type spectacles and dressed, bizarrely, in white with his bare feet sticking out at the bottom. The rough, weather-beaten skin of his face gave the impression that he needed a shave.

Seeing him laid out in his coffin brought to me a great earthquake of excitement. I had lost the good aspect of him as well as the painful trauma of his abuse. I had wished him gone and he *had* gone and the guilt came from this and my excitement and sense of loss at viewing the mighty fallen, slumbering in that coffin in the room where I had been born. I was not that clear on the full meaning of death and felt that he could have still 'got me' if I revealed our secret. As he lay there in his box that day, I was puzzled that he was ignoring me, as if he'd deserted me, and I hoped he would see me later when he was 'better'.

After this brief viewing, I was whisked back to bed in the other room and, thereafter, he disappeared from my life, leaving behind the stark memory of the uncertain fact of his disappearance. I was told that he was in heaven but I knew not where that was. It soon dawned on me, however, that he was, in fact, locked inside a box and buried six feet under the ground. Also, in saying that grandad had 'gone to a better place', they seemed to be saying that what had happened to him and his fate – entombed underground – was a *good* thing, though it horrified me. The confusion was fixed when he departed this life for ever: if this (death) could happen to him (being so tall and strong) then I feared it, too, could happen to me.

It is a most horrifying admission to make that the only tactile contact I had, in my early formative years, was the painful and confusing, paradoxical embrace of a paedophile. In the family mind, however, he was someone beyond reproach and mass family eulogies showered his memory with glory. The received wisdom was ever-present to quell my doubts and feelings. He lingered in my subconscious like a dark ogre waiting to spring to the fore on psychologically dark nights. Grandad was walking with God while his undead corpse slept in a pine box, six feet under Inverallochy cemetery (I never did see his grave and no one ever took me there). He did, indeed, have an afterlife and he lived it in my head.

The house at 47 Academy Road returned to the shrill bustle of strident, organising women. My grandmother and aunt slept in one of the two bedrooms, and my mother and we three small children in the other. There were now no adult male influences in the family household. As I grew, I would wander away from the house at every opportunity, probably trying to find my grandfather. I felt real loneliness within myself as I had no outlet for proper mourning, nor any real understanding of the situation, and I searched to have my needs gratified in the remembrance of the attentions of my grandfather.

At infant school, I was terribly shy and withdrawn. I felt frightened and intimidated by the preponderance of spidery, shrill 'school ma'am' spinsters who ran and controlled the large classes. Even the school doctor was a woman. I lay, useless and inadequate, under the lash of Miss Grant's strident demands for excellence in quick-fire mental arithmetic questions and I made my mark only in art. Not long after I had arrived there, one of my paintings of a Viking longship had been selected for display at an exhibition in London by the British/Czechoslovakian Friendship League and I received an ornate invitation to attend the exhibition with my parents. None of us, however, was in any kind of situation where we could attend; Strichen was 500 miles from London and I was a million miles from realising my dreams.

As a boy, I became more and more aware of my round shoulders, which gave me much cause for embarrassment and shame. I felt awkward and inadequate in myself. My mother took me to see an orthopaedic specialist in Aberdeen who came to no firm form of therapy other than a vague reference to 'exercises', after which my mother's interest in it vanished.

There was a kind of female passiveness about me and I felt a deep, hidden awkwardness in not wanting what other growing boys seemed to want. I liked the chatty company of girls but my main, emotional focus was on selected other boys. I had always accepted that my half-brother, Olav, was more beautiful than myself and I envied his fair hair and began looking up to him. As we shared a bed, I imagined his body – being in close proximity to mine – as attached to another boy created in my imagination and I was drawn to feel his soft skin, as he slept, half-remembering the intensity of being regularly felt and fondled by my grandfather.

• • •

In 1954, my mother was given a high tenement, two-bedroom council flat in the downtown area of Fraserburgh where she moved with her single-parent brood of three. There followed a spell of relative happiness for me as I mixed and played with the local neighbourhood boys. I was willingly accepted as a viable member of this peer group and the memories of my grandfather seemed to recede and fade.

When we first arrived at 73 Mid Street, Olav and I were enrolled in the Scottish equivalent of the Cubs – called the Life Boys. The uniform was navy-blue short trousers, jersey, socks and sensible shoes, topped with a dark Royal Navy sailor's cap. But all we really did was mess around in the Macaulay Hall doing drill and things pointlessly ritualistic.

There was a line of sheds along the far end of the huge backyard of the estate, used for the mending of fish nets. My grandmother worked in the shed on the extreme right-hand side to supplement her widow's pension. I would regularly visit her as she worked away at speed and with a deft skill, cultivated in the blood through generations of fisherfolk.

Next to the estate was a dairy and the cows were herded and milked by a man named Jackie 'Murdie' Murdock. He was wont to let us kids ride with him in the cab of his lorry and go with him to collect chicken eggs from a large battery nearby. I always had a love of animals and I built a pigeon box on top of a concrete air raid shelter in the backyard of the flats and reared two fledgling pigeons until they returned to the wild. But, in the mid-fifties, I did something which thoroughly ashamed me, then as now. In a deserted and dilapidated toilet, behind the football field across the road from the tennis courts in Fraserburgh, I slipped a wire around a friendly cat's neck. I pulled up the cat by the wire attached to the cistern pipe and watched it struggle under its own weight. After it was dead, I prodded it and turned away, disgusted by my cruel behaviour. I wanted to see the reality and process of killing and death, though I wasn't excited sexually by the act and I have that guilt still with me today in its original, raw intensity.

Coming back from my long jaunts over the dunes and the golf course, I was able to snatch a brief sight of how the other half lived. The middle classes of Fraserburgh confined their outdoor activities to the golf course and the tennis courts. Middle-class children didn't play with us working-class kids and they invariably 'went away' for their summer holidays. The different classes even attended different churches; the poshest being the English Kirk, the Episcopal Church.

My mother, meanwhile, having freed herself from the inquisitive chains of her tied domesticity at 47 Academy Road, took to looking for a mate. Cruising around the local fairground, she met a semi-literate council labourer of even temperament. Adam Scott hailed from the village of New Pitsligo and was a good, simple man without malice, guile or selfish calculation. He was honest and hardworking but had no artistic finesse or charisma and Betty dominated him absolutely. I, however, became more disturbed by this sudden family disequilibrium and the new, male presence, which struck me as being the return of a new Andrew Whyte.

Adam was transfixed and besotted with my mother. Being in her thirties, dull Adam found that she was a good catch, in spite of her baggage of three children, probably sired by three different men. It was easy to see how the passive Adam could have been easily seduced by the domineering Betty. She calculated that he could serve her as a financial anchor to her life and provide a measure of stability and respectability. Together, they made a mutually viable social item – opposite poles attracting – but there would be no confusion concerning who wore the pants in that relationship. I felt both resentful and sorry for this man who had to cycle eight miles to Strichen quarry every day to work in all weathers. I can still see him in his armchair in front of the fire in the evening, asleep, exhausted by yet another hard day's labour.

In September 1954, I moved to Fraserburgh Central School where the boys were segregated from the girls in separate playgrounds. Miss Mackintosh would regale us with stories of Victorian heroism, which kept me spellbound with rapt concentration. She was a woman in her middle years and there was an air of tragedy hanging over her. I remember her telling the story of Captain Scott's fateful expedition to the South Pole; she was in tears by the end of it. As she was unmarried, I fancied that, perhaps, her love had gone the way of so many young men in the Great War of 1914–18.

Quite soon, I became obsessed by a boy I saw in the playground. He excited me from the first moment I laid eyes on him and I can only describe him as beautiful. I never spoke to him nor could I remember his name (if I ever knew it at all) but I watched him from afar in an obsessive state of fixation. I thought about him all the time but was too shy to even catch his eye. I felt warmth towards him; protective, with a need to hug him and I hung in sullen, meek, frightened silence in the shadow of his existence. It was a new feeling of a vibrant and all-consuming, intense love. But we were all made well aware that such feelings were not only wrong but abominable; the sort to get one into hell, fast, and I realised that my feelings – in a hostile climate of absolute social homophobia – must be kept secret. I had nobody to confide with; nobody at all.

• • •

In 1956, my family suddenly upped sticks and moved to 16 Baird Road, in the small country village of Strichen, eight miles south-west of Fraserburgh, where Adam had been granted a council house nearer his work. My mother could shake off some of the shadows of her past at a fresh location as 'Mrs Scott' and, after their registry office wedding, there came a succession of half-siblings: Violet, named after Adam's mother; Andrew, after my grandfather; Gordon, after Gordon Scott (the current actor playing Tarzan) and Maurice, after Adam's stepfather. Adam wanted his own family – of his own blood. At the time, I believed it was imprudent to expand the family brood to seven children on a low labourer's wage but, to his credit, he did a lot of extra work at weekends, labouring on farms. He gave up his Capstan full-strength cigarettes and began to smoke cheaper, hand-rolling tobacco, Golden Virginia, and cut down on his intake. He was not a boozer and we had that to be thankful for.

In Strichen, I missed my friends from Mid Street and I missed Fraserburgh (known, locally, as 'the Broch') and its surrounding land and seascape. Strichen had a slower, almost comatose, pace compared to the bustle of the Broch. Strichen was agricultural and rooted firmly in the land whereas Fraserburgh was commercial and industrial and allied to the sea; eight miles, but a world apart. As kids, we would straggle along through the woods in exploratory treks, passing the time of a summer's day. The trees around the hydro lake were young, dense and concealing. We'd build hides with the foliage and would rummage around the burns and we'd bathe in the River Ugie, which flowed past the village. Fishing was available for those who had the patience and Adam was a regular – if solitary – fisherman with rod and line. He also kept ferrets and a single-barrelled, 12-bore shotgun for shooting rabbits, which he sold to the 'knackery man'. Adam also brought home the occasional trout.

We once spent a weekend in New Pitsligo, getting acquainted with Adam's parents who lived at the near end of the village at 8 Low Street. Maurice Marnoch (Adam's stepfather) kept racing pigeons and worked for British Road Services as a long-distance lorry driver. His wife, Violet, seemed to be always singing along to gramophone records of the musical, *Rose Marie*, but the poor dear had a speech impediment, which made her sound a bit weird. She kept a henhouse in the long backyard and they were never short of eggs.

Soon, family visits to the Marnochs abruptly ceased. It all came about with a great slight against Betty; something (to her mind) so serious that the two families became estranged for all time. Adam's stepsister, Rosy, was to be married and the Scotts got an invitation which stipulated only Adam, Betty and Olav attend. The two bastards born out of wedlock (my sister, Sylvia, and I) were not invited and Betty viewed this as a public affront to her past. The Marnochs remained unbowed and wouldn't relent, resulting in the whole family staying away from the wedding. From time to time, Adam would visit his mother on his own but, as a family, we had no more social dealings with them. Perhaps it was a case of the pot calling the kettle black because Violet had given birth to Adam by a man surnamed Scott; a man she had not been married to.

Olav and I joined the Boys' Brigade at Strichen Kirk but there was a marked lack of enthusiasm for the BBs there and, through lack of recruits, the whole operation soon folded. Thereafter, none of the family attended any kind of church. Betty had lost her faith but had gained a nineteen-inch, black and white, single-channel TV set which, like most things we had, was second-hand and paid for in instalments. I remember one night when the whole family was watching the TV, a sequence of ballet came on. The male dancer wore tights that emphasised the huge bulge of his well-endowed genitalia (which drew my secret, rapt attention). My mother suddenly raised her voice in eruption, 'Take that dirt off, it's just dirt!' She spat out the words like a gin-sodden whore; her voice filled with loathing and disgust. She tried to make it sound as if she thought the piece was boring and uninteresting but it was clear to us that it was the sudden intrusion of obvious and unavoidable male genitalia in her living room which had given rise to her outburst of embarrassment.

Just before we'd moved to Strichen, I had taken my eleven-plus examination at Fraserburgh Central School and failed it. My educational future was, therefore, set at Stricken School and, later, as future factory fodder with few prospects of advancement in the local community. I was set in a class under the sole tutorage of Miss Lee who lived on Whitestripe Farm (hence her nickname, 'Stripey') and attending her class brought me my first great opportunity to travel beyond the confines of Aberdeenshire. We were invited to go to a summer school camp in Meigle in Perthshire. The fee was £2 10s. per child but all that my mother could afford was 10 shillings and, I guessed, Miss Lee had made up the difference from her own pocket.

I made the (for me) long journey and we were housed in double-bunk dormitories in Belmont Camp, an affair of neat wooden structures. The new change of scene and diet made me feel a bit ill and I was troubled by a boil on my neck. We visited the birthplace of J M Barrie, author of *Peter Pan*, who had died twenty years earlier, and we toured a jute mill and places of historic interest in Dundee. The climax to the visits was a trip across the ferry from South Queensferry to Fife and back where I had a good view of the Tay railway bridge and the stone stumps of the old bridge, which had so tragically fallen in a storm, bringing down a train and all its passengers in 1879. In the dorm, a fight broke out between a white boy and an Asian boy who was picked on because he was different. It was my first encounter with racism. The Asian boy was getting the better of the other boy when the masters broke up the fight. In my mind, I declared him the winner. I remembered thinking he couldn't hide his difference, but I could conceal mine.

Back home, the household was noisy and crowded with nine people to three bedrooms. Money was also tight and Olav, Sylvia and I felt obliged to supplement the family income. I had a paper round after which I delivered fresh rolls and milk for the Co-op, where I also worked on Saturday mornings. For the paper round,

I would have to get up at 5 a.m. and trudge up to Strichen railway station on the hill and collect all the string-wrapped bundles of newspapers. I would transport these back to the chemist's shop (it was always the chemist's shop that sold newspapers in those small villages) and sort the individual newspapers into the various rounds. I'd then take my own round and deliver the papers to the house of the subscriber. As my mother had her hands full with four very young children, we older kids would also get on with our chores in the house: hoovering, washing up, etc.

I did all this on a couple of slices of bread and a mug of tea. There was plenty of broth and bread with jam but, for any growing boy, it was an inadequate diet. Potatoes were the central commodity in our food but the absence of vitamin C left us vulnerable to various infections. When school started at 9 a.m., I was relieved to snuggle up near the classroom radiator and I frequently dozed off, feeling tired and run down, unable to give my lessons their full attention. One morning, I was so ill that I couldn't get up out of bed. Dr Harkins was called and I was rushed to Aberdeen City Hospital where I was diagnosed as suffering from double pneumonia and pleurisy, and was contained in isolation in a single room 'at death's door'. I was there for some weeks towards recovery and when I returned to Strichen, I did no more paper rounds or deliveries. I had also fallen behind in my lessons and in the maths curriculum – taught in a brisk fashion by the headmaster, Mr Keith. I had lost the plot entirely. I didn't have a clue what he was talking about.

In the movement into the senior part of the school, I was allocated to C stream, the lowest. Miss Duthie taught music, Miss Ritchie, French, Mr Bruce, geography and Mr Barron taught woodwork and metalwork. Science was taught by Mr Watt, who had the reputation of being a bit of an ogre and terroriser of children, while his sister, Mrs Laurence, acted as the headmaster's secretary. Art was my métier, though in this class, there was a succession of short-term teachers. My history teacher, Mr Shanks, had a habit of requiring us to remember ten new history dates for each new lesson. The trouble was that if we got more than one incorrect, we were belted. He would call the offender out in front of the class and, ceremoniously, deliver three strokes of the leather strap to the outstretched hand. The pain was bad but the humiliation was much worse. In their turn, all of my teachers had frivolous cause to belt us kids with Miss Duthie being the sole exception.

There were few boys of my 'class' with whom to associate. Most of them in the C stream were farmers' sons who travelled home at the end of each day while I was a town boy with no empathy with farm talk. Added to this, was the fact that they were all Tories while the Scott household were traditional Labour voters (though Labour got few votes in Conservative-ridden Strichen). There were a couple of boys in my class who actually lived in the village but these were only very young children and were smothered by their mothers, fearful that they might fall under the socially retarding influence of us poorer, working-class kids.

Our family rarely mixed, socially. Even our next-door neighbours felt and acted superior to us. On one side, we had the local stationmaster, Mr Barry, and on the other side, Fred Fenty; genteel, pretentious and unemployed for health reasons. My mother was envious and venomous against the Fentys, whom she regarded as scroungers. Work was the baseline of respect in North East working communities where we were all supposed to be imbued with the protestant work ethic. The Low family lived opposite with Jimmy Low having the high status of being the janitor of both Strichen infant and Strichen secondary schools. Next to the Lows were the Radomskis. The father was an exiled Polish diplomat, further estranged from the small Scottish community because he was, like most Poles, a Roman Catholic ('they're Catholics ye know,' my mother would say in hushed, conspiratorial tones, as if the mere mention of it would damn her to hell for all time).

Village life fed all sorts of malicious gossip and its attending prejudices. Noses were forever being parked behind thin, net curtains and my mother could have a vicious tongue when she was riled towards some point of self-righteous indignation. When she exploded in a tirade of a temper, she would exhaust herself before her fury slowly abated. She was not a woman to verbally cross swords with, as many other wives found to their cost. Adam could never hope to prevail against her when she had made up her mind, with her hackles up. She was an unholy combination of economical wisdom and ignorance and she struck me as being more a household manager than mother.

Our living room was full of ornamental kitsch with her interests being popular music on the radio and reading *Titbits* or *Weekend* magazines. Her life had been shaped by her circumstances and by the usual struggles against material poverty and the need to raise herself up to a higher material plane. Artistic planes were of an alien priority and she was stuck in the groove of always trying to make ends meet, which I respected. My mother was too hard and too strong and I could not sense any tenderness in her, nor any possibility of a warm, tactile embrace. To me, she was emotional ice.

She would explode in a stream of verbal abuse at us Nilsen kids as a release from her troubles. A recurring theme was that we were the cause of all her misfortunes and that, if we didn't watch our step, she'd have us put in a home (i.e., into care). She would rant and rave at the top of her voice, with a set monologue, starting with the wickedness of Olav Magnus senior and usually ending with the notion that the burden of us all was going to kill her. We all sat in the kitchen in guilty silence as she thundered on.

I had this beat into me when Adam got home, where Betty would cajole him into hitting us for all our imagined sins. She would taunt him with the phrase that hitting us was 'his job'. I once took a pound note from my mother's bedroom wardrobe and went to watch the film *The Dam Busters* at the local picture house. Halfway through the film, I was pulled from my seat by Adam Scott, taken home and given a good hiding. The otherwise quiet Adam reluctantly did as she bid. One winter's night, with hard frost on the ground, her ranting got so bad that me, Olav and Sylvia left home and set off to walk to Fraserburgh. We ended up knocking on my grandmother's door at 47 Academy Road and aroused her from her slumber in the early hours.

My mother once shouted at me that I wouldn't know my father if I met him in the street. As he had gone for ever back to Norway, it seemed highly unlikely that I would have met him in the streets of Fraserburgh anyway and it suggested that my *real* father might have still been living in the town. He may well have been a married man. Could he have been the same man who begat my sister, Sylvia? Possibly. I did resemble her more than I resembled Olav.

In her more gentle, reflective moments, my mother would say that, during her 'wild' youthful times going to dances during the war, she was friendly with some local policemen and mentioned one of them by name: Inspector Burns of Fraserburgh constabulary. She once even said to me, out of the blue, that my father was a policeman. I assumed that she'd meant that Olav Magnus senior had been a policeman in his civilian job before the war, despite my birth certificate stating that he was a clerk in a tobacco factory.

It is, perhaps, significant that my mother had proud photographs of herself and her firstborn, Olav, as a small boy but no photographs of me exist, save for a snap taken by my Aunty Lily in the backyard of 47 Academy Road when I was five or six years old. There were no baby pictures of me. What could she say? 'This is my little bastard boy, Dennis!' No reminders please. In a fundamentalist, religious climate, a bastard was not someone to be advertised. Perhaps I was a constant reminder of the incidence of my conception and the traumas attending it. I haven't ruled out the possibility that my mother might have been the shameless victim of a rape during one of her frequent forays to local dances.

Behind the respectable veneer of staid, village life, lurked a long-running soap opera charged with all the usual social passions and domestic drama. Strichen slept on with its single policeman, PC Smith, though nothing notorious had happened since the murder of a young woman in nearby New Pitsligo during the war. In the 1950s it was the sort of community where people *did* leave their doors unlocked and neighbours frequently dropped in on one another for social chats. Only in the rich, big houses were they cold, aloof and distant.

Once a week, one of us kids would walk up to Burnett's chip shop and bring home our family's tea meal of 2s. 6d. worth of chips, wrapped in a huge newspaper parcel (you could get a lot of chips for 2s. 6d. in those days). In the mid-fifties, Burnett's had a side-room café with a couple of tables and a new, high-fidelity Wurlitzer jukebox at three pence a play. The older boys and girls used to hang around there and Buddy Holly records came to provide my emotional subtext. I pined for his 'soul' when he vanished, silent, in that plane crash of 1959 and couldn't imagine how someone, who had created such sweet sounds, could be capable of being dead.

It was at times like this that I began to question the existence of a God. I could not begin to accept that my personal misery was, somehow, all part of God's plan for the world. But with one last throw of the dice, I became embroiled in my final religious phase. A caravan came to town carrying two young ladies from the faith mission. They were to make stops at various villages and spread the Gospel and I was soon affected with their exhortations to be 'born again'. Maybe things would change with 'the miracle healing power of Jesus' and I would, indeed, be 'saved' from my misery and delivered from my juvenile attraction to other boys. I enjoyed the jolly company of a bunch of kids singing happy hymns and was ripe for change in my life. We were told that a requirement of being 'saved' would be to renounce all the pleasures of the world: cinema, pop music and all unhealthy distractions from concentrated efforts, for the 'Lord alone'. It seemed a good idea but there was something missing from their doctrine and it soon dawned on me that this was just another authoritarian power, bent on thrusting itself in control of every aspect of our lives. Our fervour didn't quite outlast the departure of the caravan over the hill to new pastures green and we were left with still waters.

At Strichen School, a new boy arrived to join my sister's class. His name was Adrian Eales-Whyte and he was the son of the English Kirk vicar. He was slim, fair-haired, studiously shy and stood apart from the group. It was my experience at Fraserburgh Central School all over and I was in love again. He shimmered like an intensely emotional shrine, within the approximation of my middle distance, which produced both hurt and exhilaration in equal measure. But all such feelings were suppressed, of course, and any fruitful expression was impossible and I had no outlet for any kind of discussion. Girls could chatter together about boys, and boys about girls, but there was no social formula for boys to share their desires for other boys. It held, within it, a taboo as damned as hell itself. I longed to proclaim, to the world, my love for the loved-one but my instinct for survival was always much stronger. Necessity demanded that the core of my emotional being should remain secret from those around me.

In Miss Ritchie's French class, there was a drawing of a (fictional) French boy, named Pierre Duval, in one of the French textbooks. I used to buzz with inner excitement while looking at that picture. The drawing depicted the face of a pretty boy standing confidently, one leg straight with the other slightly bent at the knee. He was wearing a perfectly fitting school jacket and tie and very short, body-hugging trousers which clung to his hips and the top of his thighs. He wore sensible dark shoes and socks, which came halfway up his calves. As it was a black and white drawing, his skin was flawlessly marble white, and I couldn't take my eyes off his bare thighs where they met the grey material of his shorts. There was something else in his pose. It seemed to me to be faintly teasing, as if he were seducing me.

Because my homosexuality had to be essentially hidden, I was well on the road to reliance on a fantasy existence. I would fantasise about other boys I'd seen and would spend much of my time alone or with others in the woods and all the wild places around Strichen. There was the play of peer group fantasies of adventure and there were the personal fantasies when I was alone.

In that small bedroom at the front of the house, on the top floor of 16 Baird Road, my brother, Olav, and I went to the bed that we shared, and the light went out. We turned away from one another and I waited and waited until I knew him to be asleep. In the silence of the room, I was patient for the telltale signs that his rhythm had lapsed into deep breathing and I'd wait for some minutes or, perhaps, an hour or so. I'd wait, no matter how long it took, to hear this sign of his deep breathing. Then, with microscopic slowness, I would inch my hand towards where he lay next to me, having already carefully turned towards him. My fingertips touched, feather-lightly, on to the material of his pyjama trousers, a situation that was often made more complex if he was wearing underpants beneath. I carefully undid the cord on his pyjamas before delicately turning down the flap, millimetre by millimetre. He would often turn in his sleep, as his body registered this subconscious agitation, which changed the tempo of his breathing, and I would not proceed until his breaths returned to their deep mode. This way I was slowly, but systematically, able to peel down his pyjamas and, if necessary, his underpants as well, stopping at various stages to explore where I was in the process and how much of him had been revealed. I gently handled his penis and ran my fingers over his buttocks. My goal was to move his nether garments down so that I could have full access to his entire body over which I would softly run my hand. My heart rate was at speed during this ritual. Then I would re-dress him in the reverse order and retie the cord, which was always hard to do under the blanket-covered circumstances.

One night, he showed signs of an erection, at which point I

assumed he must have been awake. He never tried to stop me, nor did he ever say anything, even when it was clear that he was awake, and we never openly acknowledged what had been going on. At least, now, he had some idea that I might be homosexual but it was never to have been spoken about nor discussed.

He was my first sexually-related contact and, at that time, I was achieving my first erections. Soon after, he began to openly nickname me 'Hen' in front of the other kids. A funny name was just a funny name, and no one asked for an explanation, but he and I knew.

Out playing in the woods one afternoon, there was a sudden thunderstorm and us kids sought shelter in an old workmen's hut on wheels. In our group was a boy called Jimmy Gibb whose company I liked because he was so camp and was an excellent mimic of female character voices. His real name was Jimmy Cairns and he'd been adopted by the Gibbs who had changed his name. In that huddle against the downpour, outside, he began to talk about 'cumming' – had any of us ever 'cum' and did we know how to 'do it'? Not waiting for a reply, he started to masturbate, to show us how it was done. His small, limp penis gradually grew and I was mesmerised by the sight of Jimmy's hand working away to get some penile response. After strenuous effort and a long time pulling, he excreted a small dribble of milky white substance. I could barely see it and believed it was there only because he said it was. Much later, in the privacy of the lavatory at home, I tried it myself and, after a tiring sequence on the hand, I ejaculated for the first time.

Jimmy seemed happier playing with the girls and, prior to that particular occasion, he had little to do with us poorer boys imbued with the real rough and tumble of lower working-class life. Of all the village kids (and I say this with hindsight), Jimmy Gibb was the best potential for sharing my secrets with. Perhaps, at that age, we were both insecure and afraid.

The boys that I became visually fixated by were visions in 'real' form of an ideal that I'd imagined in my mind. And they were based on that positive tactility I'd had with my brother, Olav, and my physical intimacy with sharing a bed with him for so many years. It was his discovery of my interest in him, and his ridicule and rejection of my need for tactility with him (and his omnipresent risk of exposing me), which encouraged my further drift into fantasy. It seemed to me that, because of the proscriptions on same-sex relationships, I could only be physically intimate with boys if they were deeply asleep or unconscious. In order that I could express my power of intimacy over them, they would have to be powerless.

I had neither the will nor the means to induce unconsciousness in any boy so I took to the need through my imagination and through the manipulation of my own, young body. Outside, alone, I would seek out a spot, concealed by much foliage, lie down on the grass and imagine another boy fondling my body and I, his. I would simulate this with my own hands, though I didn't remove any of my clothes. This 'fantasy person' would only undress me to the limits of undoing my fly buttons as I was always in fear of imminent discovery. The fingers of the loved one would slide and trip stealthily over my erogenous zones to arouse me in the dawn of my sexual awakenings. I was thrilled by the presence of a phantom person as a substitute for real intimacy. At that prepubescent stage, I had no desire to have sex with other boys, just to have physical intimacy with their bodies. This was the beginning of my ritual cohabitation of a two-in-one mind and body; the birth of my imaginary companion.

I detour at this juncture to examine the movies and the central part they played in my fantasy life. I didn't have a dad, therefore, I invented one, finding him in role models up there on the silver screen of the cinema. I suppose James Stewart was one of the first but, later, I began to look upon him as an imaginary confidant and pal because my view of him altered due to one incident when, in a western, I found myself being drawn to stare at his crotch and bottom as he mounted his horse and sat astride it. My attraction to him became sexual rather than parental. I was also horrified when he threw himself off the bridge into the river in *It's a Wonderful Life*. John Wayne was another, strong father figure but I wondered if he would have sympathised with my feelings. I suppose that the most truly correct father figure, to me, was Gary Cooper as expressed in his roles in *High Noon* and *Man of the West*. I felt that I could tell him my troubles and he'd understand.

I always warmed to the antics of Stan and Ollie (Laurel and Hardy). At eight or nine years old, I felt good about being smarter than those two comics. They were like a couple of kids, without malice and, as they were always in trouble, I felt protective towards them.

My moments of real happiness were at the picture house and I took the language of the cinema out into my life to make it tolerable. Cinema became such a central focus in my expanding fantasy life, that when I was on my own – and in adventures in the great outdoors with other kids – I imagined that I was in a movie. I approached my situations and surroundings from the point of view of the movie camera and, in my inner eye, I granted titles and even music. Life looked better through the oblong frame of the movie screen format and this preoccupation consumed the greater part of my young life.

On the screen, I could see traits of my mother and Aunty Lily in Betty Hutton's portrayal in the title role of *Annie Get Your Gun* or Doris Day's role as *Calamity Jane* (both domineering womenfolk, always 'on the go'). I could identify with the situation and emotions of the character, Dorothy, played by Judy Garland in *The Wizard of Oz*. In the movie, she had a reason for returning to 'reality': a warm, loving family. I had no such reason and had no wish to leave my fantasy land where I could be in the movies just by viewing myself in the mirror's frame. If nobody appears to love you, you can always love yourself.

• • •

Life pottered on and, in the high summers of heatwaves, little bursts of glory fizzled. The womenfolk took us kids down to the beach for a picnic while the greater populace of workers basked on the sand in a huddled mass. Young men and girls swam while the kids paddled in the near shallows. The grown-ups remained, respectably, fully clothed in their deckchairs and benches on the promenade or on towels or blankets spread out on the sand. It was a world of ice cream, lemonade and blistered skin. The sea, sky and sand looked positively Hawaiian and, now and then, a massive black steam train puffed its way past this tableau of summer tranquillity.

Full of youthful energy, us kids departed the throng of beached adult whales and sprang away, on eager limbs, to explore the miles of sand dunes stretching all the way along the bay to Inverallochy. Exploring all the rock pools below the cliffs, west of the lighthouse at Kinnaird Head, drank up the summer hours; that and fishing off the rocks. We would run to the piers when the herring boats came in; flocks of hungry seagulls following, screaming in their wake. The holds of the boats held a sea of silver herrings, which cascaded into the huge, metal drums waiting in rows on the lorries. I had never seen so many fish in a never-ending harvest of extreme abundance. Such was this overproduction, that most of it went to be processed into fishmeal (today, the herring has passed, overfished, almost into extinction). We were never more alive than when the weather was bright.

One lazy, hot day, Olav pulled a girl down on the grass and sat astride her, pinning her arms to the ground. She put up a pretence at struggling but lay quieter when he put his hand inside her knickers. That was all there was to it. I just stood and watched in a measure of excitement before they both got up and the group carried on as if nothing had happened. It marked the girl's sexual awakening and marked a feeling of rising male potency in the boys.

Older boys sometimes 'sighted' younger boys. On one adventure, we were joined by an older boy, Michael Laird*. We'd been separated

* *Not his real name.*

from the other kids and, being bigger and stronger than I, he pinned me down on the ground and sat astride my body. I struggled fiercely but couldn't move. He had undone my shorts and fondled me, which excited a frisson in me; a mixture of rage and pleasure, the rage being attached to the fact that he had overpowered me. On another day, I did to another boy exactly the same as Laird had done to me; the difference being that I didn't undo his shorts but reached his privates by putting my hand up the inside of his thigh. It proved my power over another boy when I could render him powerless to prevent me grabbing his privates. It was an embryonic sex act... perhaps a rehearsal.

It also occurred with a beautiful (almost delicate) boy called Ewan Lennox* who lived close by but didn't normally mix with us poorer kids. He was about a year younger than me and he had a feminine quality about his appearance. Like me, he was no football type and there seemed to be something vaguely understood between us. I had him on the grass after a brief struggle – his arms pinned down above his head – and he was completely helpless. We were both sweating profusely and I could feel his heavily breathing body under me as I sat astride him. His eyes looked up at mine and there was a brief moment of mutual recognition as we both panted, exhausted. I cared for him and I didn't want to hurt him. I felt a great wave of excitement at our close physical contact and that I'd overpowered him; a member of a superior class, beautiful and so seemingly untouchable. We didn't speak as I held him there for at least a minute; the only language being in our eye contact. Slowly, I stood up and it was over. I hadn't attempted to gain any sexual intimacy with his private parts and I let him get up and asked him if he was all right, before we went our separate ways.

In my long treks over the sand dunes of Fraserburgh Bay, I always came upon the dark fascination of that concrete, slit-eyed pillbox where strange things had happened between my grandfather

* *Not his real name.*

and me; the half-drugged, tired child being stripped of his clothes and fondled by the dirty old man. We boys from the backyard would adventurously explore the multifaceted fabric of Fraserburgh harbour, where we took risks to life and limb that no sane adult would take. Once, we took a rowing boat out beyond the protective breakwater of the harbour into the dangerous swell of the North Sea. The boat was loaded with boys and girls in their summer clothes, with no lifejackets, as the craft sank low in the water. The eldest was no more than eleven and the youngest about seven as we rowed valiantly out to sea. Well beyond the point, we could feel the power of both the waves and the current. Some of the younger ones had begun to cry but we brash, working-class boys believed we were on a great voyage of adventure and discovery and that, in our collective comradeship, we'd live for ever.

My mother had taken out life insurance on her three kids. She'd expressed 'nightmares' of me drowning at sea because of my wild adventures and, curiously, had dreamed that she would only be able to identify my body through recognising my underpants (which I found as weird then as I still do now). After my funeral expenses, my death might have left her with one less bastard to feed and with a small profit. There was a dark side to my mother as there is in all of us. I guessed that if she had firm evidence of my moral degeneracy, in being passionately attracted to other boys, she might well have shunted me off to an institute for deranged juveniles. There was some inbred, mental instability in the family lineage and my homosexuality could easily have been fixed on another expression of the curse of this hereditary trait. In the 1950s, much of society, the church, the law and medicine, toyed with the possible notion that equated homosexuality with mental illness.

The fact of sudden death was never far from both child and adult in a North East fishing community and such facts bred depression. Billy Skinner was rough and tough and came from the council estate and, while still a teenager, fell to his death and drowned off the rocks we had used as our adventure playground. My half-brother, Olav, attended Skinner's funeral and described, without prompting, how Billy looked in his coffin. Another time, old Mr Ironside had gone missing from his home during the night, being a bit senile and apt to wandering off. Scores of villagers were out looking for him and, in the evening, some of us took to searching along the banks of the River Ugie which flowed past the village. By chance, I met up with Ewan Lennox on the stretch of river behind our school and I spotted something floating, under an overhanging, bushy tree, eighteen feet away on the opposite bank. Ewan said it was probably just an old sack but I wasn't so sure. Some nearby labourers stretched a metal ladder out into the river and Ewan, being one of the lightest of us kids, carefully crawled along it and the body of an old man was slowly dragged on to the grass bank as we all gawped at it. Mr Ironside, still wearing his cloth cap and otherwise clad in pyjamas and wellington boots, was loaded on to a waiting Land Rover. He was as stiff as a board and reminded me of my grandfather. He eventually found his way to Strichen Kirkyard cemetery where the history of the village and its past was engraved on its stones.

What had gripped me, from the incident by the river that evening, was not the husk of Mr Ironside but the indelible vision of Ewan Lennox in his shorts and plimsolls feeling his way, precariously, along that metal ladder; so beautiful, so vulnerable, yet so brave. Our eyes met fleetingly with that knowing secret and, with hindsight, I guessed he might have been subconsciously 'proving' himself to me, the older, stronger boy.

I had dark thoughts and nightmares about drowning in the sea. I was particularly sensitive to stories from the other boys about decomposing, drowned corpses and I had an awesome respect and fear of the mystery of the sea, which had supreme power over us puny mortals. It had, after all, taken my 'strong' grandfather. I began to be strangled by a recurring nightmare around the notion that my grandfather would try to stop me rising to physical maturity, by causing me to drown, so that he could have me with him in the ground. I became wary of deep water because I thought that his force would linger there and pull me down by the ankles until I drowned. At other times, I believed that he could command the sea to do his will and engulf me, likewise.

In one nightmare…

I am swathed in netting tangled up on the beach, stone-cold, drowned and wearing my yellow swimming trunks. He is shouting angrily but I cannot make out the words. The next thing I know, he is putting me over his shoulder and walking up the shore to his cottage in Inverallochy. Then he says, 'You wait until I get you home,' in a rough, forced whisper as I feel his fingers tugging at my yellow trunks, which he pulls down to my ankles.

In the cottage, my immediate family and extended relatives are crowded into that small room. Added horror comes from the stark fact that they are all immobile and made of wax. In the middle of the room, on trestles, there is a Dennis-sized coffin, lined with white satin padding. I feel his hands gripping my lower thighs as he pulls me off his shoulder, lowers me into the coffin and closes the lid.

I would wake up in a cold sweat with an erection at that point and wonder why I should want to be subjected to a kind of feminine, passive role unless there were two sides of my nature, split only because the pair (myself and my grandfather) held a relationship inside the one body? In the course of a single dream, both roles would frequently oscillate for prominence in which I would view events as both myself and as my grandfather.

Another incident provides further sexual illumination. On a crowded holiday beach, one hot summer, I saw the lifeguards rescue a young swimmer. I was fascinated to see this seemingly strong, young man being carried from the sea, limp and almost naked and given artificial respiration. Then my eyes opened in wonder as he 'came alive' and started to breathe again.

Not long after, I took a solitary walk beyond the crowds on the sheltered beach and its green pavilions; out towards the more desolate, sandy expanses; out there along its two-mile crescent length in the direction of Inverallochy to the south. About a mile out, I stood at the water's edge watching the waves creaming the sand with its endlessly insistent invasions just up to my toes. Hypnotised by both the presence of the mighty ocean and my own emotional predicament, I began to move forward with the sea now covering my shoes and socks and whooshing around my ankles. Ever forward, I walked up to my knees, then up to my thighs. Deeper and ever slowly forward, the cold wrap of numbness carried me steadily on, deeper, past my waist where I was now feeling the weight and power of the ice-cold water.

The sharp cold was gone as I stepped onwards out of my depth and I sank into the clear-green, peaceful world of endless slow-motion. Soothing drones of murmurings sequestered my hearing and filled my mind with the slow, bass beating of my heart and its rushing pump of lifeblood. That 'everlasting instant' of peace was supplanted by that vital 'intrusion' of the will for survival; involuntary and vital. A few seconds more, in that embracing peace, and there would have been no return. I broke the surface into a waking dream as I was pulled unconscious from the sea. In reality, I was staggering, wet and traumatically exhausted, towards the shore and I imagined the thrilling vision that I was being carried by the young man I had seen being rescued himself, a few days earlier.

I flopped down on the hot sand in a hollow in the dunes and imagined him undressing me (while undressing myself). With my face to the sky (while effecting limp immobility), 'he' slowly denuded my body of its soggy garments. I explored my own nakedness (revealed with my own hands) while imagining that it was being done by 'him' and by 'his' hands. In this ritual, a great, relieving wave of peace rolled slowly over me.

Snapping back to the practicalities of life, I was anxious to conceal my nakedness and I laid out my clothes on the sand to dry out. The dunes were expansive and I remained there, for a time, before dressing in my damp clothes. I'd hoped that the best course was to let them dry on me and I spent the rest of the day wandering around.

By the mid-fifties, Olav had gone back to Fraserburgh to live with my grandmother at 47 Academy Road because it was easier for him to finish his final years at the high school there. He was to attend Fraserburgh Academy because my mother always felt that Olav was the bright one who would get on in life. I, by contrast, remained in the lowest stream at Strichen School for the duration of my school days and was not expected to amount to very much.

The year before I left school, my sexual notions took a new turn concerning another beautiful boy when I was in the grip of puberty. His name was John Beech* – a year younger than me – and I almost collapsed into a fainting spin when I saw him in white shorts, socks and PT vest. His beauty sent my pulse racing and I ached for physical intimacy with him. However, being shy and withdrawn, I couldn't even summon up the courage to talk to him, let alone go some way to express my feelings, which had, thus far, been confined to playful wrestling bouts with other boys and exploring my half-brother's body when he was asleep. I longed for contact and the very thought of John Beech made me sickly dizzy.

At one point, I teetered on the brink of criminality but drew back, shocked and afraid by my own ambition. I imagined that if I hit him on the head from behind and knocked him unconscious, I could have him to caress. I raged at myself for such a thought, not because of any injury it might cause him but because of the risk of being found out and exposed as being gay. I had a vision

* *Not his real name.*

of him lying there, oblivious to my actions, as I pulled down his white shorts and fondled his unconscious body. His would have been just the physical body of an imaginary friend created in my mind. The aim would never have been to harm him but to express tactile tenderness towards his physical body. Perhaps this was how my grandfather had viewed me.

These thoughts began to stimulate my erections more and more and I fought and ashamedly tried to force them from my mind. I knew that these thoughts and dreams were wrong and that it was undoubtedly bad to hit anyone on the head and knock them unconscious. I was trapped in a primary, dreamlike stage of emotional development, unable to progress, needing human contact but, at the same time, fearful of rejection. There formed a concomitant emotional barrier to 'protect' myself from the risk of hurt and to distance myself from my vital need. The full potency would come from the fact that these thoughts were half imagination and half physical reality where the imaginary component supplemented the physical enactment. When I would lie, hidden in the grass, fondling my own body, I would be viewing the tableaux from the aspect of all the players, rapidly oscillating from one to the other, in order to appreciate the whole, and I'd develop scenarios that would cause me to be in this situation; I would imagine, for example, that I'd been, somehow, knocked out.

An old man approaches. He kneels by me and checks that I am unconscious by raising one of my eyelids to check for a reflex [in reality, my own hand checks on my own supine body]. *When he finds that there is no reflex, he lifts one of my limp wrists and lets it flop back on to the grass* [again, physically acted out by me]. *Satisfied that I am helpless, he unbuttons my short trousers and fondles me.*

I enacted and experienced both parts and found each part equally exciting. Over the years, the plot became more complex and refined, getting me deeper into it and, devoid of remedy, it assumed a vital importance in my sexual and emotional development. There seemed, at the centre, a longing for tactility but nothing came along to break the cycle.

• • •

In the final summers of my childhood, us kids would play out and about all day long. We drank river and stream water and it was crystal pure, the sort good for distilling whisky. I had an old, heavy black bike and I cycled extensively. We would sometimes collect spent .303 bullets, empty cases and mortar tailfins from around the army firing ranges near the gentler slopes of Waughton Hill which rose to form Mormond Hill. Later, when I joined the Strichen platoon of the Army Cadet Force (ACF), I would find myself firing a Short Lee Enfield rifle (which was nearly as big as me!) and Bren gun at these ranges.

In 1959, I attended a summer camp with the local Strichen troop of the Gordon Highlanders ACF at Pinefield Camp, just outside Elgin. I remember during night guard duty, one of the adult sergeants from another unit gave me a huge two-litre bottle of beer to drink, to 'prove' – at thirteen – that I was a 'man'. He took an interest in me and loaned me his wristwatch – the first one I had ever worn. He had sent all the other boys out on patrol and ordered that I stay in the guardhouse and I think he spotted me for a shy loner from a flock that I didn't belong in. I didn't remember him drinking anything himself, just him giving me beer and refilling my mug as it emptied. I'd previously never as much as tasted alcohol and, after I had heartily downed the stuff, I passed out.

In the morning, I woke up with a thumping head on a bed in the guardroom and had a notion that he'd taken advantage of my senseless condition. I remembered voices mumbling in the night and bright lights but nothing else. The watch had been removed from my wrist, as had my tie and boots. But I was fascinated by the speculation on what else might have been done in my senseless condition. My uniform didn't feel right and I wondered if any of it had been removed. What brought on these frisson thoughts, for months afterwards, was that I had noticed, later, that my underpants were on inside out. A suspicion based on strange circumstances was one thing but not enough on which to build a case of fact. There might have even been something else in the drink. Just because I felt no pain the next morning didn't mean that I hadn't been raped. Such things were unspeakable of in the buttoned-down 1950s but it remained there silently stewing in the dark recesses of my mind.

School days became a routine chore in my final year. The long days passed like the tolling of a great, ponderous bell and I had no clear idea of what I would do when it stopped. My future seemed, as sure as hell, to get a job in one of the local factories, a prospect that increased my sense of misery. To be attached firmly in my place, in a socially hostile environment for ever, was my true definition of hell.

Everyone else seemed to be fixed on some path towards good, future possibilities while mine was a high, blank wall of brick. Strichen struck me now as a kind of trap. It was as dead as the silver granite of which its dwellings and its tombstones were made. As a boy, I feared this living entombment where personal aspirations for real change would always amount to zero. What there was for me to find, would have to be found elsewhere.

I sat and pondered these things inside the antiquity of Mr Shanks' history class at Strichen School. The desk at which I sat bore the ravages of time with a hundred sets of initials cut into it. It was old and its mixture of iron and dark, disfigured wood had served many generations of scholars going back to the nineteenth century. It was hard, heavy and Victorian. Boys – their heads packed with rote learning – had gone off and died in two world wars. Their lives were to have a quantity of learning but little quality of life.

The classroom overlooked the railway line going south towards

Aberdeen and I increasingly saw those tracks as a lifeline to a better life. In Strichen or Fraserburgh, I would always be 'Betty Whyte's bastard' and all the whispering would keep me in my social place and see me through to my grave. In the North East of Scotland, you were what your parents were in the social pecking order.

I left Strichen Secondary School at fifteen, knowing that my personal predilections would satisfy no future in the tight prejudices of Scotland. I wanted to escape from that household and that cultural locale and so I signed up for nine years' service in the British Army. Betty was only too keen to sign the consent form; now she could be rid of me with one less mouth to feed. Components fitted together in my young mind: me plus railway line, plus train, plus the army equals a prospect of escape. For once in my life, I was beginning to feel happy. There *could* be life after Strichen.

I had a few weeks to kill until the start of term at the army apprentices' college in Aldershot so I got a packing job in McConachie's fish-canning factory in Fraserburgh, for which I was paid about forty bob a week (£2) for forty hours' hard labour. My supervisor, Hector Watson, was a long-time server of the firm and I worked with a boy of my age who had come up from Birmingham to live with his grandmother. He was different and held, for me, a new perspective on the world and we were friends for that short, summer duration of 1961. He was proof of another world over the horizon and beyond the narrow, social straitjacket of the North East of Scotland.

Before I left for the army, I saw Hitchcock's movie *Psycho* (in those days you had to be sixteen to see X-rated films but I was tall at fifteen and never had any difficulty getting in). I warmed, sexually, to Anthony Perkins who played the disturbed central character, Norman Bates, though I could never understand Bates' fixation with his mother. I was particularly gripped by a frisson of sexual excitement after the shower killing was over, from the close-up of Janet Leigh's staring eyes to her being put – clear-plastic-wrapped

– into the car boot. The image of her being carried was the most intense of all. It was not the Janet Leigh figure that aroused me but a vision of myself in this extreme state of passivity, juxtaposed with me as Anthony Perkins as well. In my deeper imaginings, I refined and expanded on the script to suit:

We start with that angled, close-up shot of the staring eye. It is my own eye. The more unblinking and still it is, the greater the illusion of its extreme passivity of the subject: me. I see through this eye but I cannot react. I can also see what Perkins is seeing and I can also see the scene from a third-party vantage point.

I am hanging half out of the bath, naked, and Perkins is free to do as he pleases. In my version, there are no knife wounds on me; they have magically vanished. Norman turns off the water. He hovers over me, just looking. Next, I feel his hands under my armpits and he gets a grip on my totally limp body. He drags me over to a large piece of towelling on the bedroom floor on to which he gently lets me flop, lifelessly. He kneels over me, changing his gaze from my eyes to up and down my naked, exposed body. He then stands facing and astride me before heaving me up, over his shoulder. My vision is now upside down.

He carries me up to the house and I feel his arm around the back of my knees keeping my naked body secure and my thighs firmly together. I am now being carried upstairs in this forbidding house. He lets me slide off his shoulder on to his mother's bed. He hauls me on to my front and I can hear him masturbating with one hand while he fondles my bare buttocks with the other.

In spite of a total lack of encouragement, I went forth, as dreamers do, helped by the peculiarities of past experience and a genetic configuration which had projected me in ways so different from the norm. There were no tears on my departure and I was never, ever homesick for the North East, nor my family. They seemed to me to be bit-part actors from a past tragedy. I carried my home with me inside my head. I didn't hate them, nor was I envious of them, nor did I covet anything that they had. In a way, I felt sorry for the fact that most of them would remain on the uninspiring treadmill of their fixed roles in the local community. Of course, even with all their ups and downs, sadness and personal disappointments, they would end up the richer, while I would end up richly multifarious in intellect, as a hollow man.

On the way to join the army, I had to spend a couple of hours in the city of Aberdeen waiting for a train and I walked around the Aberdeen art gallery. My mind was instilled with a great burden of guilt: guilt for my feelings of pain at the hands of my grandfather, guilt for his death, guilt for the poverty and misery of my family, guilt for the 'abomination' of being attracted to other boys, guilt for my artistic aspirations (on the basis that *real*, responsible people sweat at honest toil for a living), guilt for my non-existent father, guilt for my 'lazy' inability to do well at school, guilt for being useless at team sports, guilt for having shabby clothes, guilt for not having had the same things as other boys had, guilt for being sick, guilt for letting down the family by giving up my paper round…the list seemed endless.

I left Strichen, to start a new life, in September 1961. I was fifteen years old.

2

Army Life | 1961

The camp at St Omer Barracks in Aldershot, Hampshire, held the accommodation for about 500 boys between the ages of fifteen and eighteen. It was one, big military complex of many barracks. Across Basingstoke Canal from St Omer Barracks was Mons Officer Cadet School. The whole place was dwarfed by the great Victorian edifice of Cambridge Military Hospital at the top of Gun Hill.

Only two adults actually lived in the barracks: Eric Day, a warrant officer class 2, who taught the culinary skills at the Army School of Catering, and Drum Major Gosling. All the other instructors lived in married quarters or in the out-of-camp officers' or sergeants' messes, while the civilian instructors commuted daily to and from their own, private homes.

On my arrival, I was billeted in a long room with about another eleven boy recruits of my own age. We were V squad and this was to be my style of military domestic life for the three-year training period. At that stage, I was shy and slightly aloof but what made me acceptable to the group were my height (a boy not to be bullied), my intelligence and my expressive humour.

Our Junior Tradesmen's regiment had a sporting ethos dominated by rugby and cricket, reflecting the tastes and traditions of the officer public school class. I had no affinity for the rough and tumble of team sports, preferring the solitude of cross country running.

Each morning, Eric Day – or 'Q' as he was referred to – joined us in our ablutions as we stripped to the waist and washed. He never removed his vest and his braces dangled down over his service trousers. Q ran the regiment's variety club and that was the true love of his life. His great friend in real showbiz was the music hall comedian, Arthur English, whose daughter, Clare-Louise, was often recruited as principal boy in the shows he ran. The camp concert was always a social highlight of the regimental year and played to a packed, juvenile house and I thought it was good for what it was. For the boys, it was a contrasting break from the realities of dull, clockwork, military routine and was pure escapism. I didn't have enough confidence to join the variety club until my final year then, even in this, I operated as no more than a stagehand (it was also too late to have any part in the long-rehearsed shows). The idea of performing on a stage in front of a crowd of people terrified me.

Eric Talbot, a fellow boy soldier whom I fancied like mad, suspected there was something 'funny' about Q. 'If Q asks you to his room for a cup of tea, don't go.' Was he speaking from personal experience? There was always a forlorn sadness in the demeanour of Q. He seemed quite alone lodged within a sea of young bodies unsure of themselves and regimented to 'button down' emotionally.

There was no privacy at the army apprentices' college; it was communal life, controlled and ordered. Private refuges for masturbation became the toilet cubicle or bathrooms and there was no stimulating pornography available as our kit and lockers were subject to continuous inspection. What there was, had to be secreted and shaped in the mind. I retained my images from life; the texture of a warm, smooth body could be enjoyed by closing my eyes and fondling myself. The only partner I'd ever had was a fantasy creation whose baseline was my brother, Olav.

I did form a kind of attachment to a boy in my squad called Brian Brasher. He was smaller than me, slightly effeminate and delicate and wasn't really able to compete physically with the rest of us when it came to rigorous, hard training over the assault course. He was generally viewed as an ill-fitted member of the squad because of his physical frailness and had only joined the army to please his father who'd been a corporal in the Royal Army Service Corps as well as a regular soldier.

That first Easter, me, Brian and a couple of other boys took a tent, sleeping bags and rucksacks from the stores and made off to camp in the countryside. Our destination that year was the New Forest. On one particular trip, we'd pitched our tent by the road at night and, as daylight broke in the morning, we awoke to find ourselves on a hill overlooking the Broadlands estate of Lord Mountbatten. An estate manager drove up and once we'd explained our situation, he politely gave us time to eat our meal and move on at our convenience. He didn't throw us off, probably because of our army credentials and the fact of our predicament.

Another time, we'd been joined by a fellow apprentice called Chris Innerd, with whom I shared a bivouac tent. It was pure heaven in our sleeping bags with the rain and wind howling outside and my heart skipped a beat when he undressed down to his vest and pants to get into his bag. There, in that cramped, two-man tent, almost on top of me, he exposed the sheer perfection of the pale, flawless, hair-free skin of his bare thighs and legs. The loose material of his green underpants then fell open and briefly exposed the fleeting secret of his most private parts; a sight and revelation that gripped me with a power unsurpassed. The vision struck me dumb with fevered excitement and at that moment he was the purest being on my planet. We slept close, huddled together for comfort through the grim, element-racked night and I wondered if it had been like this often in the trenches, during numerous wars, facing death. In a time before fences and protests, we camped on the open ground near Stonehenge and when the sun rose, we walked casually and unrestrained amongst the great, timeless stones.

I could sense that Chris was unhappy inside himself, as I was unhappy inside myself. We talked but we couldn't communicate; only a sudden flash of pained guilt in the eyes. There must have been many queers in the Junior Tradesmen's regiment just like me: afraid and alone. We were tortured by the macho drives for brisk, unfeeling conformity. We dressed, got in line and marched off cold but in correct order. The nearest that we came to emotional release was in the convivial gatherings around the campfire; eyes red from the smoke and defences loosened by the ingestion of a huge bottle of brown ale (forbidden to us in barracks), which brought us to the shared experience of soft, warm, male comradeship, close to tears. I was in love with Chris Innerd but, as such things were criminal offences, I had to keep my feelings secret.

When I laid on my back on the gymnasium floor, doing exercises with the other boys, I would catch sight of Chris lying near me. When he ran at the vaulting horse, I watched him perform in slow motion. My eyes would be the lens of a film camera and what I viewed was rectangularly edged. It was this vision that I took into the bathroom with me as I fondled myself, remembering the thrill of the feel of running my hands over Olav's thighs, belly and buttocks while he was asleep.

What I couldn't have, had to be wholly created in my imagination. This configuration became a controllable commodity, which I could summon up at my convenience and my need for emotional, human interactions became less and less necessary and compelling (in any case, such emotionally expressive interactions were impossible for me, as a gay man, without risk of personal destruction). I had two separate lives: the real life and the fantasy life. When I was with people, I was in the real world but in my own private mind, I snapped easily into my fantasy life and I could oscillate from one to the other with instant ease. Before I went to sleep at night, I would even go as far as to plan my dreams. I would slowly drift off with the warm, wondrous thoughts of my imagination all framed, of course, in the movie camera's lens.

A recurring, comfortable format featured me and Chris, naked under fur blankets in a cosy log cabin, looking into the harsh, blizzarding world outside where it was twenty degrees below zero. We would stay there in warm comfort, together, for ever. We never talked in the dream and would only, occasionally, get up to eat good food, silently, before a blazing fire, and we'd listen to the outside world on the radio. It was bliss; naked under those furs in each other's arms with the smooth, warm softness of his skin against mine. That was the full expanse of my sex life during my days as a boy soldier.

As time passed, I became a junior corporal and was given command of a room section of more junior boys. In my new room was a thin, delicate and beautiful boy who was made fun of by some of the other boys because of his lack of machismo. One afternoon, I found him in his bed space crying and at the point of breakdown. I took him to one side and talked to him, gently and reassuringly, like a 'mum'. I wanted to put my arm around him but there were other boys around and tough corporals just didn't do that sort of thing. Another time, a cheeky boy came over and sat on my knee in front of everyone, surprising me completely into inaction. I tried to behave nonchalantly and, while feigning disinterest, I inwardly thrilled to the feel of his warm, heavy thighs and buttocks pressing on my lap. I calmly asked, 'What is it you want?' whereupon he got up, having failed to excite my cool. I was bubbling with lust for him, inside, and if we'd been alone, I would have probably called his bluff.

Cruelly, there were examples to be made of anyone who openly displayed traits of homosexuality. One of the more senior boys was the subject of a flood of gossip and was socially ostracised. When he was checking around all the barrack rooms before lights-out, it would pain me to hear shouts of, 'Here he comes…arses to the wall!' The coward that I was, intent on career survival, I kept neutral and silent but as a sop to my conscience, I would always answer the senior in polite, correct tones, if spoken to.

At my final passing out parade in front of a general – graduating after three years' training – all the proud parents were assembled to see their sons off. I, of course, had nobody to cheer me on and congratulate me (but for the heroes in my dreams). It was the summer of 1964 and my mind was on the green grass on the far side of the hill. I had obtained the army Certificate of Education (1st Class) and, thereafter, we all departed on leave.

I embarked on the long train ride on the Aberdonian Express from Kings Cross to Aberdeen and then by bus to Strichen and felt thoroughly hollowed out, having to return to a situation where I felt out of place. It was a cold, but significant, comfort to me to retread the wild secret places from my past. I avidly enjoyed the company of my Uncle Bobby who had married my Aunty Lily a couple of years before and they had moved in with my grandmother at 47 Academy Road. It was the only wedding I was ever to attend in my life, with my official role being as an usher with my half-brother, Olav.

Uncle Bobby was a hi-fi enthusiast. He possessed the finest equipment of its day and was also a classical music lover. From the beginning, I was emotionally afflicted by the sublime sounds that issued forth from those Leak speakers in full stereophonic sound. I could be captivated by the tones of the great composers and I experienced the release of my full range of emotions, suffused with images reflecting my love of cinematography. I had, at last, through Uncle Bobby introducing me to classical music, found the strength to weep.

September 1964 found me back, briefly, at St Omer Barracks where we gathered to await our postings to regular army units and where we were to put all our training into practical operation. Then we took our awkward leave of one another and I departed to the British Army of the Rhine (BAOR) in Germany. I was eighteen.

• • •

My first posting as a regular army private was to the 1st Battalion the Royal Fusiliers (the City of London Regiment) where I was stationed at Belfast Barracks in the town of Osnabrück in Westphalia, Germany. The regiment was soon to be commanded by Lieutenant Colonel, the Earl of Morley (Parker). Having also trained as a chef, I took my place in the main kitchens. The cooks were a hardworking, boozy lot and our catering clique spent most of its off-duty time drinking, and I was certainly never a social loner during those Osnabrück years.

Our group consisted of Lance Corporals Mickey Duke and Ginger Watson, Private 'Pissy' Pears, Bob Howitt (nicknamed 'Dumbo'), Paddy Aherne (nicknamed 'the Brigadier' because of his cultured accent), Bernie Harper, Paddy Dougal and me. We would start drinking that wonderful German beer in the camp NAAFI bar, before going loose on the town.

After one particularly heavy night at a local beer house, I awoke the next morning, upstairs in bed, with a rather stout young German called Hans Reinhardt. He must have carried me – unconscious – upstairs, undressed me and taken me to bed with him. I remembered nothing of the night before and kept away from him after that, though the thought of what might have happened excited me. I speculated, with a frisson of excitement, on a fantasy of how he had ritualised my young, naked, eighteen-year-old body while I was unconscious. Whatever it might have been, I wouldn't have minded but was regretful that I'd not been aware enough to enjoy it.

Tactile exploration of other males would only be possible through the effects of drunkenness – inducing unconsciousness – both for me and for others 'interested' in me. I would often be just drunk enough to feign unconsciousness, as to experience what others would do, while having full control over me, and that was as near as I got to any conscious, physical intimacy. I had the occasional 'honour' when one or two of our group was out cold and I had to put them to bed. It didn't happen that often and it wasn't something I consciously looked out for, or anticipated, but within the dulling of alcohol, I did experience a mild transitory buzz while undressing one or other of my young comrades. Sometimes they would perform the same service for me but with a difference. Once, way after midnight, I'd flaked out and, later, opened my eyes to realise that I was being carried over an older soldier's shoulder. I felt his arm holding me around the back of my thighs with my head and arms dangling down his back. Right there and then I decided to feign unconsciousness in order to appreciate and enjoy being in a totally passive state and, thus, able to offer my body at his disposal. The result, however, was a great disappointment because all he did was plant me on top of my bed and leave the room!

By late 1966, I was a suspect in a murder investigation (along with almost everyone else in the regiment). A local taxi driver had been shot dead, one night, and the police had reason to believe that the killer had come from our camp. All our fingerprints were taken 'for elimination purposes' but Lance Corporal Leslie Grantham was eventually arrested, court-martialled and found guilty of the murder. I knew him from drinking in the Corporals' club and from feeding him three times a day. We were both about the same age and though I found him a good-looking kid he was a bit too aggressively extrovert in personality for there to have been any social rapport beyond the normal pleasantries of military etiquette. After serving eleven years in prison, Grantham emerged to become a famous TV actor in the mid-eighties.

In the new year of 1967, I returned to Aldershot to be told that I was being posted to the strife-torn British protectorate (colony) of Aden (South Yemen). One movie had finished and I had walked on to the set of a new and completely different one.

• • •

I arrived in Aden by non-stop VC10 airliner, stepping from the bitter cold of a British January into the searing heat of Arabia. Everyone seemed intent on killing everyone else in terrorist warfare, with the terrorist groups united only in their common ground of wanting to kill the British. For the first time in my life, I was faced with the reality of a military situation in the field.

For a while, I was stationed at Al Mansoura, a prison and detention centre for terrorist suspects and, in my off-duty time at the safe recreation area at Steamer Point, with more than a few drinks inside me, I would wander off into dangerous areas of the colony and take enormous risks. One night, I was out drinking at the Mermaid Club and I missed the armoured car (affectionally known as the 'pig'), which left at 10 p.m., sharp, to bring us back to Al Mansoura. Undaunted, I made my way back on foot and hailed a local, yellow and black taxi along the road. It stopped for me and I got in the back, drowsy, but still awake. When we'd crossed the causeway and had been waved through at the checkpoint, the driver turned off into a side alley in Sheikh Othman, muttering something about the engine being hot. As I turned around to survey my surroundings through the rear window, he must have coshed me on the head because my next recollection was waking up, naked, in the boot. The taxi stopped and I thought my best hope was to fake unconsciousness. I heard the door slam shut and my heart raced then my spirits rose slightly as my hand touched the cold, hard metal of a tyre lever. The boot lid groaned upwards and I could hear him muttering in Arabic before, huffing and puffing, attempting to raise my limp weight up into his arms. I was now half out of the boot and I seized my last opportunity. I grabbed the steel tyre lever and dealt him a sickening blow on the head. He went down like a felled ox as I got to my feet as keen and alert as a cat.

I frantically and fearfully looked about me but, in the still of the night, there was not a sound but for my own, fast breathing. With the lever still in my hand, I stood over my fallen assailant and prodded him for movement but there was none. I retrieved my clothing and quickly dressed as a dog barked somewhere and my mind reached fever-pitch. I dragged the taxi driver to the boot and bundled him in then wiped the tyre level with an oily rag I'd found in there before slamming it shut, which sounded like a pistol shot in the night. 'Fucking idiot,' I thought. 'You'll wake up the whole neighbourhood!'

I wandered around the small dwellings of Sheikh Othman until I found the familiar sight of the main road then, after a walk of some twenty minutes, I was brought into the prison by a foot patrol. I made my excuse of 'missing the pig' and was given a telling off by the guard commander who was more concerned that I'd got back OK rather than my default in procedure. I was too ashamed to mention the incident and didn't know if the driver was dead or not but, if he'd survived, he was hardly likely to report the incident because of his own criminal actions. It was just another traumatic puzzle for speculation.

In moments of inactivity, I would slip into my dream-world and speculate on a scenario that might have been. In the safety of my own bed, I was aroused by the tableaux, juxtaposed with fear for my death, in a frisson of fearful contradiction. What would the taxi driver have done with me afterwards? What would have been the sequence of events? Was he intent on other extremes; to dismember and eat my flesh? All these horrific wonders rushed through my imagination with escalating rapidity. I had feverish dreams of him, moustachioed, à la Saddam Hussein:

He has me sitting upright on his lap with my ankles bound and my hands tied behind my back. A plaster is firmly over my mouth and I am wearing white Y-fronts. As I struggle to work free of my bonds, he pinches my nose closed with his fingers and I really begin to struggle, frantically. My staring eyes look up into his and they are the terrible eyes of my grandfather. My struggling body begins to lose consciousness but my 'soul' pops up, out of my head, to watch the scene from above.

My head is moving rapidly from side to side to escape his vice-like grip on my nostrils and the front of my underpants shows wet and I defecate as my entire, straining body goes limp.

He holds the naked rag doll in his arms where it rests and he rips the plaster off to reveal a half-open mouth. He kisses me and gently fondles the front of my wet underpants [in the fantasy, I have accrued an erection at this point].

He bends me forward and undoes the goatskin band around my wrists and my arms flop, limply, to the side. He reaches over and unties my ankles. As I loll in that posture, the Arab speaks to me but it is the voice of my grandfather: 'You've been a bad boy, Dennis, making a mess of yourself like that. I'll clean ye up and we winna tell yer mither… we'll keep it between oorsels.'

Grandfather's voice fades and the Arab hoists me into his big, hairy arms. He stands there for a moment looking down at my loose nakedness; my arms and head and the bottom half of my legs hang, limply, down as he holds me under my armpits and under my knees.

The taxi driver carries me into a white, tiled room and lays me, gently, on the gleaming, white floor. He deftly rolls my body over on to its belly as he kneels beside me to look at my face. Grandfather speaks: 'Bide quiet loon [boy]*, I'm nae gan to hurt ye.'*

From above, I see him ease my briefs down over my buttocks and thighs, pausing at the knees, then they slide slowly down to my ankles and over my feet.

Although I am dead, I can feel the weight of his strong hands and arms as the Arab washes my naked body. He attempts to turn me on to my back again but I slip from his hold and flop back on to the floor with an uncomfortable thump. 'Oh, ma poor wee loon…did I hurt ye?' he intones, sympathetically.

He eventually succeeds before reaching over and gingerly placing my legs full apart. 'There's something nae quite right about ye, Dennis.

I'm gonna make ye bonny,' he says and, with that, he begins to shave the silky down of hair from my legs and arms. I am turned over again and he removes what hair there is on my anus and buttocks, leaving only a small, neat triangle of light, pubic hair and the hair on my head and eyebrows. I look like a fourteen-year-old version of my twenty-year-old self.

He has my wet body back in his lap as he towels it dry; my non-comprehending head nods to his rough movements with glazed, blue eyes. He sprinkles me with large quantities of Johnson's baby talcum powder, which he smooths into my pale skin. His final, decorative flourish is to expertly apply bright-red lipstick to my lips and a touch of mascara to my eyelashes. He re-dresses me in small, white, silk shorts and a white, silk singlet before sitting me in an armchair and standing back to admire his handiwork.

In the dream, I then go through a wedding ceremony, where I 'marry' my grandfather and, thereafter, become his 'legal property' before my grandfather carries me up to the bridal suite.

He begins to undress my body then stands back and looks, longingly, down at my exposed flesh, now in a perfect state of nudity. He sits, naked, beside my body on the bed as he strokes my hair. He moves my head slightly towards him to give the impression that I'm looking at him then, softly, he gets on to the bed and manhandles my unresisting body on to his, and a kind of one-sided wrestling match ensues, in slow motion, as his hands caress, stroke and fondle me.

He releases all his frustrations on my helpless, naked body; he licks it and spanks my bare bottom. After making love with my inert form, he lets my young body slip on to the carpeted floor. He rings a push bell on the wall and the Arab enters. 'Get rid of this,' he says, pointing to the body of young Dennis on the floor.

The Arab heaves me over his shoulder and leaves, putting me beside him on the front seat. When he arrives at some desolate spot in the desert, he takes a shovel from the boot and digs my grave, which is only about three feet deep. I am dragged to the side of the hole and flopped on to the sand. He rolls my corpse into the hole in the sand and fills it in. Back at barracks, the great mystery remains: whatever happened to Corporal Nilsen?

Dreams and fantasies had infiltrated my psyche and I was overtaken by the traumatic events from the past. I didn't dwell on it in Aden, as it drifted away to sleep in my inner recesses due to the sheer force and fatigue of hard work at the all-consuming duties of running a kitchen.

In the middle of a quiet lunch break, quite casually and unexpectedly, a private at the prison said he had something interesting to show me and, having nothing better to do, I went with him. He unlocked the gate and we crossed to the bulk of the main wall building, a distance of no more than ten yards. There, he unlocked a set of double doors and we entered. The cobbled floor fell away to the back wall, near to the outer wall, where light streamed in from a solitary, high window and I followed him down the slight incline. The place seemed to be empty except for what looked like a six-foot-long, shallow, concrete sink, about four inches deep, along the left-hand wall.

At the end of the room, we climbed a wooden staircase, which led on to a high platform under the window. I was still puzzled and asked, 'Well? What?' He pointed to the floor upon which we could see a seven-foot-long trap door with three white squares painted on its rough wood. I looked up and saw a single, thick wooden beam with a looped noose attached to it. A single lever, like a railway points lever, stuck up from the floor. It was the prison scaffold, something that hadn't entered my mind before that time and would only have been immediately obvious if you'd been looking for it.

'Does it work?' I asked my companion. 'Yes. It's one of my jobs to check it from time to time,' he answered. He invited me to hold on tight to the noose as he pulled the lever. 'Take your full weight on the rope…you'll be all right,' he said. Apprehensively, I secured my grip standing on tiptoes (for some inexplicable reason) on the centre, white square and he pulled the lever. The long, door-sized trap snapped away from beneath me and swung with a sharp crash. I fell about a foot into the black chasm of the pit. In spite of what I thought was a secure hold on the noose, my arm joints ached as I heaved myself back up to secure a hold on the stout, wooden floor. I was buzzing with fear and excitement as I regained my stance; my eyes drawn to the gaping, black hole of eternity.

We stood for a few moments, in silence, as the noose swung across the void. The shafts of bright, white light radiated into multicoloured existence by the clouds of fine dust set airborne by the brief explosion of the mechanism. The noise of the trap repeated itself in my ears; all this darkness amid so much light in an all-bright, matt white room. It excited me that I had taken 'the drop' of one of Her Majesty's gallows and was still around to appreciate it. On the way out, it dawned on me that the flat, shallow, concrete sink, with the single water tap at one end, was the post-mortem table for the examination of extinguished meat.

By the end of June 1967, I found myself on an Argosy transporter plane heading for Sharjah, one of the Trucial States in the Persian Gulf, now called the United Arab Emirates. About three months later, the British abandoned Aden and left the rival factions to fight it out for the prize of power, and I heard that the Al Mansoura gallows erupted into regular use in the new People's Democratic Republic of Yemen.

• • •

At Sharjah, my first allocation was in the Commissioned Officers' mess and, for once in the Middle East, I had an air-conditioned room to myself and a team of native cooks. My role was mainly to plan menus, supervise and do all the paperwork but I also had access to a boy servant who I was expected to pay 5 shillings a week. These boys were exceptionally deft at domestic chores and each one worked for several officers at the same time. They also, of course, provided 'extras' (the services of boy prostitutes) and it didn't take any kind of special skill to seduce me.

I was dozing on top of my bed when I heard a knock on my door. It was the boy again, asking if I wanted anything before he went home. I told him that I was a bit tired and would give him something to do the next morning. Then suddenly, almost in panic, I realised that I was, more or less, hinting that he could go, so I quickly added that he should have some money for his trouble. At this, he shut the door and drew down the venetian blinds. He came over to the bed where I lay and sent my mind reeling into space. 'Have you Vaseline?' (a common lubricant) he said, with all the ease and normality of asking for a light for a cigarette. I stuttered, taken by complete surprise. 'No, I've never used it… Look, I'm not used to this.'

Perplexed, he enquired, 'You no like nice boy?' My brain was playing the 'Hallelujah Chorus' as I stretched out my hand. 'Come over here,' I intoned. I stood up, put my arms around him and held him close and he nestled, warmly, against me. My hands moved down to caress his buttocks. 'Come and lie on the bed. I'll take off your clothes,' I said, as I steered him to the crisp, clean bed. He laid on his back and looked up at me with those deep, brown, doe-eyes, which he closed, contentedly, as my hands moved to the waistband of his shorts. I pulled them down, slowly savouring every moment, and off. We made love there in my room then laid side-by-side for a few minutes, saying nothing.

The boy became a regular visitor but, inside the space of a couple of weeks, I was moved to a new post in the vast growing military complex and found myself back with the troops with my own room at the end of a barrack room. There was no private entrance;

therefore, my short foray into native boys was over and my boy servant was most upset when I left the Officers' mess.

The huge, brand new kitchen was not yet complete and there followed a period of relative inactivity, devoted to lazing about. I travelled by taxi to the city of Dubai, fifteen miles along the coast, every other night. The Gulf States were 'dry', because of the strict Islamic laws, though alcohol was permitted for westerners in military establishments and in the Carlton Hotel in Dubai. The main lounge bar was frequented by oil men, businessmen and diplomats and I found it a pleasant watering hole where I could meet interesting people and enjoy good conversation. I would listen, rather than talk, because I didn't have the confidence of age and experience but I soon felt irritated that, always being plied with drink, I was probably regarded as nothing more than a rent boy or an opportunist looking for a sugar daddy, as I was often invited to the rooms of half-drunk, horny, American oil men. Consequently, my visits to the Carlton Hotel soon petered out to nil.

A few of us 'rebel spirits' formed a kind of group at the Flying Kunjah Club in Sharjah camp. We were a motley crew of specialist cooks, engineers, signallers, drivers and one was from the RAF Desert Rescue section. The great character I remember was a Scot by the name of Davy Crockett (yes, his real name). He was the king of the wild frontiers of our boozy, social gatherings every night and from whom I learned many entertainment skills. Sometimes we'd take a truck up the coast to an isolated spot to bathe and lie in the sun where I'd admire the beautiful, bronzed physique of a young lance corporal in the Royal Electrical and Mechanical Engineers called Smithy. He was small, slim and smooth-skinned and was a bit shy, only emerging after a few drinks in the evening.

One late night, Smithy – with some drink inside him – fell off a moving Land Rover and died of a broken neck. The group was never the same again. He was buried in the sand, in the middle of the camp, near our accommodation; just a small square of ground, little bigger than an average backyard. A couple of nights later, three of us cooks, staggering back drunk from the new NAAFI, stumbled around Smithy's grave and just stood there looking down at it. We never uttered a word but the tears ran freely down our cheeks. I knelt and touched the sand and thought of him underneath – so near, yet so far away – and he stayed in my memory – young and beautiful – for ever more. From then on, I remained, more and more, by myself with no best friend.

In 1967, the Sexual Offences Act was passed that permitted two consenting males over twenty-one years of age to engage in homosexual activities in private. But this new, partial freedom did not extend to Her Majesty's Armed Forces so, for me, there was no change. I was damned to continue the secret habit of concealing all my feelings at the core of my gay orientation. So, the fantasy world that I had developed over the years became a 'safe' and necessary alternative to living in a void of almost total, emotional isolation. There was a lot of growing pressure building up 'in there' and not entirely as I had planned or wanted.

In my room was a very large mirror and I came to be ever admiring myself in it. By positioning it at an angle, I could look at myself lying on the bed and I'd become aroused by my relaxed body. I imagined someone (the mirror's view) looking at me and lusting after my body. This was, of course, practical and visual nonsense and there needed to be a second party. Therefore, I took steps to pretend that the image in the mirror was, actually, someone else. I repositioned it so that my head couldn't be seen reflected and I imagined myself in the dominant role, as well as the passive body in the mirror. The problem was that it just looked like me pretending to be asleep. I, therefore, had to make the image in the mirror look as unlike the real me as possible (and be as truly passive and helpless) for the imagined man to act dominantly upon it. I decided that the most passive and opposite from the real, 'living' me was the 'dead', helpless me.

In the mirror, the man dominating my body had no face but he was always a dirty, grey-haired old man; the polar opposite of the beautiful, smooth-skinned young man of my dreams. He would be in many different costumes and disguises but it would always be that filthy, drooling, ugly, old man and I could make those scenarios seem real through my sheer need and willpower (though the process took some months to unfold and develop).

On an afternoon off-duty, I would lock my door, telling the lads that I was completely exhausted and wanted some peace for an afternoon's sleep, whereupon I would draw the blinds and enter the fantasy. They took many forms and I couldn't possibly describe all the variations here but will relate details of one that was obviously influenced by the recent death of Lance Corporal Smith.

I stripped my bed and put the mattress on the floor. I wore my khaki shorts, desert boots and bush shirt. I sprinkled a lot of talcum powder over my hair, face, hands, legs and clothes to simulate dust and sand and to erase the colour. I rubbed charcoal under my eyes then rubbed them to achieve a bloodshot appearance. I put three holes in a T-shirt and soaked them with a mixture of cochineal and saffron to look like I'd been shot dead. The mirror was in position and the light level in the room was low. I laid, staring-eyed, on the bed in front of the mirror and made saliva foam and drip from my mouth as I stared in fascination at the shot body of me in the mirror. I stepped outside myself in detached imagination.

Night has fallen in a wild, desolate part of the desert where a shot-up German tank lies wrecked and abandoned. Nearby, there is a single, wooden cross sticking in the sand. An old Arab arrives with a donkey, takes a small spade and starts to dig in the shallow grave and soon mutters his approval when he reaches something underneath. He kneels and brushes away the sand with his hands, until he's uncovered a pair of booted feet. He secures the body around the ankles, pulls it out of the shallow hole and drags it along the soft sand, its arms stretched out over its head. He lets the legs flop on to the sand, lights a small lamp and places it near the body, muttering to himself all the time. He has dug up the body of a young, blonde-haired, German soldier clad in shorts, jacket and boots who looks like he's only been dead a few hours.

He pitches a small tent nearby and lays exotic blankets on the floor, then goes back to the boy's body and squats at the side of it. He slips his arms under the boy's shoulders and knees then lifts him up into his arms and stands there, admiring the boy for a few moments, as the head and arms dangle helplessly. He moves towards the tent and looks down at the boy's lower legs, swinging freely with the walking movement, and he feels his hand holding the soft thighs together. He enters the tent and lays his limp, young burden on to a blanket then straightens each bare leg in turn, laying them together again.

He pours out a small basin of water and places it by the boy's head. He lifts the head gently with his splayed hand cupped under the base of the skull and, with his other hand, wipes the face free of dust and blood. This done, the old man unbuttons the front of the tunic and pulls it down over the boy's, now bare, shoulders and he washes the neck and smooth, hairless chest, dabbing each nipple in turn. He changes his position and removes the boy's boots and seeks to expose his small, white feet.

The man grunts contentedly and rolls the youth on to his stomach. He washes the shoulders and back, down to the waistband of the shorts, then sits back and ponders the boy. He moves his trembling hands to the waistband and eases the shorts down, carefully, almost delicately, over the firm, pert, young buttocks, down to the feet and off. Now, the youthful boy lays under the man's eyes in a perfect state of helpless nudity.

The cheeks of the boy's bottom wobble as the old Arab wipes them clean and his cleansing caresses travel down to the thighs and the calves of the legs. This done, he pulls the unresisting, naked boy on to his back again where he lays mute and fully exposed. He softly washes the boy's vulnerable secrets with his old, gnarled hands as the young body lays naked and oblivious to the world around it.

The man stands up, never taking his eyes off the boy, and lets his own loose garments fall away. He slowly squats, crossed-legged, on the carpet and grasps hold of the boy's wrists and drags him towards himself. He forces himself upon the boy and makes love to him until, with a long sigh, he loosens his hold on the boy's back and legs and his naked form flops askew in limp rest. He pushes the boy off, who rolls on to the carpet like a rag doll.

As the old man ejaculates in the fantasy, I, as the bodily boy, would ejaculate, as I was held in his lusting arms. I was the old man, mentally acting upon my own body, which was imagined as the boy and, at my ejaculation, they became 'one'. It has to be noted that the old man was not responsible for initiating any violence but was the willing beneficiary of violent circumstances.

That particular fantasy ended with the old man wrapping the boy's naked body in a white sheet and laying him over the donkey's back before taking him into the dark alleys of the ancient city to find a rich buyer for the boy's body. It was, therefore, possible to begin the next 'episode' at that point. The boy's body was never allowed to show any effects of decomposition; he needed to be pure and extremely helpless, to the extent that he could not respond to the man at all. However, the boy would be fully aware of the appreciating power being exerted over him. In effect, I played three roles: the boy, the old man and a third-party observer of the two characters 'in action'. Afterwards, I'd return the room and myself to normal, freshen up and emerge to my comrades as if I'd been sleeping all afternoon.

• • •

In the January of 1968, I arrived back in England like an alien from another planet. It was cold and inhospitable as I stepped from the plane looking like a foreigner with my deep-bronzed tan and sun-bleached hair. I was posted to the 1st Argyll and Sutherland Highlanders at Seaton Barracks, a modern complex on the outskirts of Plymouth, Devon, where I found the easy-going drawl of the West Country people most amiable.

The Argylls were commanded by Lieutenant Colonel C C Mitchell (the infamous 'Mad Mitch' of Aden who had been the subject of much media hype around the time) and I was employed as NCO in charge of catering in the Officers' mess (again). I had my own room in the ordinary accommodation block and didn't live in the Officers' mess building itself and, because there were – to my annoyance – no locks on the doors, I didn't engage in any mirror fantasies there.

The only practical, lockable place was the bathroom, where my fantasies would enjoy a new (albeit limited) variation on the usual theme: old man on desert island fishes out body of young, drowned sailor and carries out the usual rituals, where I actually went as far as immersing myself in a filled bath, clad in my jeans and T-shirt. It was a sexually stimulating feeling, lying in wet clothes on the solid, tiled floor with the material hugging my skin (it was also a novel method of washing my jeans and T-shirt).

On TV, I watched good, acknowledged classic films, documentaries, news and current affairs programmes and comedies. At that time, I still rarely read books, though I thoroughly enjoyed *Puckoon* written by the comedy genius, Spike Milligan, an ex-soldier with whom I had much spiritual empathy; him being a loner, like me.

Throughout my life in Plymouth (as everywhere else) I was still 'living in a movie' and I embraced it to the extent that I was constantly aware of the imagined camera and lights around me. I even visualised how I might have looked on camera. This consummated lifestyle was fed and nourished by the real movies up there in full 70mm Panavision. The films I enjoyed at that time included Lindsay Anderson's *If*, about a trio of boys rising to rebellion in an English public school where a pretty, younger boy called Bobby Phillips joined the rebels and formed a homosexual/spiritual relationship with one of them. The film expressed how I felt at the time and it buzzed with more than just the usual homophobic innuendo. I also enjoyed John Schlesinger's film of the Thomas Hardy novel *Far from the Madding Crowd* and Fred Zinnemann's film of the Robert Bolt play on the life of Thomas More, *A Man for All Seasons*.

While I was living in another part of the building, away from the cooks, I encountered my only graphically sexual event at Plymouth. It didn't directly involve me at all, though I may have been an accessory to a crime for which, later, I felt guilty for my moral cowardice. I'd been watching TV alone in my room and I left to go to the toilet. Coming back, I was startled to hear a whispering sound coming from one of the four rooms. I entered the dimly lit room and was amazed to discover an upset, young girl sitting on a bed, whose blood-stained panties were pulled down. I could also see blood on the sheets. A soldier appeared from the shadows and said, 'Do you want some, Corporal? You can have her next.' I turned to him, frightened, and said, 'No, no, I want nothing to do with this. Get her out of here before we're all in the shit!' As I left to return to my room, someone else was carrying her – still whimpering – into another room and, for all I knew, the whole landing may have had her.

The next morning, I was able to rationalise my feelings of guilt by reasoning (probably correctly) that the girl had been 'smuggled' into barracks of her own free will. She may have been a young virgin who, after the drink had flowed, found that matters had wandered out of her control. As there was no official complaint of anything alleged by anyone against the soldiers, I thrust the matter from the front of my mind. Perhaps I was worried that the soldiers taking part in the incident would suspect my true nature, by not wanting to have sex with the girl with the rest of them, but I still believed I'd failed her.

. . .

The Argylls were nominated 'Spearhead Battalion' and we were on standby to be posted anywhere in the world at short notice. Suddenly, we were flown, by Hercules transporter, to Cyprus but the rut of the future yawned before me as we returned to England after having spent only a few short months there. Word had come from the Ministry of Defence that it was being proposed to abolish the Argylls as part of defence budget cuts. The regiment became involved with the 'Save the Argylls' campaign, which was a topical subject for media interest. I was part of a large company team, which drove from Plymouth to Helensburgh where we were part of an exercise up there in Dunbartonshire. I visited a submarine at the Faslane Base and we also gave filming facilities to the *This Week* current affairs TV programme who did a piece on the regiment.

Eventually, the regiment was posted to Berlin, which I supposed was to get it outside the immediately visible line of direct public controversy. So, by the side of the encroaching winter, we all departed on leave, pending our move to the divided ex-capital of Germany in the new year.

. . .

On the long rail journey from London back to Aberdeen, I was travelling with a pretty young private from the Argylls called Stewart*. He was slim, smooth, boyish and of slight build. As we were into the festive season, we spent the first part of the journey drinking in the buffet car. Just before it closed, we bought some cokes to go with the bottle of Remy Martin Cognac I had in my

* *Not his real name.*

suitcase in our seating compartment. Back there, we hit the nectar with a gusto only found in drunks and servicemen. In those days, it was nearly an eleven-hour overnight journey from Kings Cross to Aberdeen Station and, by the time the bottle was almost gone, Stewart had flaked out in his seat.

The lad suddenly retched and began to dribble green vomit down the front of his suit. It was an unsightly mess and others in the compartment made noises towards me for a solution. Stewart was practically unconscious by now so I stood him up and we staggered towards the toilet compartment in case he was sick again.

I had meant to wipe down his jacket to remove the vomit stain but, with him in a drunken state locked with me in the toilet, my mind raced into sexual overdrive and I realised that this desirable position would not occur often. Had I not waited for years, dreaming of this situation? I had to make sure that he was totally out of it so I half lifted him up and then let him fall against the wooden compartment. His head took the impact and he fell in a heap on the floor. I picked him up and sat him on the seat again where he swayed, slightly, to the motion of the speeding train and, carefully, I examined his head. I was satisfied that there were no visible cuts or injury and I pulled up one of his eyelids to check that he was truly unconscious (in case he was shamming). I stroked his pretty face with a slightly pouting mouth before kissing him fully on the lips, as I ran my fingers through his short, silken hair.

I removed his tie and undid the buttons on his white shirt and held my head to his bare belly, listening to the gurgling noises of digestion inside him. I unbuttoned the front of his trousers, pulled them down to his ankles and thrilled at the sight of his smooth, bare legs. I stood him up, close in my arms, and ran my hand down inside the back of his underpants to feel the round orbs of his buttocks. He felt warm and good and I liked the smell of him. I laid him back on the seat and began fondling his bare thighs, belly and privates. My penis was in full erection all this time and I would have put it into effect if it hadn't been for the persistent knocking on the door by passengers wanting to relieve themselves in the toilet.

Fear took over and I hurriedly dressed him and washed the stain off his jacket. I put him back in his seat, in our dimmed compartment, and both of us slept soundly until we awoke just before arrival.

At Aberdeen, he knew he'd flaked out but believed that he'd slept there in his seat all night, though I told him that I'd tried to wipe the front of his suit before going to sleep myself. He complained of a throbbing headache but put it down to a hangover (and not a fall). We parted at Aberdeen and I took a bus to Strichen as I watched the bleak, grey landscape and the faces of the drab people on the bus. For weeks afterwards, I daydreamed about the contours of Stewart's young, naked body and would masturbate at the memory of it; so warm and so available.

Back home, my sister, Sylvia, had already married the eldest son of one of the local dairy farmers when she had been sixteen and Ian McKenzie, twenty-three. Soon after, they had emigrated to Canada and started a family. My half-brother, Olav, had married a Geordie lass, with whom I had no rapport, and I had only slight, incidental contact with them.

• • •

Back at camp in the new year of 1969 after my leave, I avoided contact with Stewart due to the shame at my impositions on his body without his consent. Fear and frustration had come down to virtual rape and I hated myself for this desperate scenario.

The regiment became ensconced in Montgomery Barracks in Kladow, West Berlin, and I remained in the Officers' mess; in fact, I even lived there. I had a civilian chef to assist me called Ernst Krutch (pronounced 'crouch') who was good natured and wholly reliable, though sometimes temperamental (as most chefs are). The civilian catering assistant, who washed the dishes and cleaned up, was Frau Kopp. She had been a teenage girl when Berlin had fallen in 1945 and had also been subjected to multiple rapes by advancing Russian soldiers, an experience which had unhinged her mind. She was a nervous, kind woman and I felt both outraged and saddened at her past predicament.

I enjoyed the experience of being in Berlin and returned to the boozy, wild, night life with gay abandon. One night out with the lads, I was so drunk that I ended up in a seedy room with a prostitute whom I screwed – or, more precisely, she screwed me. She was obviously an experienced woman and, as I lay on the bed in my usual, half-dazed condition, she pulled my clothes off and, with practised hands and body, she fucked herself with my penis standing at rigid attention on my passive body. Apart from the wonderful shock of ejaculation, there was nothing in that set-up for me.

By this time, I'd purchased a movie camera and had begun filming everything that moved. I remember being tear-gassed and sprayed from a water cannon while off-duty, filming an anti-Vietnam War student demonstration, in downtown Berlin. I was against American involvement in Vietnam and the Argylls had to take their turn in guarding Rudolf Hess in Spandau Prison. I asked if I could go and film him tending to his garden, though the powers that be dismissed my idea as if I was a madman.

In early 1970, I was sent to cater for the Argylls' ski farm in Bavaria at a village called Bodenmais, ten kilometres from the Czech border village of Bayer Eisenstein, where I also learned to ski. The locals liked me and it disturbed my sense of morality that there was still a very strong pro-Nazi feeling in that part of the country (while at Osnabrück, we had been sent to visit the site of Belsen concentration camp). I went to a local dance, one night, dressed perfectly in Bavarian national costume, and felt good in lederhosen (short leather pants) and I even got snogging with a beautiful young girl who reminded me of Natalie Wood. Her family's own chaperones, however, angrily separated us as it may have been felt that, as a soldier, I had only one thing in mind.

My real passion was for a young Argyll on the course named Ronnie Mann. The eighteen-year-old had a pretty, peach complexion, smooth skin and just enough puppy fat to make him (to me) cuddly and lovable and he reminded me of that first boy I felt attracted to in Fraserburgh. I loved being in his company and I made him smile a lot with my jokes and anecdotes. I enjoyed seeing him happy and he looked more beautiful than ever through the rosy glow of the drink and the lights while we were out. At closing time, one night, we decided to walk back to the ski farm at Kottinghammer but Ronnie was very unsteady on his feet and, after a few hundred yards in drifting and deep snow, he could hardly stand. He wasn't going to make it without help. I took his arm securely around my shoulder and, with my other arm around his waist, we trudged resolutely through the snow. Just holding him was exciting enough by itself and I thrilled to feel his body close to mine. I was disappointed when the journey was over and, at the farm, I just plonked him down on his bunk, unmolested, as there were no private areas at all in our crowded accommodation.

After an ancillary visit to Munich, the Bavarian ski exercise finally folded and I returned to Berlin. By this time, my hobby of film-making was well advanced and I toured all the historic sites in the city making the appropriate record in Eastman Color.

As the summer of 1970 approached, I was issued papers for my attendance at a twelve-week intermediate management course at the college at Aldershot, and I was off.

• • •

When I arrived, I was surprised by all the changes, which had been implemented in the six short years since I'd left. They had built a new training school and new soldier accommodation for the boy soldiers, though we, on the course, were to be lodged in the old, red brick, Victorian barracks up near North camp. Each cold, draughty barrack room still had an old, iron, coal stove at its centre with little having changed from the nineteenth century; the whole complex reeked of decay from a bygone age. I took a walk into my past by wandering around the old, wooden barracks where I'd spent three years training as a boy. They were now all uninhabited and, I presumed, were awaiting demolition. The shadows of youthful ghosts pervaded my senses; the laughing, smiling, clean-limbed boys of yesterday. There was a sadness of an appreciation of life moving slowly on towards death; an endless whisper, softly in one's ear, from the Common Prayer Book, 'In the midst of life, we are in death.'

I enjoyed the management course and did well on it but its ending coincided with the regiment's move out of Berlin to Fort George, just outside Inverness. So, I returned to Scotland with my sergeant's course under my belt.

· · ·

Bleak, cold, grey Fort George was a complete change of scene from bright, bustling, crowded Berlin. It had been built as part of the government's policy to police and subdue the Highland clans and their culture after the final defeat of the Jacobite rebellion at Culloden in April 1746. After the battle, the British soldiers had gone on a tirade of rape, murder and mutilation upon survivors of the battle itself as well as any likely civilian who came within the auspices of their lust or rage. I felt a bit uneasy being lodged in this citadel of British imperial power and its murderous redcoats and I never really settled in at Fort George. It was like living inside a depressing museum.

Then the news came in that the Argylls were to provide the annual Royal guard for the Queen's summer stay at Balmoral Castle. The guard commander was nominated as Major 'Paddy' Palmer and I was nominated to be in charge of the guard's other ranks' kitchen at the local (Victoria) barracks at Ballater, a few miles from the castle. We had to attend highland dancing classes because, near the end of her holiday, the Queen held a gillies ball (sounds painful) at the castle, to which all ranks of the guard were invited (I was excused the classes because I'd learned it all at school). Doing my bit on the Royal guard was interesting and out of the ordinary. I'd seen the Queen only once before at close quarters; at the Aldershot garrison church centenary, in the early sixties, when she had passed me to take her seat for the service in the church. This time, I was to march past the monarch who 'took the salute' afterwards.

My colour movie camera worked overtime as I filmed the royals and the Braemar Highland Games. Apart from a few ceremonial duties, the main function of the guard seemed to be to act as beaters for the numerous grouse shoots, which pleasured the royals and their guests. On shoot days, I shipped the grouse-beaters' lunch out to the moors. It ranged from stew to individually wrapped fish and chips, all sent out in insulated boxes known to the squaddies as 'hay boxes'.

Over the Christmas period of leave, which I painfully spent in Strichen with my family of aliens, news arrived that there was to be a policy compromise on the proposed disbandment of the Argylls. The regiment would stay but would be reduced to company strength. So, most of us were surplus to requirement and we awaited our new postings.

• • •

I left the port of Aberdeen in the late January of 1971 on the steamer, *St Ninian*, for the overnight voyage to Lerwick, Shetland Islands. It butted, uncertainly, out into a great winter storm of cruel winds and high seas. In my pit, in the great iron belly, I was rhythmically heaved from the fifth floor of motion to the basement, in one, long vomiting cycle, meaning my supper of scrambled eggs and baked beans didn't stay down for long. I spent the best part of a sleepless night exhausted and sick as a dog and the vista was no better on deck as we pitched and smashed into gigantic, forty-foot walls of grey, angry water. There were crates of sheep and poultry on deck and the poor critters looked terrified, so I fortified myself with the notion that if they could take it, then so could I. Thus, I was steered into hope and fortitude and the ship docked at Lerwick in the grey, misty light of morning.

When I arrived in that desolate quasi-Scotland, the Up Helly Aa festival was in full swing (where the islanders celebrated their Viking ancestry). In many ways, I fitted like a glove into that bleak, colourless and treeless landscape of solitude with its long, dark winters and long, light summers. The locals were very trusting and friendly but, I suspected, too set in their old ways. With my suitcases, I piled into a Royal Signals Land Rover and set off south for the sixteen-mile journey to the southernmost tip of the mainland at Sumburgh.

There was a golf course, a hotel and a lighthouse, designed by Robert Stevenson in the nineteenth century, and a scattering of dwellings with the small army complex of accommodation for about twenty people situated at the fringe. Oddly, it had no external markings to identify it as a military site. Each day, the Signals shift would travel from Maybury up to the station at Mossy Hill with its conglomeration of radio telescopes.

Social activities were centred in the Maybury Club where the bar and lounge were attached to the living and dining accommodation by a corridor. On our occasional excursions to the 'big city', we imbibed at the Commercial Hotel or Thule Bar in Lerwick while, up the hill, was Boddam Town Hall, where there were periodic dances accompanied by piano, squeeze box and fiddle. Rock 'n' roll, it seemed, had passed them by.

Movies were sent up from the Services Kinema Corporation, so we enjoyed a range of films from the latest blockbusters to a catalogue of stalwart classics. Sergeant Gerry Wilmot was the trained projectionist at Maybury who showed me how to use the equipment in the projection box and I stood in for him more and more, especially when he began courting a local girl. In 1972, when I'd been the working projectionist for several months, the army discovered that I'd never actually taken an official projectionist course, so it was decided that I'd have to attend one at the Services Kinema Corporation training school at Beaconsfield to get the certificate.

As the projectionist up there, I exhibited many films. There were three particular movies that remained in my mind, while a fourth became permanently etched upon it. *Oh! What a Lovely War* was a musical, anti-war indictment of the wasting destruction in the trenches in World War I. It had the ability to make me cry; I was probably weeping for the loss of all those millions of beautiful young men. Another was the musical version of *Goodbye, Mr. Chips* with Peter O'Toole as the ageing 'drudge' of the title. I was extremely touched by his love for all his generations of boys. He was like a lost father of the kind I might have imagined or hoped for. Sam Peckinpah's *The Wild Bunch* lingered like a brooding depression in my eye and in my mind. The 'ballet of death' sequences were filmed and edited in such a way as to make the blood, pain and violence of death, itself, look beautifully artistic. It presented a totally pessimistic view of humanity and it ground its action, inconsolably, on to a vision of a kind of mass mutual suicide for humanity. It was a depressing fantasy on a theme in dark, endless dirges – like much of my life – and I found its power exciting in its passive aggression.

In the fourth film, however, the old explosion of sexual excitement came like a thief in the night, from an unexpected quarter. My brain was hit, straight from the screen, in the middle of the ordinary John Wayne movie, *True Grit*. To me, a relatively short scene struck me like pure pornography and invited the opening scene of my recurring fantasies. It occurred when the Marshal, Rooster Cogburn (John

Wayne), was bringing his load of shot outlaws into the settlement. The boss wanted to see who they were and there followed a lifting of the heads of the bodies, draped over the back of their horses. Nearest to the camera was the body of a teenage boy and the sight of his limp, top half being lifted by the hair and then released to flop back down again sent me into inner spasms of sexual frisson. It was the fantasy of the old man and the boy again, brought to life in living technicolour, as surely as if it had happened before my eyes in real life.

In its high-performance imagery, it stimulated the 'what happened next?' question in me. And in tune with the theme, I was able to talk my mind into taking me where the movie had left off. My fantasy followed the predictable ritual of stripping the boy and washing his naked body. I was the man, the boy and the observer of the ritual and it was a bittersweet conundrum of estrangement from the complexities of real, human relationships.

I spent a great deal of my free time filming wildlife in the seascape wilderness on the south end of the island mainland. I loved my long walks out, especially in the summer, where the high, northern extremity saw twilight fade and dawn break in a short space of darkness. In summer, it was milder than one would imagine. I would spend hours setting up the filming of puffins that made their nests in burrows in the side of the high Sumburgh cliffs or Atlantic grey seals with their pups. One of my favourite walking destinations was the great cliff overhang of Fitful Head near the western end.

On one trip, I found a young herring gull, which had fallen from its nest. It was no chick – having a four-foot wingspan – but I took it back to Maybury and built a small enclosure for it outside my window. I did my best to emulate its parents, regarding feeding, and fetched some Birds Eye fish fingers from the deep freeze and washed off the breadcrumbs. I then chewed the raw fish in my mouth until it was soft and pulpy, repeating the process until there was a slimy mass in a small bowl. I prised open its beak and prodded the pulpy mess down its throat and it worked! Soon, it would open its beak in expectation of food and, in no time, it was following me around like a duck. Later, it was making short, hesitant flights, each becoming more distant than the last, until that call of the wild saw it linger on the roof for a few minutes before it departed for good.

• • •

In the hazy mist of closing time, one night at the Maybury Club, I found myself accepting an invitation for some more drink at the home of a Department of the Environment employee called Frankie*.

He was near middle aged and was a quiet, well-mannered and solitary individual and a regular drinking visitor to the club. We stumbled off into the darkness and arrived at his antiquated, small house where he lived alone. The interior was dimly lit and the whole place had a shabby appearance; it might well have belonged to some Victorian granny. Frankie produced a black bottle from somewhere and the whole atmosphere made me feel uneasy. He watched me drink but said little as I'd run out of things to say in his uninviting precinct. As I made to leave, I suddenly felt dizzy; my co-ordination started to give. I could hear his voice droning slowly in the background and, though I attempted to walk to the door, my legs gave out and I found myself on the floor – on my back – as the room around and above me geared into slow motion. I couldn't move and stared up as his face loomed over me. Even his speech had slowed down. 'Des, time for beddy-byes…'

I'd woken up the next morning, naked in bed, with him naked too, and I dressed like an express train before dashing home. The bugger even had the cheek to mumble, 'Des, come back to bed.' Once back at Maybury, I pieced the evidence together and drew my own conclusions. I felt sore in several places; there were bruises and bite marks on the back of my neck and near my nipples. Grease and gunge were in my

* *Not his real name.*

underpants and there were marks on my buttocks where he may have bitten them or strapped them with a belt. My penis was swollen and very painful. So, it appeared that I'd been raped and abused. It was not an experience that any man could share with others due to sheer shame and embarrassment. In any case, people would always be bound to say that there was no smoke without fire, implying a degree of consent. Thereafter, I avoided Frankie and he kept well clear of me. Had he done this before or was I his first time? I would never have suspected him of such a thing because he seemed so quiet and docile.

I had a dislike of being sexually used without my consent or knowledge but, thereafter, I would relive the encounter, embellished in my imagination. The Aden dreams reoccurred in truncated form:

Frankie is undressing me on his floor while mumbling to my unconscious body. 'Des, I've had my eye on you for weeks. I didn't tell you that I have a taste for slim, smooth, young men. I couldn't ask because that's just not done up here. They wouldn't understand; you wouldn't understand. So, now you're fast asleep, where's the harm in that? What you don't know, you don't care about,' slapping my unconscious face with a sharp 'thwack'.

He lifts my nodding form upright into his arms, drags me across the room and drapes me, face down, over the back of the old settee. He pulls my pants down to my ankles and lashes my buttocks with his belt before raping me. The pain wakes me up.

Part nightmare, part sexual fantasy, I was now locked into a life with 'silent partners'. I'd always aspired to engage with the real thing but, in my circumstances, the real thing seemed extremely risky, if not impossible. And so my predicament might have returned to slumber within the dull military routine, if it were not for the next defining, traumatic event.

I was eating a meal in the other ranks' dining room when the Land Rover returned from Lerwick. From it, walked Private Jamie

Foster* into my life and I was captured. It was love at first sight. He was about eighteen years old (eight years my junior) and hailed from Wales. He'd been posted to my kitchen and, in the realm of working together, we came to know each other quite well. We drank together and I trained him on the projection equipment. We went on long walks over the dunes and Quendale Bay up to Fitful Head and my life was now full of pleasure and developing expectation.

I had a stills camera and it was he who took that published photo of me with one of my movie cameras, on a tripod by the wall, in Maybury. So that I could capture the beauty of his moving image, I often filmed him in slow motion, running and jumping. I filmed him climbing and in the full range of usual situations. In one, he feigned being shot and as he fell, I tracked the camera to where he lay 'asleep'. I lingered the shot on him for a full five seconds and was excited by the passive image of him. Later, when he wasn't around, I would watch the footage of him and go to the bathroom to masturbate. I never imagined Jamie Foster dead, as had been later suggested. The whole idea of losing him horrified me. Everything alive about him stimulated my libido.

I was desperate to prove myself to him in a balance of physical and intellectual potency and I wondered if he'd suspected that I was trying to seduce him by stealth. One hot afternoon, we went for a run from one end of Quendale Bay to the other and back. I arrived at the finish line and stood confidently, legs and arms akimbo, awaiting his arrival. He staggered over the line, weak-legged and completely exhausted and fell in a heap on the sand, cramped and spent and I dropped down beside him for common cause. I eased the cramp in his legs with my massaging hand and thrilled at the intimate touch; the contact; the closeness of him; his smell; the whole presence and vision of him. I 'accidentally' brushed my fingertips against the inside of his thighs, though he responded by turning over, whence I

* *Not his real name.*

massaged the muscles on the back of his legs, stopping just short of the inviting swell of his buttocks.

It was an altogether new phase in my life; one of extreme attachment to a real person, and I was powerless against the drive to be 'one' with him. It was a challenge to my world of fantasy and the simulated relationships with unreal situations that I'd created in my mind. It was, in fact, a last grasp to be part of the world of real people and positive interactions. I needed to express to him how I felt and I hoped for some measure of reciprocation. It was something which I'd have to play carefully and assume a gradualist approach while waiting for a suitable opportunity. In the meantime, I would let matters drift at normal sea level.

When he was on early breakfast duty, I would ask him to wake me up in the morning. In reality, I'd wake before he came in and arrange myself in a prone position – naked – under a white sheet seductively draped over parts of my body as though it had become thus disarranged by the natural tossing and turning in my sleep. I'd hear the door quietly open and I would hear him pause for a moment, presumably looking at me, before putting his hand on my bare shoulder to wake me up. It wasn't Last Tango in Paris, but it was better than nothing at all.

One night after the bar had closed, I found Jamie sitting by himself in an armchair in the TV room, looking most forlorn. I sat down beside him and we talked about him and his feelings. Then he began to weep and seemed to be in a great emotional state; calm but weeping. I told him that I knew how he felt and that I had often felt the same. Then suddenly, sitting side-by-side, I took his hand and our fingers became entwined in a finger-by-finger clasp in which he reciprocated. It was the sort of union which time itself could not have dissolved. I was besotted with him but we were both trapped inside our own personal restraints: rank, class, sexual orientation, tradition, the law, religion, culture, peer group pressure, professionalism, distance and routines.

I stood him up and put my arms around him and we held each other close for a few, long moments. Then I steered him from the deserted TV room and down the silent corridor towards the living quarters. As we were coming to the laundry store, I suddenly said to him, even taking myself by surprise, 'We can go into the laundry store, as I've got the only key. We won't be disturbed.' But he replied, 'No, I don't know what's happening.' He pulled himself away and darted out of the outside door into the black night. 'God!' I thought. 'You've really done it this time. You've lost him for good.'

I returned to my empty room to reflect and have a smoke then decided to go to Jamie's room to see if he was all right and, perhaps, to apologise but he wasn't there. I became worried and walked out to search for him. Far into the long grass, I saw him lying there. I approached cautiously and knelt beside him. His tear-stained eyes looked up at me in humble resignation and I brushed my hand down his cheeks to wipe away the tears. 'I've got to get you inside. You can't stay out here all night,' I intoned and, without more ado, I put my arms under his knees and back and lifted him straight into my arms where he nestled, quite contentedly, still awake. My penis was as hard as it could get, as I carried him towards the door.

The whole fucking establishment built seemingly insurmountable defences against homosexuals in the forces. All the service and contributions I had given would count for nothing against the damnation on my queerness. How was a man expected to live his whole life encased in the greatest lie; a flat denial of who and what he was, right out of nature? Imagine the hell involved in a life where one could never embrace someone of the same sex and say the simple, but profound, words, 'I love you.'

In the morning, there began a drifting apart of me and Jamie Foster, which continued until the relationship exploded before my departure from the islands. A fat, closet queen sergeant from Signals arrived and began to 'chase' Jamie. He had a big car and started taking Jamie into town, shopping. I paced the site – mad with jealousy – when they drove off for the day together. I even lost my appetite for food and was not that pleasant after I'd drunk too much. The sergeant didn't want to be seen with the kid in our bar and, after one particular dinner and dance, I confronted him outside the hotel and told him that he wanted only the one thing from Jamie Foster. Obviously, Jamie had told him about me because he intoned that it was for Jamie to choose who he should go with and not me.

Never before in my life had I felt so cut off from everybody. I even climbed to the overhang at Fitful Head and sat, reasonably deliberating whether or not I should throw myself off in order to end the humming pain inside me. After duty one day, I directly challenged Jamie to come out and fight me and we squared up, out there on that barren, windy hill. I had no intention of raising a finger against him but wanted him to see that I was hurt and angry. After I had taunted him, verbally, some more, he came at me with fists flying but I didn't even try to punch him. I just grappled with him to stop the wild, flailing blows. He wrestled me to the ground and got on top of me but I acquiesced and it burned a rage in him.

With blazing eyes and no words, he put both his hands around my neck. I stared mutely up at his wild expression and saw the red fever in his eyes as his grip tightened. I couldn't breathe and my whole body began to struggle, involuntarily, which seemed to excite the strength of his hold on my throat. He held on and on and I could feel the fearful desperation of having no air. I was suffocating and my whole, conscious existence strained against the great outré. Suddenly, he let go and I lay gasping for air before he got up, still saying nothing, and strode off down the hill. It was all over: finished.

It wasn't the only thing that was done. I had already decided that I'd let my current term in the army expire without enlisting for a further three years. I wanted a better life for myself and could see no workable future as a homosexual in the British Army. I had outgrown living out of a military kit bag and moving around like a gypsy. I was also ashamed by the conduct of the army in the Bloody Sunday massacre where, earlier that year, the Parachute Regiment (from Aldershot) had murdered thirteen civilians in the town of Derry in Northern Ireland. At twenty-seven years old, I felt that I was still young enough to find a new life and direction in the outside world.

One of my last acts on the Shetlands was to get drunk and burn the reels of film I'd made since 1969. I couldn't bring myself to burn the images of Jamie Foster, whom I still loved, but was resigned to never seeing again. The day I left, I gave him my sound film projector and a thirty-minute reel of film containing all the footage of him. That lesson in unaccustomed humility took him by surprise and left him speechless. I didn't say goodbye to him before I left for the plane, and he never approached me.

I flew out of Sumburgh Airport in a Vickers Viscount turbo prop, headed for Dyce Airport outside Aberdeen. I had to report to Edinburgh to be officially released and so, after eleven years and eighty-four days, I walked, calmly, out of the camp gate.

That self-supporting career, with its accommodation and meals provided, had enabled me to escape from my fixed, social position in the North East of Scotland. It had rejuvenated my educational opportunities to the extent of five O level equivalents and numerous trade qualifications. I doubted very much that I would have ever had the opportunity to travel as widely, learn to ski, rock climb, sail, ride or learn orienteering skills, nor to meet so many different people from different classes, ethnic origins and religions, if I'd remained in the North East.

On the minus side, I guessed that nothing much had really changed in my level of total happiness because I took all my problems with me in my head. I had exchanged the homophobia of civilian life for an emotional climate much more severe. No person in the forces was able to effectively develop any kind of healthy, emotional life if he or she were gay. There was a total absence of any kind of emotional or social counselling in the armed forces where big boys were not expected to show feelings or cry. It encouraged emotional detachment and there was always the danger, with the passage of time, that that detachment would become ingrained in those subjected to it. The army was an institution every bit as damaging to those subjected to it as a children's home or prison. I had spent my youth and young manhood socially isolated in the dependency cocoon of service life. There were few social links with the community or the real world of society and its performances. Individuality was discouraged, while uniformity was demanded as a base essential, and all the structured, social occasions were centred around drinking.

I left the army an emotional cripple as a continuation of my boyhood. My time in the forces had not healed that festering wound inside my inner, psychological recess, which continued to fester away, burying itself deeper. I was cast out into society, about to enter – as a novice – the co-habitational sociability of the outside world.

The catering sergeant, Paten, his wife and small daughter, all of whom I always got on well with, saw me off at the airport. In those last days before leaving, I had been immersed in the bottle and the Moody Blues album, *To Our Children's Children's Children*, all of which acted as an expression of my emotional condition and, as the Vickers Viscount banked over Quendale Bay and past Fitful Head, I could hear one track playing over and over in my head. Not only was my life about to change but the lives of the islanders would soon change too as the Shetlands stood poised on the threshold of the great North Sea oil bonanza. Life for all of us would never be the same again. As we reached for the outward clouds on the flight south, I could hear the words from the Moody

Blues' 'Question' ringing in my ears as the past slipped further and further behind:

'I'm looking for someone to change my life. I'm looking for a miracle in my life.'

3

Civilian life | 1972

I moped about in Strichen and Fraserburgh with a past somewhere else and no future in the North East of Scotland. I walked into the Station Hotel for a drink and saw some of the country boys whom I remembered from school. They were men who had long-since met their limits and, as I recalled from the classroom, their limits were not very wide, even then. I suppose they'd found their own level of happiness, fully integrated as components, knowing their place in rural community life and they played dominoes and supped their pints of ale with the mutual, common security of farming talk.

At 47 Academy Road, Fraserburgh, a distant cousin, Dave Smith from Detroit, Michigan in the USA, was living in the spare room, as there was only my grandmother left in the house. He'd come over to work in the North Sea oil business on one of the rigs and I got on well with him. My sister, Sylvia, and her husband, Ian, had also arrived on a visit from Canada and I was pleased to see that I had two, little, fair-haired nieces and I was now an uncle; it was odd listening to them chattering away in that Canadian accent.

I was still angry with my half-brother, Olav because, on a previous leave, he'd sought to humiliate me in front of his friends. On that occasion, he'd invited me around to his temporary house off Broad Street with his wife and another couple of like-minded proles. A movie called *Victim* was showing on TV and it was the first Irish film to portray some of the difficulties facing homosexuals in a homophobic society, highlighting the criminalising effects of the law and of how gays were being blackmailed. Olav sneered and jibed at the 'poofs' and 'queers' all the way through the film in a mixture of loathing and ridicule. He, and he alone, knew that I was gay and he used the power of this knowledge to devasting effect. Behind it all was, perhaps, the guilt in remembering that it was my fondling of him when we were teenagers that had stimulated his first erections.

Two weeks in Strichen was long enough for me. I'd sampled the wider world and the North East of Scotland offered few, real opportunities and too many restrictions for someone of my sensibilities, as a gay man, so I decided to try my luck in London.

Before I left, I spent a few days revisiting my old haunts as a child. I climbed Mormond Hill to the old ruin of the seventeenth-century Hunter's Lodge where, on the grass, Michael Laird had pinned me down and fondled me between the legs. I looked out west on that crystal-clear day and could see the great ragged peaks of the Grampian mountain range, which brooded for ever over the land of Macbeth and the Highland legends. I took the hill road to the old Strichen cemetery and looked down to the river at the spot where we'd found old Mr Ironside. It was the same all through my mind; trying to remember the past and contemplate the full, fatal horror of the passage of time.

I entered the well-kept lawn of the cemetery and found the grave of Brian 'Braddy' Strachan who had been killed in a motorcycle accident when he was eighteen. Coincidentally, when I was eighteen, I had also been in a motorcycle accident in Aberdeen while on leave. My head and shoulders had dented the right front door and smashed the window of the car I'd hit. I was concussed, but nothing else, and I contemplated that it could have been me lying in that grave.

I remembered Braddy laughing and smiling at school. I

remembered us all, stripped and bronzed-skinned, jumping, exuberantly, into the wide bathing shallows of the river, a mile out of town. Braddy and his brother, Patrick, had fixed up an old car and we would all pile on board while it spluttered and banged its way through Strichen Wood. It was really only a chassis with an engine and a seat for the driver. Ten years after his tragic death, I wondered how much 'bodywork' was left on Braddy as he lay contentedly in his terminal cot in the ground.

We never really live except in brief, momentary flashes and we never really die so long as a human is alive somewhere. Was it possible to love and fear the idea of man's mortality? I didn't want to die and yet I didn't want to live for ever. I didn't believe in an afterlife but still, I didn't want my conscious existence to end with an old box full of putrefying slime. All my life, I'd been searching for an answer to the questions, 'Where had grandad gone?' and 'Where was I going?'

• • •

In London, I stayed at the Chevrons Club in Dorset Square and got myself an interview at the Metropolitan Police recruitment centre at Paddington Green Police Station. I was called in for the medical examination but was exempt from the educational exam because of my education certificates from the army. I figured that the Metropolitan Police was the best, and most logical, transitory step from the army as I was fearful of making the switch to civilian life in one, cutting stroke. It had been suggested to me that I might consider working as a prison officer but I ruled that out for a number of reasons, one of them being that I had no urge to order people around. As a policeman, I thought (in my naivety) I would be serving the people and the law and, prior to joining, I had a high opinion and expectation of British police standards.

The Hendon Police College was in a state of flux; twixt

locations in a new building project. We trained at the old school but lived in the new accommodation tower blocks. I was in A block. My colleagues on the course were mainly young and well-meaning people who drank up the theory of policing 'by the book', though we were to be sorely disabused on finding the reality on the front line, especially in an inner-city patch.

We all attended New Scotland Yard in Victoria for a mass swearing in and our warrant cards were issued. Robert Mark was the commissioner, with a special mission to stamp out corruption in the Metropolitan Police. He toyed and tinkered, and a few token arrests followed, but the mess within the Met proliferated, relatively unchecked. For bent coppers, it was business as usual.

The classroom work was intense in the sense that there was so much legal detail to memorise and years of running kitchens had detached me from addressing legal concepts. The positive thing, which came from the training, was that it increased my skills in thinking on my feet and taking decisions concerning complex, human situations and interactions. Knowledge gave me the confidence to appear in public – and in court – and make articulate, reasoned arguments on a focused train of logical thought.

The centre of my sexual attentions at police college was in sporting activities. After our sessions of physical training, I experienced – for the first time in my life – the joys of the communal showers afterwards. What had I been missing all these years? My heart leapt as I stood, soaping myself, inches away from all those wet, beautiful, young, male bodies glistening in the hot, steamy atmosphere. Buttocks, thighs, bellies and penises of all shapes and sizes crowded, delightfully, in on my own nakedness. It was the arena of quick, furtive glances in an air of studied nonchalance and I did my best to 'pose', without seeming to pose, in the hope that one of them would find my body sexually stimulating.

By the end of the course, I was engaged in basic lifesaving and, as luck would have it, I was given a nice, young man to rescue. The whole operation had me buzzing with extenuating excitement. Getting him out of the water and on to the tiled floor, then giving him artificial respiration, sparked, within me, a throbbing tension you can well imagine. I thrilled at the power and control that I had to lavish my strong, but gentle, attentions on this beautifully passive young man. I now fully accepted the fact that the main inheritance of my life was an ingrained sexual perversion, which thrived on passive male bodies. It was, of course, secret but I felt that I could keep it in check.

The training term broke up for Christmas in 1972 and I found myself in Strichen for the very last time. There, I found a letter and photo from Jamie Foster saying that he had just married a local girl in the Shetlands. That was the last contact he ever had with me. Such a rushed, desperate affair, I thought, though he would not be the first – nor the last – man who saw heterosexual marriage as a cure for feelings of homosexuality.

Back at training in the new year, a few of us, forsaking our 'homework', took a visit to Soho, the red-light district in the West End of London. We were spectators, not participants, but when one of our party showed his police warrant card at the door of a strip club, the doorman let us all in free of charge. It was the first intimation I had of the corrupt relationship that existed between those of the criminal subculture and officers of the Metropolitan Police.

One weekend, I was out with another trainee called Toner, doing a bit of sightseeing around Haymarket. He hailed from Liverpool and had acquired the affectionate nickname, 'Scouse'. As we walked, I noticed the man behind us was wearing a dark, Dracula-like cape. We turned into a side street and there he was again, behind us at a discreet distance. 'I think he's following us,' observed Scouse. We took the next available turning and, sure enough, he was still there. I said, 'Look, after the next turning, get in a shop doorway and see what he does.' We did just that and he passed us by so close that

I recognised him immediately as he marched, boldly on, down the street, while we doubled-back on our route. The man held himself in such a regal manner with his dark cloak and hat that it was as if he owned the street. I said to Scouse, 'That's Sir John Gielgud, the great Shakespearean actor.' Toner was an ex-Guardsman and I could pass for a tall Guardsman. And as Guardsmen were notorious for 'entertaining' classy gentlemen of a homosexual disposition, I wondered if Gielgud was generating a bit of danger and excitement in casing what he thought were two young Guardsmen, on the game, for suitable patronage. He certainly had a long-established reputation for being a bit of an old queen. As a parting shot, I said to Toner, 'I haven't seen his Coriolanus or any other part of his anatomy!'

I'd heard, from police training, that gay people would hang around in the Earl's Court district of London. The instructor had said, 'You can spot a queer a mile off; they all wear white, polo-necked sweaters, red corduroy trousers, Hush Puppy shoes and usually go out taking a white, French poodle for a walk.' The following weekend, I took the Tube train to Earl's Court and, after checking the high street for any 'interesting' pubs, I ventured into the Coleherne.

In one bar, there were lots of men of all ages in leather trousers, jackets and caps. I transferred myself to the crowded, larger bar and I knew, instantly, that it was a gay bar because everyone blatantly looked me up and down. To ease my unaccustomed paranoia, I began to down pint after pint and I watched everyone out of the corners of my eyes, not wishing to stare.

The first time in such a bar was a bit unsettling and I didn't know what to expect or what to do; I wasn't familiar with the special language of the thriving gay subculture. What I did understand was body language and I found myself chatting to a slim, young man who was eyeing me up. To this day, I can't remember a word he or I said because I was so high on the excitement of this unique occasion and all that was going on in the bar.

At closing time, he asked me to go back with him to his place. We ended up entering a house a couple of Tube stations down from Earl's Court and he told me not to make a noise as we tip-toed into a side room. I sat on the single bed and prepared myself for fulfilment while he had momentarily slipped off into another room. Suddenly, I could hear loud voices arguing and I went to investigate. To my utter surprise and embarrassment, I found him with a young woman and a baby in a cot: his wife and child! Obviously, she had taken great exception to me being there and it seemed as if this sort of incident had happened before. I apologised to her and told them both that I should go. He argued with her that if she threw me out, then she'd have to throw him out as well. 'Come on,' he said, and we both left.

It was around midnight and I wanted him like I wanted nothing else. I hailed a passing taxi and off we drove to my digs in Hendon where I took him up the fire escape stairway to avoid the caretaker's glass-fronted office (it would have been obvious to anyone that he was no policeman – with his long hair). After the long day, the drink, the various journeys and climbing the seemingly endless flights of stairs, we were both exhausted. We stripped naked and, as we fell into bed in each other's arms, a wave of peace and comfort swept over me as I felt his warm, young nakedness against my skin. He snuggled closer to me and we both fell fast asleep.

I must have awakened less than five hours later, like a child who couldn't sleep on Christmas Eve, knowing that he would soon get his presents. I lay there appreciating him sleeping in my arms in that small bed. It felt good to run my hand over his whole, soft beauty and down to the natural gem of his buttocks. I slipped my hand down and held his penis that had helped to create that small child and I wondered on the mysteries of life and all the problems people get into. I thought about that letter and the photo from Jamie Foster; in his desperate hope, did he need the scourge of his homosexual feelings to be wiped away by marriage to a woman? I was lying in bed with a similar young man who was living a great lie, with all the attending miseries and problems that thwart all our good intentions. I could see that he needed to get away from his situation for a few hours and I was happy to have someone warm to cling to in the barren desert of that heartless, British police academy. We had no sex and we didn't say a lot that morning; there was no need to. Later, I saw him off in a taxi and our paths never crossed again. That night, I returned to my lonely and empty bed.

• • •

Having successfully completed my exams in the spring of 1973, I was posted to Willesden Green Police Station in Q division, based at Wembley. It was like being smashed into a hard, stone wall. The general advice was, 'Forget all that shit they taught you at training school, here's how we do things now!'

It was then the custom to attach a new officer to the guiding hand of an experienced PC and my 'parent' constable in this case was Pete Wellstead. He was well-meaning and basically moral but was also battered and bruised by a lifetime of experience on the front line of police work and he steered his own surviving course within the unholy mess of police practice. One had to switch off a lot of one's personal emotions just to get by from day to day.

The tapestry of a normal shift was fraught with human drama: suicide, sudden death, gruesome traffic accidents, fires, interpersonal violence, drink, sex and drugs and rock 'n' roll. Willesden comprised a multicultural mix of indigenous white, subcontinental Asians, Africans, West Indians and Irish. There were rich, middle-class areas on the patch living in uneasy coexistence with inner-city deprivation and it was the deprivation – not the racial mix – which gave rise to the levels of crime, whereas people, generally, seemed to get on all right with one another.

My whole, waking existence revolved around my police duties

and I always seemed to be tired; night duty, court appearances the next morning, a short sleep snatched and then back on duty. My social life was practically nil and we single men, living in the police section house, 'lived for the job'. Talk was 'shop' talk and, even off-duty, one surveyed society and its street scenes with a policeman's eye. I was never off guard and, in many ways, it was an 'us' (police) and 'them' (public) situation.

One did not achieve career success in the Met by helping old ladies to cross the road. One was noticed and advanced by growing reputation, leading to promotion through 'crime knocks', i.e., arrests and convictions; one had to be pushy, loud and extrovert to get on. The ambitious were not seekers of the truth but engineers of 'results' (expressed as convictions) and many weren't too morally concerned about how they got those convictions. This, therefore, exposed ambition to a whole field of malpractice.

Willesden Police could enjoy free, after-hours drinking at the Spotted Dog public house, as well as numerous other collective and individual gratuities. Crates of drink would mysteriously appear at the station, at Christmas time, from 'grateful' local publicans and off-licences. The abuses were rife and a recognition of police power over local businesses prevailed.

One day, Pete Wellstead took me and another new policeman, Ian Johnson, up to Brent Mortuary. Ian was visibly pale-faced and shocked but it affected me less so in some ways, though more so in others. The 'sudden dead meat syndrome' didn't bother me in the least, having seen it all in Aden. I had also trained and qualified as a butcher; I could dissect a carcass of mutton down into its component joints (chops, saddle, etc.) in less than twenty minutes.

What shocked me, upon entering the 'butcher's shop' of Brent Mortuary, was that the dead bodies were treated with the same skilled and decisive casualness as carcasses of mutton; it was exactly like an army butcher's shop. It was the first time in my life that I'd been fully confronted with the behind-the-scenes official view of dead people, treated like commodities of dead meat to be processed. Such realities collided with a bedrock of romantic notions in my psyche.

The scruffy mortuary attendant reminded me of Dr Frankenstein's assistant, Igor. He had long, greasy, unkempt black hair and he wore a plastic apron to keep the splashes of his enthusiasm off his scruffy clothes. He ushered us into a small room containing four stainless steel trolleys, upon which lay the naked corpses of three old men who had been opened up from neck to navel and had had a square of ribs snipped out to give unrestricted access to the heart and lungs. A section of their skulls had been sawn through to allow removal of the brain and it all generated a hot friction of opposites in me.

I looked at the old man on the trolley nearest to me and pondered the conflict. He had lived through two great world wars. He'd probably worked, fought, loved, married and conceived children. In keeping with the conventions of his time, he would have inherited the English reserve of being properly dressed and of knowing his place. He would probably have been acutely embarrassed to belatedly have noticed that his trouser buttons might have been undone. He would have held his teacup the correct way and performed all the prissy acts of glum, English etiquette. A smudge of shaving blood on his white collar may well have incensed him with anger and frustration. And now, here he was; his dignity smashed, lying supine, naked and exposed with his privates private no more and his innards inside no more, reduced to the status of a butchered animal carcass.

Here was the stark proof and answer to the question, 'Where has grandad gone?'

This pessimistic offering of the reality of death was juxtaposed with another reality that met and married in the exploding heat of their contradictions. On another trolley, lay the naked body of a sweet, pretty young girl. She had obviously just been stripped and 'Igor' had not yet got around to cutting her. She laid there as if she were having a short nap and I noticed that a small comb was still in place in her flaxen hair. Someone asked the attendant how old she was and he pulled her right wrist off the trolley, by a small plastic bracelet label, and read from it. 'She's five.'

Now, what produced a surge of sexual excitement in me was that when he released her wrist, he let it flop, limply, against the naked thigh of the old man on the next trolley, which was hard against hers. It was, for me, a very potent image. It was the invigorating contrast between the gutted, wasted, hairy, old nakedness and ugliness of the man against the pure, young, new, virginal softness and beauty of her small hand lying on (of all places) his naked thigh. It was the old man and the boy all over again.

As we left, that image stuck with me. Added to this, was a short, daydreaming fantasy which had, as a proviso, 'Igor' – after we'd left – spending his lunch hour playing with the girl's naked body and having intercourse with it, before he was forced to eviscerate it for the pathologist that afternoon.

There were no mirror fantasies at all while I was staying at the police section house, so I would expend my energies going to gay pubs in the hope of meeting someone. My true aspiration was to form a stable, gay relationship in spite of all the difficulties.

The more I got to know some of my police colleagues at the section house, the more I despaired that I was, perhaps, in the wrong line of work. As time and experience progressed, the police and the villains began to look much the same. The CID brought the traditions of police criminality to a fine art. They were the worst of all and seemed to be entirely a law unto themselves. They put a few people away but I often wondered if they'd put the *right* people away. In order to get a result, all the 'arts' of conviction could be deployed: perjury, planting evidence, forced confessions, etc., and if a prisoner questioned police integrity, they could invoke, in court, a man's previous convictions to prejudice the jury.

I was shocked by violence against suspects in Willesden Green charge room as the guys doing the kicking were members of the

CID. I was, of course, advised to hold my peace if I knew what was good for me. One went against the flow at one's peril. The whole scenario depressed me and I began to lose pride in my job.

To be fair to the police, the great mess of inner-city deprivation was not of their making. They were in the middle of it with the role of trying to hold the line of good order with little input of action, other than reaction to events on the ground. Prevention was ideal but seldom was it a reality. The PC on the beat, with his whistle and truncheon, has no legislative powers and feels as desperately hopeless as the victim on the street. His job is always picking up the pieces of social disorder and he becomes emotionally hardened to all his experiences. I became a part of all this and my total involvement in the duties and the lifestyle did me no psychological good. But in all the time I was a policeman, I never took bribes, tendered false evidence, perjured myself or assaulted suspects. I was certainly an odd copper.

As time moved on, I began to frequent London's gay haunts and nearly always succeeded in picking someone up – though, more often than not, they would pick me up. On one occasion, I went to a gay centre, in a small hall in Marylebone, run by a curate of the Church of England. There, I met a young man in his late teens or early twenties who hailed from Dublin. His name was Michael Aherne* and, one night, I booked us both into a small, respectable hotel off Dorset Square where we spent the best part of the evening drinking Scotch whisky and talking in our room.

Eventually, I began to think of going to bed because I could no longer match his alcoholic intake and I didn't want to flake out and miss a promising evening but, when I returned from a visit to the toilet, he was flat out cold on the bed. I wasn't particularly worried because I would service him awake or asleep. I stripped him and registered slight disappointment that his legs were hairy but, apart from that and a little dark hair on his young chest, he was

* *Not his real name.*

'available'. I fondled his privates in the hope that he would revive by my attentions but I soon gave this up as it was clear that he was most definitely deeply asleep.

I lifted him up into my arms and just stood there for a moment, savouring the power I felt over his helpless, vulnerable nudity. In his resting, uncaring sleep, he belonged there. The hardness of my penis, at that point, was so rigid that it didn't feel like flesh at all. I placed him on the bed, rolled him over and slid my hands down either side of his prone nakedness and drew myself into him. Afterwards, I laid panting on him, kissing his neck and shoulders. I looked at him, still sleeping there, and felt my libido beginning to rise again. To my surprise and joy, this time, he began to respond to my attentions and I revoked the tiredness in my body with a will as I stirred him up faster and stronger. Exhausted, after this second time, I rolled off beside him and gazed into his happy face, gurgling to itself in some erotic dreamland. I returned to my own bed and we smiled and gazed at one another until we both fell asleep.

I often visited the King William IV pub in Hampstead where the clientele was of a more sedate refinement than in some of the rough houses of alarming repute. It was there, one evening, that I met a young man called Paul Waring who I later discovered was in his early twenties; although he looked about sixteen. He took the bar stool next to me and, in a buzz of mutual excitement, we eyed each other up.

He was smooth, pale and slim with long, silken, fair hair and he reminded me of my sister, Sylvia. I was instantly his slave. Instantly! He radiated a quiet, shy confidence with momentary bursts of camp. As he was living with his parents in Swiss Cottage, we took a taxi to my place. I suppose he thought that I was living in a hostel or something as it was late and there was no one about. We had both had a few drinks to add to the unreality of the situation and the all-consuming concentration of my sex drive had thrown caution to the wind as we entered my little, unlockable room at the section house.

I put a chair up against the door to deter intruders and we made the most passionate love throughout most of the night.

I woke early for the morning shift, dog tired, and felt his nakedness against me and I cursed the fact that I'd soon have to go on duty. I saw, lying next to me, a composite beauty. Paul Waring was my sister, Sylvia, my boy brother, Olav, Adrian Eales-Whyte (the elusive fair-haired boy from Strichen School), Chris Innerd, the Arab house boy, Ronnie Mann and Jamie Foster, all come together into the one flesh. He had all the attributes of each one somewhere in his delectable form; a dream come true. I wanted no one else and would have been content to be his servant in order to be wedded to him, in bed and company, all the days of my life.

I got up and dressed in my police uniform. I put my hand on his shoulder and gently shook him awake. He slowly turned around and opened his bleary eyes and was instantly awake – with eyes wide open – at this London policeman hovering over him. 'It's OK, it's only me,' I explained as casually as I could. 'We've got to go. I'm due on duty soon.' He was highly amused by the situation. 'Is this the Police Station?' he asked, as if he were asking the time. 'No, I'm letting you off with a caution, but I must warn you that anything you say will be taken down, including your Y-fronts,' I joked.

We geared straight into humorous banter as he sprang, naked, from the bed, searching for his clothes. 'People just won't believe this,' he said, trying to get his briefs up and almost falling over in the process. I pulled him close into me. I was on a rising slope to sexual arousal again. 'We haven't got time now; I have to get to Augustus Barnett's [the off-licence shop where he worked],' he said, sensing what I was thinking. He gave me a telephone number and we would see each other again. Then, like a shot from *The Prisoner of Zenda*, we descended the grand staircase of the section house to the teeming assembly below.

There was I, resplendent in full uniform with helmet under my arm, stepping out with this slim, long-haired, young man in jeans and all the poise and air of the Queen of Sheba. As we passed by the section house sergeant, with cool desperate improvisation, I said to him, 'Sarge, if anyone else calls about the fish tank, tell 'em I've just had a caller and it's been sold.' His eyes showed great, inner relief at a puzzle solved. 'Yeah, OK I will 287 [my number].'

We walked out of the section house, down the drive to Willesden Lane and met the kerb and a constant heavy stream of rush hour traffic. 'Christ, we'll never get across here,' he said. 'Not so,' said I and I stepped out into the road and halted the great, arterial flow to the heart of London. With arm raised to keep the traffic at a stop, I beckoned Paul to cross. He smiled in half embarrassment and delight then minced across the 'Red Sea' with all the rage of the frustrated motorists looking on.

I accompanied him to the platform of Willesden Green Tube station where there would be a train every couple of minutes. As one drew up, he turned to me and said quickly, 'You know, I've always wanted to do this…' The train was in and the doors were open. 'Do what?' I asked, puzzled. 'Kiss a policeman with his helmet on.' And before I could react, he gave me a quick peck on the cheek in front of a hundred commuters then jumped aboard the train and waved to me as it pulled away down the line. I turned and walked off with all the carriage and dignity befitting a steadfast officer of the law. It was a good start to the day.

I wasn't to know, at that stage, that Paul was a wandering spirit, like me, and that his ravishing beauty would assist him to wander more easily over the higher menus of life and it was nothing unusual for Paul to have many sexual partners. In time, I met quite a few of his 'friends' and many of them were older, professional men: a doctor in Golders Green, various businessmen in and around Hampstead and masses of London's arty and bohemian super subculture types.

Paul belonged to everybody and nobody and my intensity of feeling for him was never reciprocated because there simply wasn't enough of Paul to go around. There were never any bitter or angry words between us, or emotional dramas of jealousy, but I saw him less and less as time passed and nothing was to ever match the intensity of our first encounter.

When I wasn't cruising the gay pubs or watching the omnipresent TV set, I would call at the cinema. A film that I still remember vividly was Stanley Kubrick's tale of ultra-violence, backed with Beethoven's music: *A Clockwork Orange*. It was a bold experiment in cinema and, along with his other films, had confirmed Kubrick's place as a genius of the cinematographic art. The critics who wrote it off as a piece of violent pornography always missed the point about art and saw new ideas as some kind of threat to the established order. It was the same with those who went to see *The Shining*, expecting to see Stephen King on the screen. Stephen King wrote books but it was Stanley Kubrick who made movies.

On the art front, I was fond of all paintings and sculptures featuring the nude, male figure but the only painting to give me an instant erection was *The Raft of the Medusa*; once seen, never forgotten. It featured an image in full continuity with my predilection, i.e., man with naked dead boy lying on his lap. There was a 'constant' which depicted a powerful, ugly, old man expressing his desires by lavishing the power of his will and sexual attentions on the unconscious, naked body of a beautiful boy and this painting inspired a great many fantasies in me.

In all of my fantasies, the boy is always a virgin with the old man always the first (and only) one to take the boy. The 'dead' boy is aware of what the 'dirty old man' is doing to his body but loves every moment of it, secretly, though he gives no response whatsoever to the old man – or to the 'observer'. The old man is never aware that the boy is conscious, probably because if the boy were awake, the old man would not touch him. There is an undercurrent of guilt and there is a need, by the boy, for powerful attention and sexual pleasure. There is a need for the old man to care for the boy and a need also for him to gain sexual pleasure from fucking the boy.

The two are in mutually unspoken 'tune' with one another. The need of the adult and child had been met in the one body, living out a fantasy.

I digress here, slightly, to recall that a few years after my grandfather died, I climbed into the attic at 47 Academy Road and found two, very old, huge books up there, which had belonged to him. One was a huge volume, printed in the 1880s, of the life of David Livingstone, the Scottish missionary doctor who surveyed so much of Africa. The second book was a massive history of the period in British history from Richard III to the end of the Tudors. I was too young to read and understand these weighty tomes but there were one or two memorable, full-page plates in them and I especially remember one well-thumbed picture. It showed an artist's impression of the murder of the Princes in the Tower of London depicting a couple of big, burly men standing over a four-poster bed on which lay – in their night clothes – two boys who had just been smothered to death. One of the men was holding a pillow. On the other page was a picture of other big, strong men lowering the two naked bodies – in sheets – down to the arms of another big man waiting below the stairs. The book was dated from the 1890s and, by the marks on the pictures, I surmised that Andrew Whyte had looked at it often.

I pondered that my grandfather might have been a fantasist, like me, enacting out his deepest desires, taking me out to the wild, desolate dunes and carrying me home, asleep. I was quiet, passive and shy by nature and fertile ground and a stimulus for occasional paedophilia.

After about a year in the Metropolitan Police, I was overtaken by utter exhaustion and disillusionment. One night on foot patrol, I discovered two young men in an intimate, sexual situation in the back of a car that was parked up in an alley. I warned them to 'be more bloody careful in future,' and let them go. I never recorded the incident in my incident book, nor did I do my job; the precise measure of the law required me to have arrested them both for 'gross indecency in a public place'. My conscience instructed me that it was never justified to merely obey the law or orders; there were pertinent occasions when a very bad or oppressive law or order needed to be disobeyed. We were not robots and we were, in the fullness of our humanity, obliged to make a stand. I regretted, later, that I was not strong enough to make a stand against the gross drives of my furious sexual aberration at the time.

It became clearly apparent that I couldn't reconcile my expanding gay lifestyle and aspirations while remaining a Metropolitan Police officer. I couldn't be open about my homosexuality and, if I wanted to gain promotion, I would have to adopt all the practices I detested. Their society didn't like 'blacks', 'queers', 'communists' and, in the unfolding of history of the time, they didn't like 'paddy bastards' either. I would have to protect the abuses of the subculture by turning a blind eye to routine abuses by colleagues, which would also involve me having to lie under oath in court. This was *their* normality and I wished not to have any part in it.

I resigned quietly from the police in early December 1973. They were surprised at my 'sudden' decision and tried to dissuade me. Generally, I was not an unpopular member of the team (in spite of all the revisions after my arrest, ten years later). I made the excuse that I was leaving because of the poor pay and the stress of the job. I needed a good report and reference; therefore, I couldn't tell them my real reasons. But my decision to resign cast a great pall of depression over me. I was saddened that the organisation I had hoped to love was beneath contempt and I clung to my morality like a man clinging to a piece of wreckage in the vast expanse of the ocean.

• • •

I moved out of the section house and, by Christmas, I had moved into a single room at 9 Manstone Road, just off Cricklewood Broadway, where there was a strange, nosey, old woman in attendance as a caretaker. I got myself a job as a security guard for the Department of the Environment, who provided security cover for prominent government buildings, ranging from the parliamentary office buildings in Bridge Street (adjoining the House of Commons) to the Ministry of Defence (MoD) building itself. It was boring, uninteresting work with long, lonely nights of checking 'clocking points' and reading. It provided little job satisfaction but it paid the bills.

At the MoD building, I was teamed a few times with an interesting man called Harold Sanderson. He was in his fifties and had been a stuntman and stand-in for the film industry for many years and he regaled me with tales of his work and experiences. He had now retired because of his age and a rapidly vanishing British film industry and he told me some intimate details of the lives of the greats he had known, at Elstree film studios, with verve.

The last main production he had been involved in was David Lean's *Ryan's Daughter*. Harold was always Robert Mitchum's double or stand-in for preparatory shots and they'd spent months in an old, rented farmhouse, in the Republic of Ireland, making the movie. It was, apparently, a slow, time-consuming process, working for the perfectionist Lean, for whom money seemed to be no object. Mitchum insisted upon doing all the cooking at the farmhouse himself and had a passion for cooking Italian food. Harold had Mitchum's Californian telephone number in his address book and would even still get an occasional call to visit Mitchum at his hotel, for a couple of drinks, whenever he was in London.

At the MoD complex at Stanmore, I met an odd man whose main preoccupation seemed to be to fill me with gruesome stories from his past. He told me about his work during World War II when he had had to collect up bits of 'tits, cunts and limbs' after the Blitz bombings. He was obviously a man who had been both traumatised and excited by his experiences because he needed to tell people long after the event. I only worked a few shifts with him and the only time in our conversation when I experienced a moderate frisson of sexual excitement was when he said that he also had to prepare the bodies of some young American servicemen for dispatch to the States. That, again, conjured up my fantasy of naked, young men being washed and 'attended to' by this old man.

In early 1974, I served a couple of stints at a large complex in the Strand in Central London, where I remember, during my rounds, coming across an office library. Browsing through it, I distinctly remember one book, which excited me, called *The Manual of Medical Jurisprudence and Toxicology*, and I thumbed through it, having a whole night of free time on my hands. I was sexually stimulated by some of the pictures therein. There was a black and white photo of a boy who was described as having died by drowning. He was lying down, naked on a mortuary table, with only the head and upper chest visible in the photograph. He looked asleep, with a tightly closed mouth. In my mind, I imagined the rest of his naked, limp body on the table and I wondered if they'd covered his private parts.

Another, more exciting, image was a full colour photo under the subheading, '*Rigor Mortis*'. On a crumpled, white sheet lay the naked body of a youth. His body was smooth and young-looking and, apart from the head and slightly on the naval, it was hairless and, to me, sexually exciting. The colouring of the emulsion of the photograph made the youth's skin look rosy and lacking in the pallor usually associated with death. He was laid on his back with his arms by his sides and slightly bent at the elbow with hands pointing down from his (rigid) wrists. His legs were slightly bent, with his knees slightly raised, and his small penis lay sideways and flaccid. I was almost sick with desire at this extremely potent image and even thought about stealing the book but, because it looked well-used, I figured that it would soon be missed. Even today I can still visualise that photo as if I'd only just seen it.

I spent a lot of time filling in at different posts for absences. For one such assignment, I worked at a new site at Gorst Road in North West London. It was a tripartite site; the inner sanctum was a high-security vault containing a repository store for pictures not currently on exhibition at the Tate Gallery of which I had no direct dealings. The second part of the building was a geology laboratory with a store of rock samples from every conceivable part of the world. The third part was a huge store full of stuffed animals belonging to the Natural History Museum.

Before I started work at this new location, I had, coincidentally, decided to change my appearance and had purchased a hair-dyeing kit from a shop on Cricklewood Broadway. After carefully following the instructions, I stood, naked, before the mirror and was blown away with excitement at what I saw. There, reflected back at me, was a fair-haired, young man with fair eyebrows, fair body hair and fair pubic hair. An absolute vision of perfection! I dressed and took a walk down to the bus stop and, upon arriving at Gorst Road, I found that I was to be on single duty (the other man had phoned in sick). I settled down for the night, alone in that vast complex, with the entire place securely locked up with me in it.

As I was doing my rounds after midnight, I entered the near dark, natural history store. At the far end were a selection of stuffed gorilla specimens, fixed in various attitudes, which I perused carefully. It was as if they were still alive. I touched them and the hair on the back of my head and neck began to bristle with fear as my imagination advanced. They looked fierce and very powerful… yes big, hairy and powerful. My fear gave way to excitement and thoughts of the possibilities of a fantasy scenario entered my head. My heart was pounding faster and faster and I couldn't restrain the impulse to take off all my clothes.

I stood there, naked and blonde, before the rigid shell of this huge gorilla with outstretched arms. He was half-crouched and I walked between his arms and carefully draped my naked body over his shoulders, as my erection pulsated. I hung there, limp, feeling his solid, great, hairy body against my skin. Having no mirror, I imagined the sight of me being carried off, unconscious, in the arms of this great beast and I felt a great, relaxing peace come over me as I lay there for a few minutes imagining. When I came down, I examined where his penis should have been and was disappointed by the pathetic, little, hard stump on such a powerful creature. That seemed to deflate my ardour, in the discovery that he didn't have the means to satisfy me, and the vision of his potency vanished. I dressed and returned to life without so much as an ejaculation, but my power and passive syndrome was developing.

One afternoon, on a day off, I went for a walk, along Cricklewood Lane, and stopped at a café for refreshment. A boy of around sixteen came in, walked to a pinball machine near my table and began to play on it and the sight of him provoked a hot trauma of excitement in me. As he eagerly concentrated on his task, his whole body gyrated with quick reflexes of unselfconscious abandonment. Sitting there, watching him, transported me to heaven and his vision made me more blissful than I had been in years. There were only the two of us on that side of the café and he barely registered me at all, except with casual sideways glances, as I furtively surveyed the splendour of his holy presence. Then he ran out of coins and left as suddenly as he'd arrived.

Seeing him, that day, made me the happiest man alive – and the saddest, when he vanished for ever. I've never forgotten him and his vision returns even now, time and time again. Being in my late twenties, I'd never had a relationship and was as emotionally immature as the boy myself. As I walked from that cafe back to Manstone Road, I had never felt so alone and I was aware of the reality of just how alone I was. As each attempt to form a relationship had failed, I got closer and closer to the edge of this desperation.

The vision of that boy was very real but all my emotions dwelt inside myself and my self-love. It was never going to be the case that he (the *real* boy) would sacrifice his own self – and his willing individuality – to me, for a feeling of love inside me, which I'd always owned and controlled in order to gratify my emotionally-stunted self. It was fortunate for him that the ingredients of my ritual were not chanced to be in place.

If I'd been made bold through alcohol, the subliminal acquisitive 'predator' might have kicked in, driven to desperate possession of a substance for my 'love'. Would I then have jumped in with coins – for another try when he had run out – with plausible chat lines; persuasively 'innocent' to find out his surface interests, hobbies and needs, satisfied with casual offers to 'come back and see'? None was in my mind at the time as there was no time to think beyond his overwhelming presence, in that café, which stunned out all other thoughts. In other circumstances would I have offered him a drink at my place to give him more relaxation to his innocent frame of mind?

The landlady at 9 Manstone Road kept giving me strange looks, which turned to actions, and she finally objected to me 'entertaining' in my room. I found another place to live, ten minutes away at 80 Teignmouth Road in Willesden Green, and moved in during the summer of 1974.

• • •

By that time, I was bored with sitting around on fixed security duty all night when I would rather have been out looking for 'trade'. My fling with a gorilla was no basis for sexual happiness and I wondered where my life was taking me. I had no intention of ever going back to the North East of Scotland and I fixed my future in the great, sprawling capital, which seemed to be less hostile to gays than other parts of the British Isles. I continued in this mode of inactivity for about six months until I eventually tendered my resignation. I then threw my passions – and my rapidly dwindling reserves of cash – into drink and gay bars. Like Micawber, I was totally irresponsible to believe (without helping to make it happen) that 'something was bound to turn up'. When I wasn't out drinking and searching, I was at home drinking and watching TV. In a teeming city of seven and a half million people I was as alone as if I'd been on Mars.

Soon, I ran out of money and I felt obliged to claim some financial assistance at the local unemployment office. I had sold my last vestige of connection with eleven years and eighty-four days in the British Army: my General Service medal (South Arabia) and the dealer paid me its worth, which was exactly £8. Almost flat broke, I presented myself at Willesden unemployment office but, rather than give me money, I was surprised when they employed me as a clerical officer in the Department of Employment's Jobcentre at Denmark Street, just off Charing Cross Road. It was a specialist government placement agency for the hotel and catering trades.

At work, there were a few recognisably gay men among the fifty-or-so staff but they kept their sex lives within their own private domain being, officially, 'in the closet'. A few of the girls in the office got around to asking about my sexual orientation: 'Are you gay?' and I confirmed but I was never demonstrably gay because I wasn't effeminate or camp. I got on well enough with everyone in the office but I could be unsympathetic to people who were too much of the 'mealy-mouthed clerk' mentality.

On a Friday after work, I would take a bath and shave off all my body-hair, save for a neat, but sparse, triangle of pubic hair and, of course, the hair on my head and my eyebrows. I would dry myself and stand in front of the large mirror, vainly and narcissistically, admiring the vision reflected back; an image of slim, pale, soft, hairless beauty; an image of the only person whom I could really love and who could love me. I stood, looking like a version of a sixteen-year-old, compellingly vanquishing the thirty-year-old reality. I would dress and watch a bit of unsatisfactory TV and start to drink Bacardi and Coke. Then, needing an emotional outlet of expression, I would 'congeal' into listening to classical music tapes through my headphones. With the slow but steady increase in my alcohol intake, I would drift into a virtual 'other world' centred on my imagination and my feelings that were provoked by the music.

After over half of the bottle of Bacardi was consumed, I would take to the Tube and the gay pub scene to search for an unreachable dream. One night at the King William IV pub (the Willie), I was picked up by a young businessman from South Africa. He was fairly rich and inhabited a big house in Hampstead where I slept naked in bed with him. No sex occurred, though he invited me to move in with him. I enjoyed the intelligence of his company and conversation but he didn't appeal to me, sexually, and I didn't want to lose my independence by being his live-in lover.

I had a brief fling with a writer who worked on censorship issues for a magazine called *Index*. He had a major drink problem and drained me like a psychological leech. There was also an Australian who had been a boy actor on TV but he had no sex appeal to me. I even spent one night in a Lord of the Realm's home in bed with his butler, while m'lud was abroad with his wife.

All kinds of people would come into the Willie. Peter Cook (Dudley Moore's other theatrical half) would often be there drinking with a few friends. I never met him but we did exchange glances as one was wont to do in any such social situation. One night, a bearded Peter O'Toole staggered in seemingly wanting to fight someone – anyone! Superstar or not, he was thrown out of the pub just as any abusive drunk would be. Famous people could find privacy in that pub because they were not pestered by fans.

I extended my range to The Black Cap pub in Camden, which was on most good tourist guides and which often hosted drag cabaret shows. From pickups there, I was able to find partners from a wide range of races and cultures. There was a beautiful young Israeli, an airport security policeman in the UK on holiday and a young Japanese doctor who, the following day, presented me with a little, Japanese, wooden, carved sculpture with Japanese writing on it. I also met a young, beautiful, Swedish anaesthetist who knocked me out without recourse to his profession. He never came to 80 Teignmouth Road; we would make love at the Charing Cross Hotel where he was staying as a tourist.

One night in The Champion pub in Bayswater Road, I was picked up by a well-known film director who was firmly in the closet. He advised me that if I really wanted to enter the film industry, I should seek a post as an assistant cameraman, be prepared to be unemployed a lot of the time and commit myself to a precarious, declining industry. I never pursued the idea because I felt a lack of confidence, and our ways parted, though I still followed his impressive work on the screen as I clung to the security of my safe, 9–5 job at the civil service.

It often came to pass when I met up with older men that I would accompany them back to their flats, drunk. This passive profile was always my 'plan B' when no 'sweet young thing' was available. I had a conscious desire to be used by older men and would fake passing out in the armchair as part of this conscious desire. There I would be, ready and eager to be 'domestically and sexually ministered to'. I would observe the 'proceedings' through my senses and through my almost-closed eyes, subject to my opportunistic control; eyes tight shut when I thought they were looking at my face.

On a few occasions, the man would check me out for total unconsciousness before he began his play and, for the most part, he remained relatively silent after becoming convinced that I was out cold. I never had an erection during these passive rituals because this would have been incompatible with my passive role. Lying there, I felt the exciting approach of the force of decision by this other being. I longed to be carried off and undressed. The frisson came from someone else lifting my limp, passive body and carrying me in their arms. I would thrill at my limp weight being lifted up and carried in his arms, which, sadly, didn't occur that often due to my size (though I only clocked in at about ten stone in weight). He would lay me on the bed where he would undress me and I thrilled at the notion of his total control over the totally passive me. I would imagine how he'd triumph over me and this was also *my* triumph. The enjoyment of the senses of being 'passive' was doubled by imagining the controlling pleasure of the active man. The duality of the situation magnified the frisson and the 'pleasure flow' to my brain, on these occasions, was off the scale.

One guy just sat astride my chest and wanked on to my face after he'd performed his tactile caresses and fondling. In the morning, I acted unaware and asked no questions. I was not willing to openly acknowledge the truth about what turned me on; the secret of my active and passive dual role.

In the summer of 1975, Paul Waring, completely unexpectedly, called round to my bedsit to see me. He looked slightly haggard (though to me, he was still as beautiful and alluring as ever) and we couldn't wait to get to bed on that bright, sunny afternoon. Soon after, I noticed a milky discharge, which was later confirmed as a case of the sexually transmitted ailment 'non-specific urethritis', which I believe was a milder form of gonorrhoea. I was given some tablets and told to abstain from sex and drink for the next ten days.

Once or twice over the next five years, I saw Paul in a crowd of commuters at a Tube station; though, as we passed quite close, he didn't seem to want to acknowledge me. Despite this, I loved him and would have always taken him in as a friend and lover. I love him still. He was the epitome of all my human, sexual and emotional aspirations and when I lost him, I felt that life was a bitch!

• • •

In the November of 1975, I met David Gallichan – or 'Twinkle' as I would come to call him – outside The Champion pub. I took him home and bedded him but, rather than move on, Twinkle stayed and, after a few days together, we moved to a ground floor flat at 195 Melrose Avenue in Willesden Green.

I called him Twinkle because he wasn't a very bright spark. He was a wanderer with no great sense of responsibility and needed a daddy figure to lean on. The novelty of sex with him soon wore off because he just laid there on his stomach with as much interest in the proceedings as a sack of potatoes. He was thin, with dyed blonde hair and, although he was about nineteen or twenty, he had the IQ of a ten-year-old. He was young but his bony, hairy body was not my idea of sexual allurement, though, with a few drinks inside me, he would look better.

I found my tactility with him more sexually exciting when he was unconscious than when he was aware. He had become so drunk one night that he flaked out, leaving himself to my total discretion to exploit his extreme passivity. He ceased to be David Gallichan at that moment and became the 'created entity'. I was then able to express a higher degree of physical and emotional tenderness on his sleeping form.

For a time, Twinkle and I, together with a puppy dog, Bleep, that I'd bought from the pet shop close to Willesden Green Tube station, constituted a kind of a family and I had no wish to roam the streets and bars in search of sex. But it was soon clear that he wanted to continue his life of wandering around Piccadilly and the specialised, gay night spots and he'd sometimes disappear for a couple of days, having found a new, temporary protector. One night, he brought back a boy from one of the main line stations, which was asking for trouble because it was obvious that I would make a play for his favours. The food and drink flowed freely and the three of us watched *Butch Cassidy and the Sundance Kid* on TV.

After the TV had lost its coherent influence and we had eaten and drunk our fill, it was very late. Twinkle had gone to his single bed while the boy sat on my bed and was so drunk, he didn't even appear to have sufficient co-ordination to take his clothes off. I stood him up and put my hands on his shoulders to steady him and told him to have some Alka-Seltzer, which would help him feel better in the morning. He mumbled something about feeling dizzy and I told him to take a deep breath and hold it in. He did so and stood there for about half a minute, holding it in and growing redder in the face before passing out into my arms. I laid him on my bed and rose to seventh heaven as I undressed him. He was a slim, beautiful boy with satin-smooth, pink skin. Drink was having a greater effect than usual on me, but I managed to strip and join him in the small bed. Our bodies pressed together and, with our legs entwined as one, I, too, fell asleep, being too drunk for anything else.

I woke up the next morning to the sound of my alarm clock telling me it was time for work. I did think of phoning the office and faking a cold or something but I'd done that too many times not to be noticed in the office. In the civil service, one was expected to take no more than ten uncertificated days sick leave a year and I didn't want to be too overdrawn on this privilege. The boy was stirring, with his arms around me, and I could feel his erection against my buttocks. I regretted having to leave that wonderful boy and go to work. 'Twinkle will look after you,' I told him, assuming that, once I'd left, he would have relieved his driving ambition on Twinkle. But that evening, I found that the gas and electricity meters had been broken into and the cash taken. When Twinkle came home later from working as an assistant in the Knights and Heralds bar at Paddington train station, he annoyed me with his explanation as to the cause of the thefts. The idiot had gone off to work on the late shift at 10 a.m., leaving the unknown boy alone in the flat. The boy, who was obviously a runaway from either a home or a young offenders' detention centre, had financed his next venture and left as suddenly as he had arrived.

As Twinkle took more and more to sleeping out, I found myself drifting back to the gay centre at the church hall in St Marylebone in search of more casual encounters. I picked up a small, smooth Malaysian who wanted me to assume the passive role, which didn't suit me. He was nice for close bodily contact but not for real, long-term, sexual satisfaction. I met a young Chinese medical student and, while Twinkle was off somewhere, I spent quite some time in bed with him. He would always please me by making flattering comments about my body and he made me feel comfortable and relaxed. He stayed with us at Melrose Avenue over the Christmas holidays in 1976 and, as he was a diligent student, I suppose he would have later become a fully qualified doctor.

Into 1977, Twinkle's absences became longer and longer and he had scant interest in his social and domestic responsibilities. Correspondingly, I too sought association elsewhere. I had been with many different partners and if this extremely promiscuous part of my life had happened ten years later, then I would have been a prime risk for candidature to the terminal HIV club.

Risk became hard fact when I picked up a seventeen-year-old named David Painter. He came into the Jobcentre and, in his interview, told me that he was looking for a job with accommodation, adding that he was destitute, with nowhere to stay. Later, when I called in at a local bar for a drink after work, I came across him on the street and invited him home as I knew Twinkle was out at the time. We watched TV, drank a few Martinis, conversed normally and watched some of my home movies on my film projector and I showed him my new sound movie camera.

Eventually, he got into my single bed and, after the lights were out, I put my arm around him. He immediately woke and threw a fit. He thrashed about, screaming and shouting his tirade, waving his arms about in the air. I did my best to calm him down, but he barged into the glass panelled vestibule in the communal area, in front of another tenant. Eventually, the two of us managed to calm him down until the police and ambulance arrived at my insistence (he'd cut his arm as he smashed the glass). They took him off to hospital to have his cut seen to while I was taken to Willesden Green Police Station to make a statement where I was locked up and subjected to a great deal of verbal abuse from a Scottish CID sergeant.

The police later released me, explaining that Painter didn't wish to press charges. I suspected that Painter clearly didn't want to subject himself to cross-examination in a witness box. Maybe his parents wanted to protect him from public exposure in a potential court appearance. Maybe the disinhibiting effects of the alcohol might have brought about his behaviour. What was clear, was that a few years later, the prosecution at my trial thought better of calling David Painter as a witness, nor was the incident overtly referred to at my trial. Nor did he recount the incident in the press, nor was he available to the press for interview or to sell his story. I thought his fears had been triggered by not being used to the subconscious liberating agency of strong drink and I felt bitter about that event but didn't let it deflect me from my gay lifestyle.

I still occasionally attended the cinema but there was now a wealth of good films on TV and this indulgence was more cost-effective and convenient. At home, my appreciation of a film would appear to be enhanced by a few drinks and, in *my* cinema, the bar was always open. Often, I would make my own movie images in my mind with the aid of Bacardi rum and music played through my stereo headphones. The pictures in my mind were 'edited' so that they matched perfectly in sync with the music I was listening to and my emotions and, on occasion, this would actually bring me to tears. There were some potent and disturbing images in those perceptive dreams and one, in particular, usually came at some climactic trauma in the music.

All in slow motion and in full colour, I imagine what looks like a pool of blood on the ground. I rise up from this pool, naked with my arms outstretched in the crucified position. Naturally, I am covered in thick-clotting blood, with the droplets cascading off my body to the ground. In one outstretched hand, I hold a sword, which is pointing upwards. In the other outstretched hand, I am holding a naked, living and wriggling baby by the ankles.

It was a bloody image but there was no violence and as the music reached its crescendo, the film would cut and the action would move on to something else – whatever my mind dreamt up at the time.

Other common images involved golden sunsets and me, as a boy, in wide, high landscapes. In my thoughts, just before going to sleep, there was still – after many years – the image of me inside the furs in the log cabin with the roaring fire and sub-zero temperatures outside. I still had the rifle near my hand but the naked, young man in bed with me would change to whoever I was sexually fixated on at the time.

In my vacant moments, I still inhabited my everyday life as if seen through a movie camera. Things were more potent and real when viewed through an oblong movie screen and I almost always engaged in this, apart from when I was actually concentrating on some work or was in direct conversation with another person. It was my whole life. It was probably a contributing factor as to why I was never able to get emotionally close to people; my attraction was for ideal, theoretical people who presented a simplistic relationship, free from the problems and complexities of *real* people.

I'd never encountered any such deficiency where animals were concerned and if ever I deeply loved and cared for anyone, it was for my little, vulnerable, child-substitute of a small black and white mongrel, Bleep. In 1977, she'd had another litter of pups. While I was at work I always left the back door ajar, giving Bleep full, unfettered access to go into the garden whenever she wanted. That's how she kept getting pregnant; male dogs, smelling her on heat, would scale the high, wooden fence to channel their natural urges.

I had previously given the pups away freely to the Willesden pet shop so that they'd have some chance of finding a decent home and life. I would never have considered killing them because they were Bleep's and they were so lovable in their own right.

One night when the latest litter was a few weeks old and becoming mobile, Twinkle and I had to keep an eye on them; they would stray away from the kennel, out in the back garden, and we had to return them to Bleep to stop her fretting. That night, it was Twinkle's turn for the chore, and I was going up to the shops to get some cigarettes and drink. When I returned, I could hear Bleep yelping outside and I went to investigate. To my horror, I found that three of the pups were in the garden pond with the rest being very close to the edge. I pulled them out and two of them had drowned and I was able to revive the third. I berated Twinkle for his stupid idleness in lying, like a lump, in front of the TV while Bleep was calling for help just outside the French windows. I was completely devastated by the tragic death of those puppies and blamed myself and, more pointedly, Twinkle.

After that, I don't believe I had any remaining feelings for David Gallichan and, by the summer, he had found himself a businessman sugar daddy in Central London. Apart from one brief visit, I never saw Twinkle again and, in spite of living in close proximity to him for eighteen months, I didn't really know him at all (I would read of his death, in the tabloids, in 1992).

After he left, I felt liberated and I met a young seventeen-year-old commis chef who moved in with me for a few weeks. When he was about fifteen or sixteen his adventurous, sexual curiosity had caused him to go cruising up on Hampstead Heath, one night, to see if 'the Heath' lived up to its reputation as a meeting place for queers. Two, rough-looking men had jumped on him, held him down and took it in turns to viciously rape him. He had been a virgin and the brutal assault had made his anus bleed. He was too frightened to go to the police in case they wanted to know what he'd been doing wandering the Heath, alone and late at night. He was, to a great degree, psychologically broken and I was only able to give limited comfort. In any case, our intimacy never really amounted to more than kissing, fondling and cuddling (he couldn't bear to be penetrated) and he soon moved away.

At work, though I was never ambitious for power in the trades union (the Civil and Public Services Association – CPSA), I was elected to a branch union official's post and I took my duties seriously, never treating the position as a stepping stone to other things. I was just a 'dog soldier' on the front line and that required hard work in return for little or no glory. All those duties were unpaid and made demands on my time but I knew that when I took the job. What troubled me was that the majority of members weren't particularly interested in the democratic process or the issues or business of the union. A union is only as strong as its collective membership and, at that time, there were nearly a quarter of a million members in the CPSA but few activists (activists were generally people who bothered to turn up for meetings).

There were no 'strong arm tactics' at branch level, with all elections being undertaken by secret ballot. There was no brief show of hands here! But at branch level, in my contacts with management, I expressed no view that was not the mandating instructions from the membership. I was no maverick running my own agenda and I functioned as an ordinary branch secretary.

My annual reports from the civil service were not encouraging, however. They couldn't fault my work but marked me down as not yet ready for promotion due to my 'personality' and 'attitude', which I interpreted as oblique references to my homosexuality and militant union duties, respectively. I had worked on the front line of job-placing activities, at a busy Jobcentre, for over four years and I felt that my efforts had gone unrewarded or unrecognised.

I was finding money tight after losing Twinkle's contribution to the rent and the running costs of the flat and, with my domestic, social isolation becoming unbearable, I drank, which added to my costs. In that year, I was always overdrawn at the bank and also lost some money after being robbed by another late-night pickup.

I had one or two other short-stay flatmates but their prime motivation was temporary accommodation. Then there was Steve Martin whom I met one night in the Golden Lion pub in Dean

Street, Soho. He was working as a general assistant at a club called The Cine and Arts Club in Greek Street and, afterwards, we returned to Melrose Avenue where he stayed for some weeks. I had a great lust for Steve's body, him being smooth, well-proportioned and youthful, and I enormously enjoyed having sex with him. Unfortunately, so did a lot of other men and I hardly saw him after the initial honeymoon period had expired. He was very promiscuous, and I soon discovered that I'd contracted another dose of the old 'non-specific', which I had diagnosed and treated at James Pringle House (an annexe of the Central Middlesex Hospital) in my lunch break. In the end, he moved out and, for mainly sexual reasons, I regretted his loss. His promiscuity had a disastrous effect on his young life when I read that, in 1986, he had committed suicide after having been diagnosed HIV positive.

I became despairing of ever finding a stable flatmate at 195 Melrose Avenue and was subjected to further robberies by people I had met in pubs or by 'queer bashers' out in the street. My social and sexual morale was at an all-time low.

In September 1978, on the eve of my going to Surrey University for a union branch chairman's course, I realised I had no one to look after Bleep while I was away. The night before, I had brought a young guy home after having had more than a few drinks in Camden Town. I remembered nothing about him other than that he said he was from Liverpool (which was fairly evident by his accent) and that he lived nearby, in West Hampstead.

We were sleeping on the high wooden platform that I'd built after Twinkle had left and, as he had drunk more than me, he appeared to be in a deep sleep, laid on his back. I, meanwhile, was feeling sexually aroused but didn't want to wake him with the possibility of rejection. He had gone to bed in Y-fronts and T-shirt and I slipped from under the blankets and put the orange sidelight on. Carefully, like threading a needle, I pulled up the bed clothes to expose his legs. The room was quite warm and I knew he wouldn't react to any change in temperature. I pulled the covers up further – to just above his waist – and carefully slipped my hands under the calf of one of his legs and lifted it up. As I held his limp leg with one hand, I started to ease down his underpants with the other. Changing legs, I carefully inched them further down as he continued to sleep soundly. It gave me a frisson of sexual pleasure to hold and move his limp, warm limbs. Having successfully removed his underwear, I contemplated the other things I could do but the fear of him waking up and rejecting me was more powerful than the urge to continue, so I carefully replaced his pants and the covers and joined him in bed.

Well, the next morning he volunteered to call in and feed and water Bleep while I was away at the course. The back door would be left open so that she could come and go as she wished. But when I returned a few days later, I found he had fed Bleep all right, and had even left my door key behind, but he'd also stolen my movie camera and sound projector.

By the end of 1978, the Labour government was in disarray and CPSA policy wasn't much better. The members of my union seemed to be totally indifferent to any democratic activity themselves and I was left to take the stick, in their name, without any backing or support. Everybody seemed to be on strike and I could see the spectre of Margaret Thatcher looming on the horizon. The country seemed to be in a state of doom and gloom and I was completely isolated and dejected. I would walk Bleep in Gladstone Park, drink to excess and watch TV. I'd lost the stability of any flatmate, I had no sex and I had nobody to talk to. And then the busy year culminated in the suddenly inactive void of the Christmas break, which I spent on my own, at home, drinking and watching TV with my little dog. I was never so alone.

4

Taking Life | 1978

As the holiday season dragged on to 30 December, I was desperate for some company. I'd been drinking at home before wandering out, very drunk, to the first pub that crossed my path: the Cricklewood Arms on Edgware Road. It was as far from being a gay bar as one could possibly get and was frequented, almost exclusively, by Irishmen. In my drunken haze, I got into conversation with an Irish youth whom I later discovered was called Stephen Holmes. We were both already very drunk and had a couple more drinks before closing time, after which he accompanied me back to Melrose Avenue.

When we arrived at my flat, even more drink was consumed and I remembered nothing of the conversations we had, nor even his name. By the time we'd finished drinking, it would have turned way past midnight and we both ended up naked together in bed, which was a mattress on the floor that I'd pulled from the high platform. And that was the scene when I woke up, still befuddled with drink, a couple of hours later.

I felt happy with him lying there, warm, by my side and I caressed the sheer comfort and beauty of his form. I had felt miserable during the whole Christmas break but with him beside me, I felt good. But, as with everyone else who had passed through my life, I knew my contentment would soon turn to despair. My mind was seized with the panic that he would soon wake up and suddenly depart, after which I'd be plunged back into the despairing loneliness of a bleak, cold life. I was becoming desperate with the total futility of my life and wanted him to stay with me like the boy in the furs in the cabin with the great, hostile cold outside.

At that point, he was a smooth, young body in a completely passive state and I wanted him to remain that way. I was snapping into the ritual. My mind was already buzzing with sexual, almost fevered, excitement at the warmth and vital proximity of his body but I just couldn't face him going. There was also a degree of sharp panic lurking in my subconscious, recalling how David Painter had behaved when he'd woken up and gone berserk some months earlier.

My thought processes, as narrated herein, seem slow and deliberate when taken at reading speed but this creates a false impression because all those thoughts travelled through my mind like a video player on fast forward. They were all compressed into no more than a few seconds.

I pulled the covers down over his smooth, nude body and my pulse rose accordingly. My eyes wandered to my tie on the floor and I strained against the all-pervading notion that I could cause him to stay by strangling him unconscious.

I reached over and took the blue tie from the floor. His back was towards me and I carefully slipped the tie under and around his sleeping neck. I quickly straddled him and, twisting the ends of the tie around my wrists, pulled tightly. He came alive instantly and struggled, frantically, off the mattress on to the floor, twisting on to his back, with me on top of him. We moved a couple of feet until his head was at the skirting board and under the wine-coloured padded seat of a small, steel-tubed chair. I pulled myself up to lay on top of it, still holding on to the ligature, with his head and shoulders beneath and could feel his hands clawing against my taut arms. He bit his nails, so they didn't scratch my skin.

In the space of a minute or two, I heard his hands flop on to the carpet. He was unconscious. My mind was, by that time, furious with panic and relief that he'd stopped struggling and a buzz of high-speed fear and confusion roared in my head. I stood up and pulled away the chair and found he was out, but still breathing.

'Oh God,' I thought, 'when he regains consciousness, that's it, I'm in serious trouble.'

'I'll drown him,' I thought. 'It's too late to have second thoughts now; it's all or nothing.' I ran into the kitchen and filled a plastic bucket with water and returned to the room and put it on the floor. I stood astride him and, putting my hands under his armpits, I lifted him up and draped him over the chair, resting his torso on the seat. I then lifted his head up, pulled the bucket underneath and lowered his head into it. Being unconscious, he didn't struggle and, after a minute, the stream of air bubbles stopped. He was dead and had ceased to participate in any existence of personality.

And so it was that I became a killer, to appease all the trouble and stress at that time, through the frisson of addictive remedy. If I'd known him as a person with a clear identity, outside of inhibition-removing drink, I could not have laid a finger on him and I didn't want to kill him. It was the ritual with a passive male body that I craved. But the ritual had exploded in the face of logic and morality, splitting my life in two, bearing away all that had gone before into another, refined configuration beyond and against moral and criminal law. That single act was the most intensely concentrated moment of my whole life and the power and focus of it propelled me far beyond myself.

As I looked down at him, I had become my grandfather, looking down at my own passive, naked body. I/he stood astride the boy/me. I bent over and secured him under the armpits, pulling him up to be manhandled, limply, over my shoulder. Then I caught sight of us in the full-length mirror; his young head and arms hanging limply down my back like a rag doll. I thrilled at the added sensation of his body weight, suffused with the excitement of seeing him/me holding him/me securely around the thighs with the clenched orbs of his/my buttocks – naked, passive, vulnerable and exposed. I then took 'myself' to the bathroom for the cleansing part of the ritual.

I could have carried him for miles and would still have sustained my erection. I was on a high better than anything I'd ever encountered, hitherto, achieving my maximum frisson when I was carrying his weight. His young, naked body was totally at my disposal and, at the moment of his death, he had become the central prop in my fantasy. A surface appreciation of the situation is quoted in Brian Masters' book, *Killing for Company*, but I will provide the mental and emotional subtext here:

His body formed a more appreciable substitute for my *own* body in the fantasy. However, it was still basically me. I could give full attention to the 'old man' role but my psychological apportioning of roles still stayed the same. The stripping and washing were all constants in the ritual fantasy and I still got a buzz from appreciating what I was doing to 'myself', even if it was that young man's body. I had to dismiss any thoughts of the reality that I had killed him. In the fantasy, someone else had killed him and I was just taking care of the mess.

My mind had achieved an impossibility and had created a new reality: me carrying my own naked body and enjoying its absolute passivity. I could convince myself to believe in two opposing things simultaneously where, in my imagination, the impossible had become possible. His body – as him – was dead but his body – as me – was still alive and aware of what was being done to it. I couldn't bear to think about the real individual behind the shell of this real person. That would have been defensively driven from my consciousness; another retreat from reality.

I spent a relatively long time just examining – inch-by-inch – the young naked body; the movement of the limb joints, the texture and pliability of the skin to touch, the fleshy texture of the muscles on his thighs, arms, lower legs and buttocks, and the feel and texture of his privates.

After the moral anguish of that first killing had abated, I was resigned to the fact that I was a killer and nothing could ever alter that truth. It all looked bad and it *was* bad; unacceptably bad; the high of the ritual being juxtaposed with its gross, inexcusable immorality. Call the police? Never. I still had that clear vision of the Willesden Police turning up with that Glaswegian, foul-mouthed detective and his tirade of abuse with probably a kicking in store for me down in the cells. I was too traumatised for this addition to add to the totality of the situation so I endeavoured to cover up, still in fear of hearing the front doorbell ringing to herald the arrival of the police.

At that stage, I wasn't clear at all about the circumstances of the previous night in the pub and the many questions this raised. Had he been with others? Would he be reported missing? Would witnesses come forward to identify me as having been seen with him? All these questions shimmered over me like a hanging dagger with the logical conclusion that one just couldn't meet with someone in public, go home with him, kill him and not be found out.

Then came the mystery of rigor mortis. Because I was still in fear of the arrival of the police, I wanted to hide him. But his body stiffened up like a shop window dummy, which made putting him under the floorboards (the only place I had that was large enough to hide a fully-grown person) difficult. Later that morning, I went to Willesden High Street and bought a large saucepan and an electric carving knife and brought them back to the flat. Then I thought what a bloody stupid idea it was and my notion of dismemberment was abandoned.

Eventually, I managed to get his body under the floorboards, and I disposed of all his clothing except for his fawn coloured underpants. Still not knowing his details, as he had no documentation on him, I waited, with some apprehension, for something to happen; news in the media or a serious knock on my door but a few days passed and there was nothing. From this, I supposed that he might have been a migrant Irish worker living in digs, possibly under a false name to avoid paying tax. Many such casual labourers operated on tax-free 'lump labour', being picked up and hired for the day or the week at the multitude of building sites all over London and the Home Counties.

The cold draught of January 1979 whistled through the vents in the outside wall under the floorboards and this kept decay at bay. It was like an icebox down there. I'd gone to Woolworths and bought small-sized, white Y-fronts and a singlet before taking him up from under the boards. There was a little dirt on his skin and I bathed him again and dressed him in the underwear. He showed no signs of decay apart from a slight pink hue on his face and light blue lips that widely contrasted with the pale, smooth skin of his body. I articulated his limbs and examined him, feeling the sensations of being handled 'as him' as well as experiencing the sensations of the handler. I then, again, played out the ritual on his body in its various but familiar forms, which don't bear repetition.

When he was eventually returned under the floor, he remained there until the weather began to get warmer when I brought him up for dismemberment – a most sickening and unpleasant task. I cut the blackened, putrefied body into sizable parts and wrapped them up in cloth and small plastic bags before finally burning them in a fire at the bottom of the garden in August 1979. The dust and ashes sank into the ground by the rain or were scattered by the winds. Contrary to textbook opinion, I never kept any token of that (then) nameless boy; everything left, that was connected with him, having been confined to the fire.

As his last, physical trace vanished with no enquiries in my or anyone else's direction, the emptiness in me remained unrelieved. I had no feelings of triumph about 'getting away with murder' because I knew what I was and what I'd done and there would never be any kind of escape from that knowledge. My social isolation continued and I was pushed further from finding new flatmates, especially for the time that the body lay decomposing under the floorboards; if I'd had one, he would have detected the smell and I couldn't very well have disposed of the substance of the deed if someone else was around.

• • •

The body gone provided a small shimmer of optimism that things in the future might be controlled. In October 1979, I met a young Chinese guy, Andrew Ho, in the lobby of the Regent Palace Hotel, Piccadilly. When I first saw him, my mind went 'Bam!'; he was so good looking, smooth and boyish. I invited him back to my place, despite it being the middle of the day, and we took a taxi back to Melrose Avenue.

We climbed up on to the platform in that back room. My mind was in overdrive at the sight of his smooth, slight frame and I sat astride him. I wanted to strangle him into unconsciousness and, to cover the offence, finish his unconscious body off afterwards.

I put my hands around his neck and began choking him with all my strength but he struggled like a tiger and I lost my grip more than once. Then, just when I thought I was getting the better of him, he reached out, grabbed a brass candlestick and hit me with a resounding 'wallop' on the right side of my head. I immediately let go of my hold and he rolled sideways and jumped off the platform on to the floor, six feet beneath, shouting to me to throw down his clothes before he hurriedly dressed and left in a traumatic fever. Make no mistake…I wanted to possess him as I had done with that Irish boy ten months earlier.

After Andrew Ho left the flat, I felt devastated and anguished that he had escaped me. I had imagined a more favourable result of me standing on the platform ladder and pulling his limp body over into my arms, placing it on the table and carefully stripping it naked. I was sick at the thought that he'd escaped, not so much for the prospect that I might be discovered but because of the great fact that the ritual had been denied so near consummation. I spent some months intermittently masturbating at the memory of the sight of his body and its vulnerability.

After my arrest four years later, my courage failed me at Hornsey Police Station, during my flood of confession, and the mention of the name 'Andy Ho' brought a red flush of embarrassment to my calm, controlled exterior. I was afraid that he might testify to the details leading up to the enactment of 'the ritual' and my true motives towards him. I also had quite enough on my plate with multiple homicide charges so I made the general comment to the police that I had not intended to harm him and that, by a feeble attempt to throttle him, I was only trying to teach him a lesson. Of course, this was not true. Back then, I was quite prepared to admit to murder but not to the existence of my aberrant 'ritual'. He should have been listed as an 'attempt' count.

• • •

Two months after attempting to kill Andrew Ho, I found myself chatting with a Canadian student in a West End bar on a cold, Sunday afternoon. We walked around London sightseeing and, after more drinking, we took a taxi back to a warmer Melrose Avenue where I committed my second act of homicide. Afterwards, Ken Ockenden laid back, there on the couch, and I gazed and gazed at him, wondering on the great mystery of where he'd gone and where he now was. I moved beside him and thought my thoughts to him.

Brian Masters, in his book, *Killing for Company*, wrote that I sat around talking to my dead victims in everyday conversation. But what I actually did was *think* to them – all done in a fleeting flood as one is apt to do in some situations. It seemed more appropriate than speaking to deaf ears. Those times were more dreamlike than real because sitting in their presence was a dream world to me. To stroke and caress was to like and love but what I was liking and loving was an imaginary being inside my own mind, created by my own emotional needs.

That essence of the *real* Ken Ockendon had been removed by his death and the 'dream boy' had entered the solid flesh of the 'husk'. I barely knew the real man; just a jumble of conversations, fuelled and fuddled by drink. Was his form now transformed into my brother, Olav, now no longer able to mock and reject me, passive and at my command?

There he sat, brimming with beauty and sexuality with his longish, fair hair, seeming to acquiesce and invite the next stage of 'wooing' by his 'consensual' silence. The thin, hugging material of his singlet and pants accentuated his mystery; his guarded secrets. I took his hand in mine and he didn't say 'no'. When I touched, held or moved him, he would not wake up and 'discover' me.

After my warped, human ritual had played itself out, I took him, seated in my lap, and held him. The frisson was in a relationship between me and me; one false and one real...painfully and inadequately real. He seemed oblivious as to how compellingly beautiful he was; his smooth, pale skin, his belly, his chest, his nipples, his thighs and legs – everything – but still his mute, passive power rode high over me.

• • •

The 'ritual' that I performed on his body followed a similar pattern with each victim, which I will relate here in detail. Immediately after the death, I would have an erection in anticipation of the events to come. The key indicator that the tenant had 'vacated the premises' was when the bladder or bowels had evacuated in his death throes. This gave me the 'excuse' to wash the body after stripping it free of its soiled clothing and former identity. I would then lay it on the floor and remove all its clothing. If there was faeces in the underwear, I would roll the body over and wipe it clean before sitting it upright in a chair, kneeling in front of it and, draping it on to and over my right shoulder, heaving it up for transportation to the bathroom.

If there was no faeces or urine in the clothing, I would be careful how I carried it into the bathroom. With one such body, the weight of my shoulder joint, pressing against the victim's stomach, caused a post-mortal issue of faeces. Consequently, this type of body would be carried into the bathroom by holding it, cradled, in my arms; one hand supporting it under its knees with the other under its shoulders.

The carrying itself caused a further frisson of sexual excitement and my power over the passive victim accentuated my own passivity. What surprised me at first was that when I lifted up the body, it issued a deep sigh from the lungs, as air escaped, temporarily alarming me that the victim was, in fact, still alive.

The bath would be filled with warm, soapy water and if the naked body best identified with the fantasy body in my mind, I would be inclined to strip off and get in myself, to hold and wash the body. If not, I'd wash it 'normally' with me fully clothed, kneeling beside the bath. Any ugly body hair would be shaved off using disposable razors, though the hair on the head and eyebrows were always untouched. All other body hair would also be removed, including from the anus and scrotum, leaving a neat triangle of hair in the pubic region. The subject would then be removed from the bath and towelled dried on my lap as I sat on the toilet.

The dried, naked, young body would then be given a dusting of Johnson's baby talcum powder to smooth the skin and give the aroma of scented life. It would then be carried back from the bathroom and laid out, either on the floor, the table or the bed, for examination. I would closely inspect every contour and every square inch of the smooth skin. The orange sidelights would be turned on to give the skin a rosy, lifelike hue and I'd add a further dusting of talcum powder to conceal any bruises on the neck. Later, after they'd been dead for some days, I would disguise any discoloration with the powder. I never applied any make-up to them because I just didn't have any, though I might have retouched their lips if I'd had any lipstick. I would appreciate this vision and I'd thrill at the sight of upturned buttocks, which I would knead, stroke and fondle, and I would apply the same attention to the flaccid penis and scrotum. I had become my grandfather and the dream boy had become me. I would sit astride him, with my legs bent and running close and parallel with his thighs, and I'd masturbate as I felt the sensation of his soft privates against my own, naked buttocks. I would ejaculate on to his belly and chest before wiping it off with a tissue. Then the ritual was over. For this, I killed many men and no fire in the back garden could ever erase the memory of them from those that they'd loved and were loved by. I remained pathetic.

· · ·

In May 1980, SAS men held the camera's lens as they stormed the Iranian Embassy in London. After the siege had finished, I left London for a week to attend the Civil and Public Services Association annual conference in Southport and, upon returning to London, I went on the town and met Martyn Duffey, whom I invited back to my flat at Melrose Avenue.

When I recall the events that followed, I am filled with gut-deep shame with which I viewed his passive flesh after I'd rendered his will obsolete through a quick, concentrated kill. I remembered no frisson as I strangled Martyn Duffey with a ligature, just a determined expectation charged with great physical strength and energy while being blind to everything else. I was also disinhibited by alcohol, without which I couldn't summon the courage to do the vital deed. I didn't see the act as killing Martyn Duffey but a necessary and compulsive act of removing his will and personality from his body so that I could enjoy imbuing it with my own will and my own desires.

From the rigours of the struggle, I remembered turning on the lights and seeing his body, wan and passively helpless, where he was powerless to talk or act with any smidge of resistance. I relaxed into gentle intimacy, easing his T-shirt over his torso then up and over his head, heightened by the flopping down of his limp arms. At the time, I didn't know that he was close to turning seventeen years old but I did notice that he had a smooth, boyish chest, nipples and belly. The tempo of the pounding blood, buzzing in my head, increased as I removed his underpants, imagining myself as him, thrilling to the notion and sight of having *my* underpants so removed from *my* passive body. Naked, I embraced his still-warm, naked body.

I had, again, become my grandfather, lavishing attention upon myself, supported by a prop of the desired partner. I was goal-driven; that heroin fix for the saving moment only; the one of many 'endings' for the junkie.

I recall, with clarity, the pleasant, blue sky and sunshine the following day as I was engrossed in dressing and undressing Martyn Duffey's body. He had become rigid with rigor mortis in his underpants and jeans with its heavy, black leather belt. I was aroused by his pale, smooth belly where it met the waistband of the belted jeans. I unbuckled the belt and pulled his jeans down to mid-thigh before I laid the flat of my palm on his soft belly and masturbated to completion. Then I looked at his flaccid penis hanging there under the light-brown, pubic down and I looked down at myself and we looked the same – with useless instruments. With the ritual over, I snapped into practical mode.

I'd become reduced to fondling the naked, dead body of a young man that I had liked but had killed. This was the 'diminished responsibility' on which I pleaded at my trial but, at that time, couldn't describe or articulate to my defending counsel why or what it was.

. . .

Three months later, in August 1980, I met Douglas Stewart in the Golden Lion pub in Central London, viewing him as just another potential sexual partner. The talk and atmosphere in the Lion were such that nobody, other than a complete idiot, could have mistaken it for anything other than a gay pub. Amongst other beer brands, it supplied Stewart's favourite: Younger's Tartan bitter, a Scottish beer.

When he accepted my invitation to come back to Melrose Avenue, I guessed that he was well acquainted with the form of gay pickup for the purposes of a one-night stand. At the flat, I made no attempt to ply him with drink and just gave him a single beer, though I was puzzled when he declined my obvious invitation to go to bed. There were two separate mattresses on the raised, wooden platform and he was under no obligation to sleep in my bed. In fact, he said he'd sleep for a time sitting in one of the armchairs, fully clothed. This set alarm bells ringing and I suspected that his true intention of coming back with me was robbery, gay bashing or something worse. Having had more than a few drinks, I feared going to sleep because of the possibility that he would rob me and leave before I awoke.

I mounted the platform and laid in bed waiting for him to go to sleep while he snuggled into the armchair. I knew I couldn't sustain this watch for too long as the drink would soon have an overpowering effect on me. It was then that I decided to settle the issue and strangle Stewart into unconsciousness, 'killing two birds with one stone', though I was too drunk to let a clear, workable plan form in my mind.

When I thought he was asleep, I attacked him, impractically and clumsily, from the front and tried to strangle him with his own tie, which was still around his neck. He immediately sprang to life and wrestled me to the floor and straddled me. I called out, 'Take my money, take my money!' but he said he didn't want my money and he let me up. I was still not convinced and went swiftly into the kitchen, returning with a large carving knife but I soon realised his intentions in coming back with me were, naively, innocent and he posed no threat.

With the crisis over, I returned the knife to the kitchen and we talked. He then said he was leaving and I did nothing to stop him. I didn't know what had happened to his tie but guessed he'd discarded it as soon as he'd left the house.

An hour or so later, he returned with police officers and I convinced them that we'd been drunk and that I'd thrown him out, leading them to deduce that it was probably a homosexual quarrel. They informed Stewart that if he wanted to make an official complaint then he could do so when he'd sobered up but Stewart never did.

If he hadn't been so fit and alert, I would have strangled him in the follow-through and his body would have undoubtedly been subjected to the usual ritual. My fear of what I believed was his robbery motive made it essential to neutralise him in any case. Perhaps I was just looking for a moral justification. Maybe the truth was that we were both confused that night in a drunken, hazy fog of crossed purposes. Ultimately, I could have no excuse for my conduct, which was not a one-off but was becoming habitually addictive. The ritual had become more important and compelling than all the circumstances surrounding it and it formed a clearly defined path. It was a subconscious wish to fulfil and replicate conditions in my distant childhood when I had become detached from close, tactile relationships.

· · ·

There were several young men whom I'd picked up and used as props in my fantasies without them ever coming to any harm. In the case of one guy named Steve Webster*, I picked him up flat out drunk in the street and my behaviour towards him, as I retold in my official police statements after my arrest, was correct in the extreme; I simply didn't need to kill young Steve. He was put on my bed 'out like a light' and had no idea that his passive body was the subject of another fantasy ritual. I stripped him naked but I didn't bathe him in case he woke up, forcing me to kill him. I lifted him into my arms in front of the mirror then fondled and caressed him before gently penetrating him and ejaculating. All he remembered was waking up with me in bed in the morning. In order that he'd be less inclined to suspect any sexual impropriety the night before, I put his jockey shorts back on him. I had no reason to believe that he was even gay.

When I failed to totally incapacitate men like Stewart and Ho, it was just that they were able to put up an effective resistance and escape. Others, that I'd rendered unconscious by strangulation, were used for the fantasy then let go the next morning with a plausible reason for their sore heads and throats.

There was one guy who was very drunk and with whom I tried to strangle into full unconsciousness. He went limp and, as I was taking off his trousers as he lay in the armchair, he woke up, much to my surprise, and said, 'Fuck me, please fuck me!' I was completely taken aback. He must have thought I was just playing a kinky sex game by putting a tie around his neck. He never knew the true nature of his situation.

In around 1980, I was arrested, one night, and incarcerated in Kilburn Police Station. The arresting officer, knowing I was queer, arrested me for allegedly being drunk. I was assaulted by some of the lads at the station, thrown into a cell and urinated on by one of them; my red, mohair jumper was soaked in the stuff. The next morning, I was given nothing to eat or drink and was driven to the

* *Not his real name.*

cells at St Mary's Road Magistrates' Court, awaiting my appearance before their worships. I presented my own case and cross-examined the evidence of the arresting PC, pleading that it was a clear case of animosity from an ex-colleague and that I was not drunk. I told the magistrates that I'd been beaten and pissed on and I asked, 'If I had been drinking – and drinking alcohol causes dehydration and thirst – why had I not requested anything to drink in the twelve hours since my arrest?' The case terminated with the magistrates giving me the benefit of their doubts and they found me not guilty. I was free to go but what the court did not know was that they had just released a serial killer who was already deep into homicide.

In the summer of 1981, I set about doing a last, mass dissection at Melrose Avenue, prior to my move to Cranley Gardens in Muswell Hill. Pulling decomposing bodies up from under the floorboards on to the kitchen floor, to cut them up, was a nasty and unpleasant task; the corpses were in varying stages of decay. In order to face this ordeal, I started drinking from a bottle of Bacardi rum and, by the time I was finished in the evening, the bottle was almost empty and I was practically legless. I put as much of the viscera as could fit into a space between a board and the fence on the right, near the bottom of the garden. I wrapped the other, mainly fleshy, parts of the bodies into smaller packages and put them back under the floorboards. The stench of the decaying flesh was still, even while pissed out of my mind, bad enough to cause me to periodically throw up.

In this muddled haze of booze, I took it into my mind to take Bleep up to Gladstone Park for her daily romp. There I was, with the mutt on a lead, tottering over to the park with a plastic carrier bag bulging with all the surplus entrails – stinking to high heaven – which I left, in broad daylight, by the side of the road adjacent to the park. Apparently, it was found by a biology student, Robert Wilson, who was concerned enough to call the police. The bag was taken to Willesden Police Station, where the duty old bill thought it might be butchered animal entrails and it was subsequently destroyed.

Had it been subjected to a closer examination by a qualified pathologist, alarm bells would have rung loud and clear for a death probably caused by foul play. My bloody fingerprints were all over the carrier bag and those could have been matched with mine on file in a relatively short time. But this omission delayed my arrest by eighteen months and four more deaths (Malcolm Barlow was still to die in the late summer of 1981 at Melrose Avenue).

. . .

For many years, my fantasies were presented in the oblong frame of a mirror. It was, for me, a very potent window on to a different reality. The frame was also the movie frame, which played such a central part of my psychological life and health. Although this has been mentioned in other reports on my case, it has never been given the significance it warrants. My rituals in handling the bodies were replete with the continuity of mirrors. My undressing of the bodies was nearly always viewed by me through a mirror, as this was more potent than looking directly at what I was doing. My highest peak of frisson was to stand before a full-length mirror, with the orange sidelights on, naked, holding the naked body with one arm under the knees and the other under its arms and back. The feeling would be accentuated by walking forward, towards the mirror, and in seeing the lower legs and arms sway limply to my movement. This was a very potent addition to the body's passivity.

The unblemished body-beautiful was totally divorced from the retrieved, putrefying stench later to be disposed of as obnoxious garbage. The circumstances of disposal were dictated by the means I had available. I didn't own a car, nor did I drive, otherwise I'd have taken the bodies out to the countryside in the boot and buried them without any recourse to dissection. I also thought it would attract too much attention to be digging full-sized graves in my small back garden. There would also be the problem of the dog digging up bones when I wasn't there. Putting them under the floorboards was the usual first expedient 'to sweep the problem under the carpet' as it were. The decision to cut them up and remove the guts came only from the smell problem when the weather became hot.

The dissection of decaying human meat did not have any excitement for me. It was just like butchering any carcass, though a normal animal carcass has not the repulsion of decayed human flesh.

There was certainly no suggestion of cannibalism, nor did my dog eat any human remains. When dissecting the corpses of the first two victims at Cranley Gardens (on the wooden board across the bath), I was able to reflect, rationally, on the culinary possibilities of fairly fresh, human meat but the thought only engaged me for a few moments. When I sliced through human buttocks, the meat looked just like beef rump steaks, with the colour being slightly lighter than in beef. Similarly, the pieces boiled in the pot (on the stove at my flat in Cranley Gardens, in 1981) looked just like boiled beef.

The thought of giving a small chunk to Bleep crossed my mind but I didn't want her to acquire a taste for human flesh, though she looked interested enough at the prospect of getting a piece. In any case, food was never an important feature of my life and I was content to have everything I ate served with chips; fried egg, bacon or chop or hamburger or sausage, with baked beans or tinned tomatoes. I never had the time nor the inclination (after many years in catering) to prepare elaborate meals for myself, and my previous flatmates, like Twinkle, had the same, common, culinary tastes as myself. I also figured that those young men may have been in possession of various diseases and may have been taking drugs, thereby contaminating their own flesh. Finally, and perhaps insultingly to those I'd killed, I wasn't sure of the purity of their meat (having not been passed for human consumption by a meat inspector). In total, and also on moral grounds, I didn't think their flesh was suitable or fit for human consumption.

If I'd had chemical means for preservation, I suppose I would have kept some parts of some victims. I remember one victim's hands, for example, were small, marble-white, pretty and very delicate. I may well have kept them in a jar of alcohol or some liquid preservative and would probably have done the same with all the scrotums and penises. Ideally, I'd have liked to have had sufficient skill and chemicals to retard decay altogether and preserve them by embalming them to a lifelike colour but my circumstances, being so limited, confined such thoughts to the realm of idealistic dreams.

• • •

While I was living at 23 Cranley Gardens in Muswell Hill, I had at least three contacts with the local police. The first was when I reported that I was mugged of my wallet as I was coming back from the pub. On another occasion, someone I had attempted to kill reported it to the police (they were not called to give evidence but their statements were amongst those not tendered in evidence against me at my trial).

Then, in late February or early March 1982, I called the police after taking a walk in Highgate Woods with Bleep. While walking along a dirt track, I noticed a freshly dug hole. I took a closer look and, to my amazement, I found, just below the surface, the large bulk of an object covered in man-made material, possibly clothing. Having a one-track mind at that stage, imbued with the possibility that I was not the only murderer in Muswell Hill, I thought it might be a dead body. I hurried to the phone box (by the parade of shops near the Cranley Gardens' end of the entrance to the woods) and dialled 999. Two police cars and a van duly arrived and a horde of plodding bill followed me into the woods. They all gathered around the site while a sergeant scraped away at the buried object until it revealed the body of a large dog wrapped in material, which disappointed them all. I apologised for wasting their time and told them that it might have been a murder ('you never can tell nowadays'). The sergeant assured me that, as a good, alert citizen, I'd done the right thing and he thanked me for making the call. They all then bundled into their vehicles and buggered off back to Muswell Hill Police Station.

* * *

In April 1982, I met Carl Stottor in The Black Cap gay bar in Camden, North London. He'd had a few drinks and told me he was 'of no fixed abode' and was dossing at a local hostel. His social and emotional life was in turmoil and, apart from his failure to fit into the uniform standards of society, he also suffered the contortions of an ongoing sexual identity crisis. In short, he told me that he wished that he was dead. I won't dwell on previously reported details of the events of his attempted murder but I will provide additional narrative where my fateful and traumatic encounter with Stottor should be viewed in proportion; me being just one of a succession of competing forces in his greatly troubled life and volatile personality.

I had invited him back to my flat at Cranley Gardens, where I'd been living for about six months, and in the less than twelve hours he spent in my aberrant company, he had scant knowledge of its full significance. At most, from his sore eyes and throat, he must have guessed that he'd been the object of some kinky, bondage sex involving a ligature. In reality, however, I had used his passive body as a prop in my fantasy. When I revived him, it wasn't so much a change of heart (as had been maintained) but an accident of luck and circumstances. While I was carrying him into the bathroom and while I was holding him under the water, he was in a sexually aroused state and, up to his moment of submerged unconsciousness, the milk of his seed streamed in spasmodic jerks into the warm water of the bath. But his premature ejaculation had ruined the flow of my fantasy, and so I put him to bed, and his embraceable warmth was all there was left, having exhausted my frisson of interest in him through drink and fatigue. Within the ritual of my fantasy need, he had served his passive role as a young, naked, male body to be ministered to and used.

• • •

In the festive season of 1982, I had picked up another young man in the Golden Lion pub in Soho. His name was Roy Foxton* and I lusted after him. He was temporarily homeless and was bumming his way home, up north, before I had invited him to 23 Cranley Gardens. The conditions were never right to subdue him because we were both too sober and, in the rational condition, I couldn't overcome my scruples. As we both laid together in the same bed, I could feel my possessive libido rising and there, in the dark, wide awake, I desperately wondered what to do. Eventually, he drifted off to sleep on his side, purring gently. Carefully, I eased down his briefs and fondled his privates and buttocks. He was a slim, smooth, young man and my inner fever rose in temperature. I thought of bashing him on the head with a blunt instrument but couldn't do it. I thought about stabbing him to death with a kitchen knife but could not do that either. I thought about tying his sleeping legs together and then strangling him but couldn't overcome some restraining inhibition blocking the forefront of my mind. Was it pure cowardice or was it something else? I remembered feeling it was important not to damage his body, in such a way as to mar the purity of the image in my fantasy, and I couldn't bear to think of his smashed head or any stab wounds on him; I had visions of his blood fountaining all over the walls and ceiling as he struggled, dying, against an unremitting bludgeoning. And the noise of his last, desperate screams would, no doubt, wake up the whole street.

I slipped quietly from the bed and crept into the kitchen to

* *Not his real name.*

ponder a plan whereby I could affect my purpose. It might just work. I put Bleep in the front bedroom and locked the door (at that time the bed was in the living room where the TV was). Without turning on the lights, I brought in a small, portable, one-bar electric fire, plugged it in and draped a wet towel over it before retreating into the kitchen. The idea was to get the front room filled with smoke thereby forcing the sleeping Roy to fall into deeper unconsciousness due to smoke inhalation.

After a few minutes, I checked and the room had, indeed, begun to fill with smoke. To dispel my doubt of success, I began to run the bath in anticipation of the receipt of the youth's unconscious, naked body. Alas, the enterprise failed and my aberrant drives would have to hold patient for another day in their addictive spiral. The smoke had woken him and I came dashing in from 'a late-night bath' and pulled the smouldering towel from off the fire. The light was on by this time and I was opening the window. 'Christ,' I said, 'I couldn't sleep and went for a bath. The towel must have slipped from the rail on to the fire. Stupid idiot.'

I seemed to have convinced him with my explanation and if he had his suspicions he kept them to himself. With the room clear of what little smoke there had been, I joined him back in bed as though nothing had happened. He probably thought me a bit odd because, in the early morning, I began to fondle him openly in bed and, while he didn't overtly resist, I felt that, in matters sexual, he was a bit inexperienced. I'd already guessed that he may have been struggling between orientations and had opted for a heterosexual one. Who knows? I saw him on his way the next day.

• • •

On the evening of 26 January 1983, I met young Stephen Sinclair, my final victim. We had both had a few drinks and he was a bit incoherent. It was clear that he was immersed in a drugged lifestyle, famished of social rectitude. With his blonde hair, youthful looks, T-shirt, black leather jacket and very-tight-fitting jeans, I thrilled at the prospect of having him as a sexual partner and, as the evening began to fade, we took the Northern Line underground train to my flat at Cranley Gardens. We rode in a half-empty carriage sitting opposite one another; our respective clothing standing out in stark contrast. I was wearing my grey, tweed jacket, pale blue shirt, tie, dark trousers and brown, slip-on boots. The casual observer would never have known that we were even together.

Since we'd met, I doubted that I'd understood a single word he'd said in his half-drugged Scots brogue. He struggled to stop himself dozing off on the train and, at Highgate Station, we alighted and followed the long, thin escalator to the surface before walking the mile or so to my flat.

He settled easily into the warm, convivial comfort of my room, in front of the three-bar, coal-effect, glowing fire. I poured us both a drink while he disappeared into the toilet where he spent an inordinately long time. I later reflected that he'd probably popped some pills in his multifarious addictions. When he returned to the main room, still as uncommunicative as ever, he resumed his place and, as he sat, he would casually rub his thighs slowly together as he eased and changed the position of his legs. His whole being sent a shock of excitement buzzing through me. Soon, his pale blue eyes began to close above his pretty upturned nose and soft, pouting lips; the total possession of him beckoned me.

He left with no more than the feeblest of struggles. It was the beginning of my last ritual of a possessive fantasy. In the soft, orange glow of the sidelights, the dopamine flowed as I gently removed each tattered and dog-eared running shoe from off his limp feet and the urine-soaked jeans from off his boyish limbs; that ceremonious removal of things soiled – to be cleansed into a new perfection. He was still very warm. He had fooled the onlookers into believing that he was blonde but, as I peeled his mucky briefs down, a shock of ginger pubic hair was revealed, wherein nestled a small, white, redundant penis. I also found there were deep cuts on his forearm, as evidence of recent self-laceration.

I lifted him, sleeping for ever, naked, into my arms and carried him to the bathroom. He was a bit street-grimy and whenever he had most recently bathed, this was to be his last. It was into the early hours of 27 January that I pondered and touched his powerful presence.

After bathing him, I deliberately placed his naked body, full length, on its side on the edge of the bed, in a precarious position. I had already placed pillows and cushions on the floor to break his fall, stop the noise of him hitting the floor and to prevent any damage to his body. I sat and watched as he gradually rolled over and fell on to the floor. What excited me was the movement of the limp body and limbs as they fell and laid themselves at rest when they hit the cushions.

What was missing from the bald account I wrote for Brian Masters, related in *Killing for Company*, was the emotional, thinking subtext in fuller detail. My heart pounded as I supported Sinclair's body weight over my shoulder and held him in my arms. The thrill of holding him and imagining being held by him, in this dual role, sent oscillating shudders up and down my spine. I stood there in the room just bearing his weight, one arm securing him under the armpits and the other hand holding him under his knees. This clasped his naked thighs together, forcing up his penis from its nest of bright ginger pubic hair. His skin was fair and as white as moonlight and his nakedness was smooth, warm and beautiful. His pale blue lips accentuated – with his totally limp limbs – his total passivity.

Was to fondle his beautiful buttocks, or to take his nipples between my lips, being hateful and pornographic? Are tender caresses obscene? I thought not. What was irredeemably obscene was to kill Stephen Sinclair and use his corpse for a completely selfish purpose. I killed him and I used him and such homicide was a crime against humanity.

When I returned from work that Thursday evening, he sat waiting in an armchair, clad only in his black leather jacket, and he again served as the naked boy in my sexual fantasy. By the following evening, Friday, I sought a respite from his cold presence (he would keep for some days yet).

I ventured out and took the Tube to Hampstead where I found an empty refuge at the King William IV pub. The Willie was almost deserted that early in the evening with no real talent in yet; only a few of the older regulars. The evening advanced in the hollow indifference as I casually eavesdropped on the routine chit-chat. One guy came in and told his friend that they'd shut down Hampstead Station. 'Probably another bomb scare' (in reference to recent IRA activity) was his speculative quip.

As the Willie showed no signs of perking up, I decided to decamp to the Sir Richard Steele pub, down the road. Perhaps there would be some interesting talent there. I could be reinvigorated by a brisk walk down to Belsize Park as the Tube system seemed to be closed off. It was a straight road down past Hampstead Police Station to the pub, but it seemed to be a night for obstructions as I could see traffic building up and a lot of flashing lights ahead. 'Probably a road accident,' I thought. But as I approached Belsize Park Station, I could see all the physical consternation of some kind of emergency.

A policeman, aided by colleagues, was stopping people and turning them back and I asked, 'What's up?' He replied, 'We're dealing with a dangerous man here. The station's closed.' I backtracked slightly and crossed over to the far side of the street because the single element in my concentration was to quench my thirst – and perhaps my eyes – at the Sir Richard Steele. But it was no improvement on the Willie. The Steele was not a true gay bar anyway, though I'd been well favoured in there from time to time with my straight appearance. If it was anything, it was a closet gay bar.

After a short stay, I thought about making my way down to Camden Town or maybe getting a taxi back to Cranley Gardens but, before I walked out, I overheard a conversation to the effect that they'd just arrested an IRA man at Belsize Park Station, so I hailed a taxi which took me home instead.

After I'd let Bleep out into the back garden for her final call of the day, I turned my attention to Stephen Sinclair, sleeping in his cold infinity on the floor of the front room. I lifted his soft, firm emptiness up into my arms, carried it into the warm glow of my living room and placed him in the black vinyl armchair. I tilted his head back and studied his pale, young face with the blue lips and the tousled blonde hair. His once-bright eyes were becoming clouded against humanity. 'He was better off,' I thought, 'than that poor bastard the police have just got their hands on.' Little did I realise that the cause of all the inconvenience at Belsize Park Station was David Martin, a fugitive on the run from the police and a man who I would meet in the months following my arrest.

I filled my glass and watched Stephen Sinclair through the music plugged into my brain. I sat back and contemplated what I'd done and what I'd become.

· · ·

The act of killing was never an end in itself. If I'd had access to some kind of knockout drug then it's unlikely that there would have been any deaths at all. I dressed and undressed them a lot more often than I admitted in testimony. I got a buzz from that and also from washing and lifting them up to carry. And those high spots produced a sexual tension, which needed ejaculation. I didn't remember having an erection during any of the killings and, if I had, it would have resulted only from rising sexual expectation of favours to come. With some victims, I had tried but could not achieve sexual penetration because as soon as my penis touched cold flesh my erection subsided. I never punched the bodies, cut or mutilated them, nor did I slap their buttocks or partake of any other violent act once they were dead.

Another point of great significance was that the more I was aware of my victims as individuals – with interesting personalities – the less likely they could be fit for use in my fantasies and rituals; they would have been unsuitable as an anonymous object or prop.

It's hard to believe that more men survived my attacks than were killed and I was surprised that I wasn't arrested earlier. Short of taking out an ad in the *Telegraph*: 'Come to Melrose Avenue and Be Murdered', it was never difficult to put two and two together. Even six weeks before my arrest, distraught victims were still going to Police Stations, claiming that I had tried to kill them (Toshimitsu Ozawa, for example, on New Year's Eve in 1982). Fred and Rose West were able to operate for over twenty years undetected. Peter Sutcliffe for over five. Even at the eleventh hour, I could have covered up or even fled.

I think that I'd just had enough of being trapped in a psycho-ritual, which had become more compulsive and meaningless as it progressed in its escalating extremity. I was really happy to be arrested and to begin to be released from all the building pressures that had accumulated over a whole life exposed; itself, burned out by the disease.

5

Life | 1983

When I was arrested on 9 February 1983, the police were unsure of their ground. In the interview at my flat they were fishing, tentatively, in the hope of gaining information concerning the samples of human flesh found down the house drains. Detective Chief Inspector Peter Jay told me that he thought the remains could only have come from my flat. Weary of the expected long train of questioning, I put myself – almost immediately – on their hook. I surprised the CID trio by interjecting that I would go down to the Police Station and tell them everything. Jay was still unsure about what he had until I opened the cupboard and showed him the two black, plastic bin-liners and it was only then that he became manifestly aware of the smell. In subsequent documentaries and interviews, Jay incorrectly said that he was aware of the stench of decaying flesh the moment he entered the flat. If he was, he didn't register it or mention it to me. Surely any such recognition – upon entering the flat – would have prompted the first of any detective's questions, namely, 'What's that awful stench?' but no such enquiry was forthcoming at the time.

I didn't ever recall hearing DCI Jay saying, 'Stop messing about, where's the rest of the body?' and suspected it was invented, after the event, designed to paint Jay as the textbook sleuth, homing in for the kill on someone he suspected of murder.

In the car on the journey to the Police Station I was asked: 'How many bodies are we talking about, one or two?' I immediately replied with 'fifteen or sixteen'. With that, the numbers fifteen and sixteen became, for ever, the universally accepted total of the number of men I had killed between the 30 December 1978 and 26 January 1983. Soon after, my memory rolled back the fact that the actual number was twelve (nine at 195 Melrose Avenue and three at 23 Cranley Gardens). This was widely known by 1988 but one sees no mention of it in any publication to date. The literati, programme producers and journalists had no intention of diminishing their monstrous 'property' and this stance went across the board without a single exception.

I was kept incommunicado in Hornsey Police Station in the early stages after my arrest and it was the police who gave the press all the information that hit the headlines in the first couple of days – including the infamous number sixteen. Nobody else knew the published details but for the officers on the case and me. This was to be the biggest case in all of their careers and they made sure that the entire nation knew about it when they sat down at their breakfast tables. At that stage, I hadn't even made a statement in writing. The press was better briefed than I was and I didn't get possession of a single newspaper to read in all the time I spent at Hornsey in police custody.

At my arrest the police had an identifiable dead body whose condition couldn't possibly have come about through natural causes (beheaded, halved and disembowelled). They had a name for the body (Stephen Sinclair) and an admission from me that I had killed him. In short, they had everything necessary in order to lay a charge against me, even if it was only a holding charge. But this would have placed the whole matter under the protection of *sub judice* and out of the reach of the sensation-hungry media (too much pre-trial hype and 'monsterising' speculation in the high profiles of the media colours a jury's view when the trial comes up). Instead, a clearly prejudiced picture had been allowed to form in the public's mind even before I was charged with any offence. In order to enhance their own place in the professional and public spotlight, they took a full forty-eight hours to charge me, giving the media full latitude to milk their property. This allowed the images of monstrosity to take full flight to whet the appetite of profiteering imaginators.

Upon my arrival at Hornsey Police Station, I strained for release from the years of unbounded pressure of periodic killing. I could not easily face any ordeal at the hands of the police and my past experience had told me what to expect if my full co-operation wasn't forthcoming. Added to this, was the guilt I felt for my past actions and I was in desperate need of relief.

In the first eight days at Hornsey, me and the police investigators kept each other sweet within the restricting circumstances of arrest and imprisonment. At one point they called a brief halt to the interviews when it was reported to me that a Japanese TV crew were on the roof of a building opposite, eavesdropping with high-tech sound equipment. Having a good view from the window, I didn't notice anyone and it may have been that they were becoming paranoid with the size of their investigative profile.

At my first interview, I immediately informed Detective Chief Inspector Jay that I'd be fully co-operating and I was allowed to retain my essential cigarettes and spectacles; I needed to smoke in order to calm my nerves. I knew that they required me to write their script and, in a kind of unspoken conspiracy, we began to act out our respective roles according to form. Playing the part of the villain was new to me and, being absolutely isolated and friendless, I entered into a spirit of bonhomie with my captors, which I needed as there was no one else. My treatment was correct and amiable and I struck up a rapport with the two police officers who remained with me in my cell twenty-four hours a day, though neither of them knew quite what to expect from me.

Prior to my arrest, I'd left a letter in my desk drawer at the office. On the envelope, I'd written, 'To a solicitor acting for Des Nilsen. Under no circumstances must this be given to police.' In it, I wrote a note dated 9 February 1983:

'If I am taken into police custody, I believe I am in real fear for my life. It will be expedient for them to arrange my termination by the usual method, i.e., enforced "suicide". I now state that I have not a single thought in my mind about suicide. If any violence occurs against me, it will definitely not be with my consent.'

I signed it, 'Des Nilsen'.

Previous commentators have grossly underplayed or ignored this foremost element of fear of what I thought might have happened to me after my arrest. But when gripped by fear, a man will do things which he wouldn't do under normal circumstances.

On the second day after my arrest, I was driven to Melrose Avenue to point out the site of the three bonfires I had made in, or near, the back garden there. It looked like they were holding a police convention because I never thought it possible to get so many of them into my back room. The last time detectives had stood on that spot was in 1981 when I had called them in to note the criminal damage done; the agents of the landlord had gained entry and completely vandalised my things. Back then, I remembered they took notes standing on the very floorboards underneath which were stored numerous bodies. They noticed no smell, or if they did, they kept it to themselves.

On my second evening in custody, someone in my union (the CPSA) sent a solicitor, Janice Kaufman, to see me, though I thought her unexpected appearance on the scene would have been viewed as obstructive by the police and I didn't want to dull our spirit of co-operation. I told her that I didn't want a solicitor as I would have expected one to have pressed me to remain silent. The police seemed pleased with my decision and made no attempt to persuade me to do otherwise.

On scores of blank pages at Hornsey, I set about indicting myself with the full, muted applause of the forces of the Crown. Detective Chief Superintendent Chambers asked the questions and Peter Jay wrote my answers down in longhand. I felt that Jay was a better policeman and more intelligent than his superior. Chambers was an old timeserver near to retirement and struck me as being the sort of man who fed off his brighter subordinates and took the credit for their solving efforts. He seemed to have forgotten a lot of the basic principles in police evidence gathering, in spite of his exalted rank. I give you one glaring example:

I was giving details of the identity of one of the men I had killed, and I said something like: 'One of them came from Canada. His name was Ken…' and Chambers interjected with, 'Ockendon?' Well, that was a major mistake in as much as Chambers had introduced the name 'Ockendon' into the conversation. For any confession to be credible in court, the facts of identity must come, spontaneously, from the accused and not be put into his mouth by his interrogators. However, to spare the man embarrassment, the official version read so that it had me saying 'Ken Ockendon', which I was quite willing to sign as the man that I had killed, in early December 1979, was, indeed, Ken Ockendon who had been reported as missing around that time.

My relationship with Chambers made him feel a bit awkward because, after a lifetime of dealing with routine, stereotype London villains, I was a strange bird to have in his pigeon loft. Being matey with me strained against his every police instinct. His career was being rounded off with a puzzling ambiguity, though he didn't have a lot to do; I wrote the scenario and he and his small army of investigators scuttled around trying to pick up the torrent of clues I laid before them.

Before I was due to appear at Highgate Magistrates' Court

the following day, the police recommended that it would be better if I did have a solicitor for the court appearances and they chose Ronald Moss, who was also a stipendiary magistrate. I had always regarded magistrates as great police sympathisers and thought they'd be less inclined towards the defendant's interests. But in a mood of full, unfettered co-operation, I took the police advice and allowed Ronald Moss to make his court appearance. Apart from a few brief chats with him, I didn't remember any great exchange of conversation between us and, for the remainder of the long hours of my confessions, he was present but took no active part in the proceedings. For my court appearance, Jay purchased for me two new sets of underwear, two new, pale blue shirts and a couple of pairs of socks while Ronald Moss bought me a couple of sober neckties of the clip-on variety.

A media circus awaited me that dark morning at Highgate Magistrates' Court and, before and after my appearance, I declined to hide under a blanket. Before any trial, a defendant's stance must appear to be publicly neutral and I tended to sway to the opinion that only the guilty had any need to hide their faces under a blanket; it would certainly give that impression in the public mind, based on the principle that an 'innocent' man had nothing to hide. I was guilty of killing but felt that there were facts concerning my psychological inadequacies which mitigated my offences, short of the usual malice aforethought associated with murder or cold, sober, reasoned deliberation.

The State has only three ways of looking at a defendant. They are either 'a good 'un', 'a bad 'un' or 'a mad 'un'. It seemed that if I wasn't barking mad, in a clearly observable way, then I must be held fully culpable for all my antisocial actions, though I retained my sense of innocence on the distinction of degree and degree alone.

· · ·

Eventually, the unburdening questioning was complete and, on 17 February 1983, I was packed off to HMP Brixton as a remand prisoner while the case against me was built. In my long, nine months of pre-trial imprisonment there, I was kept in the prison medical facility as a mental patient, much against my will. All patients were assigned a doctor and mine, Dr Paul Bowden, stated that I was being detained in the hospital as a suicide risk – on his authority. However, in his report for the trial – written seven months later – Dr Bowden would state that I was *not* a suicide risk, which struck me as odd; Dr Bowden was giving evidence in court that I was not a suicide risk but was simultaneously keeping me detained at Brixton Medical Block on the strength that he thought I was.

I objected strongly to having to wear a prison uniform while still being an untried prisoner but the prison department recognised no such distinctions and treated everyone as objects to be processed. Members of the Home-Office-appointed Board of Visitors (BoV) were of no help at all and told me that I should do exactly what I was ordered to do at all times, otherwise suffer the consequences.

I was surprised to find that most prison officers were unfit, overweight and appeared to have heavy smoking or drinking habits. The full flood of their imaginations seemed rarely to stray beyond the basic mentality of a small man made 'big' by a uniform, a key, a chain and the backing of all the power of the State. The older ones were as institutionalised as any of the recidivist, old lags in convicts' uniforms. They followed a routine and didn't acquire the habit of thinking for themselves and they tended to take their own inadequacies out on prisoners where they could indulge their nasty temperament without fear of redress. They covered up for one another and stuck together and, like the traditional East End gangster, they didn't grass one another up.

My contact with other prisoners was almost exclusively via conversations through closed doors. Early on, I struck up a rapport with a prisoner called Arthur Neal who'd been charged with murdering his baby daughter. He told me that he'd been on drugs at the time and was clearly shattered by what he'd done. He had cut his own throat, leaving a vicious scar from ear to ear that was still in the early stages of healing. In spite of his predicament, I understood that he was still being closely supported by his family and I had long conversations with him and tried to cheer him up as best that I could. He wanted my copy of Wilde's *Ballad of Reading Gaol*, which I was happy to swap for his *Complete Works of William Shakespeare* and I still have it with me today with his name and number in the inside cover, 'Neal 160362'. He was eventually moved to another part of the hospital and, on 22 November 1983, while I was at Wormwood Scrubs Prison, I heard that he had been found hanged at Brixton Prison the night before his trial.

In my early days at Brixton, I received several requests from journalists and writers seeking my co-operation with them in writing about my case. This ended with a shortlist of two possibilities: Gordon Honeycombe, the famous television newsreader, and Brian Masters, a renowned author. I opted for Masters as being the most learned of the two and, thereafter, we exchanged frequent letters and he visited me on a regular basis.

Writing in my cell, I filled about fifty-five exercise books with very rough notes and I wrote and sketched other, loose page work. It was the best exorcism of the past that I could think of, as I was locked up sometimes for twenty-three hours in relative solitary confinement. They were the great outpourings of gut reactions and pressure-relieving self-therapy. Many of my immediate conclusions about myself and my predicament were, however, ill thought out; fevered introspection that resulted in quick 'healing' answers. I did the best I could but held back some details, knowing that the material I produced would be used for a publication to be written by Masters. I didn't believe in censorship but I trusted the discretion of the writer to treat some of the more intimate details with sensitivity. Masters had also given an undertaking to the governor that he wouldn't publish anything I said to him on visits concerning my treatment inside. Subsequently, there was a great deal of content from my extensive 'Brixton Journals' which was completely missing in Brian's book.

During a protest against having to wear a prison uniform, after my own civilian clothes had been confiscated, I threw the contents of my chamber pot out of my cell door window. Half an hour after the incident, six guards barged into my cell and gave me a severe beating; I was punched, kicked, headbutted and walked upon before being taken to the medical annex on B wing and thrown – naked, cut and bruised – into a strip cell. To justify my injuries, I was charged with the serious offence of 'gross violence against prison officers' (two years later, during a routine dental appointment, my top jaw was X-rayed and the dentist found that my skull had been fractured above the front upper mouth as a result of this assault).

Later, at the punishment hearing, the principal criminals who had committed the assaults against me told lies that the 'impartial' adjudicators believed. The BoV sentenced me to fifty-six days' loss of all privileges and solitary confinement, after which I was locked in a cell for almost twenty-four hours a day with nothing, not even a newspaper or a cigarette. I complained to a senior governor about the general, poor treatment of prisoners and the prison's failure to even obey what antiquated and meagre rules that were in existence and he told me that I had a cheek talking about prisoner's rights with all my charges. In saying this, he was clearly stating that because prisoners were accused of breaking the law then he, as a senior official of the prison, was perfectly entitled to treat them unlawfully, as he saw fit.

Throughout all of this, I could find no one willing to help me take action against the Home Office or make a serious issue of it. Ronald Moss, my solicitor, was on holiday and Brian Masters simply didn't believe that what I was telling him was true (though he *did* believe everything I told him which was damaging to myself). I was totally alone. I later told Brian that the chapter in his book entitled

'Remand' was so poor in its reflection of prison life that the prison governor himself could not have done a better job.

Towards the end of April, I sat on the bed in my 'punishment' cell reading, as my Philips 202 radio softly sang out its beat of cheap potency. It was as hot as it could get in that special type of cell with sealed windows that admitted no air. My tired eyes moved up from the sluggish print of the book and panned instinctively to the cell opposite and my attention was drawn to some new and sudden movement.

The occupant was David Martin, the man who had been the cause of those Tube station closures and other obstacles the night I had ventured out after having killed Stephen Sinclair two months earlier. He brooded in his cell in the upmost of despair and depression.

I watched him through the sun-drenched frame of the door beyond, rising in slow motion. He stood on a chair and stretched to look, wistfully, out of the high window at the vibrant light of a different world outside. There, I viewed his brilliance too beautiful for tears. I sat paralysed by the vision of his perfection in that uncontrollable condition called human love. I was transfixed for many full minutes until he turned and slowly stepped down. He stopped as our eyes met and we both smiled and the worried, worn strain on his face melted as we came to our cell doors to talk. This was the beginning of magic and there was no going back.

Over the coming weeks, my love for him grew. In my fantasy configuration, the props were always anonymous bodies but David Martin was a real, warm, complex and lovely individual whom I fell in love with. He was no boy, old man or observer but someone I got to know fairly well. The only time we could touch was when we were showering. He would wash my back and I his, while a crew of three guards stood grimly by trying to pretend they hadn't seen what they had. I had found warm softness in a cold misery. Looking at the blank wall of an uncertain future and the iso-solitude, it was my love for him that sustained me through the darkening days before my trial. He helped me to remember that I was still a man and not a monster.

At the same time, I was becoming more and more aggrieved that my solicitor, Ronald Moss, seemed unwilling to intervene on my behalf over the illegal treatment I was receiving at the hands of my jailers. In my extreme predicament, in solitary confinement, I dispensed with his services and tore up nearly all the documents for my trial because it was clear that the process of 'monsterisation' and punishment had already begun. The trial would have no importance other than that of a piece of theatre meant to exhibit the 'majesty of the law'.

A couple of ex-colleagues came to visit me but they were brief, shallow visits of fifteen minutes where I never discussed my case. At my arrest, you could hear the loud slamming of closet doors all over the civil service and none of the many gays that I'd known in my office – and in other branches of the service and union – ever contacted or visited me in prison. Cathy Hughes, a militant activist and my successor as CPSA branch secretary at the Denmark Street office, visited me a few times, even though she was heavily pregnant at the time and, again, we never discussed my case. But despite this, it was openly being discussed in the media.

Around 25 May, I made my last appearance at Highgate Magistrates' Court to be formally committed for trial. On the drive back to the prison, the policemen on the case were in high spirits because their investigation was now over. They were in a real celebratory mood with a dinner planned for all the members of the team. I was on good terms with them and entered into the spirit of the occasion. The police officers presented me with a pile of blank menu cards for me to autograph, to which I also added a few one-liners, and, before I left the court, Peter Jay gave me a halfpound bar of Cadbury's dairy milk chocolate (which the screws at Brixton confiscated). Later, when Brian Masters visited me, he told me how embarrassed the chiefs of police had been when they'd heard about the autograph signing in the back of the police van and he asked me to be discreet about it, fearing that the press would find out.

By now, I had reinstated and sacked my solicitor, Ronald Moss, for a second time and was resigned to having no legal representation at all and to undertaking my own defence. I made appearances at the Royal Courts of Justice in connection with applications to judges in chambers for dismissing Legal Aid and applying for bail. The judges were Mr Justice Farquharson and Tudor-Price who flourished under the odd title of Common Sergeant. To the latter, I applied either for bail or to be held in police custody away from the cruel violence of the Brixton Prison authorities, but this was objected to by Detective Chief Superintendent Chambers on the grounds of public safety.

• • •

Doing my punishment on B (medical) wing, I had to witness the daily grind of emptiness and I watched the poor, neglected wretches of patients shuffling about. I wasn't completely alone, as I had cockroaches and a couple of mice in my cell. At night, I'd put down bread or a biscuit and watch the timid little mammals running out from a hole near the hot water pipe to nibble nervously at their evening meal. They were much less fearful of me than growing public opinion.

I was able to look out of my cell through the flap in the door and, one day, witnessed the hospital screws bullying a half-wit prisoner. The man was so mentally disturbed that he didn't seem to know where he was or what time of day it was. As this was going on, one of the chaplains was coming up the stairs and, suddenly noticing the screws abusing this prisoner, he turned sheepishly about and descended the stairs again hoping that nobody had seen him. But I had and I shouted after him, 'Yes! You know very well what's going on here but you haven't got the guts to face up to it. Go on, run back to your safe hole.' He scurried off about his dubious business and never came near me again. He should have intervened and stopped the abuse of that helpless prisoner but, instead, he chose to turn a blind eye.

The greatest hurt for me in solitary confinement was in being away from David Martin for long periods of time. I was desperate to see him. I'd heard from another prisoner that Dave had, at the eleventh hour before his trial, hired a solicitor to take his case, though he had initially intended, like me, to represent himself. It then struck me that if I hired the same solicitor, we'd have a point of common contact. So, I wrote to his solicitor, Ralph Haeems, and asked him to represent me.

A few days later 'Ralphie' turned up and accepted my brief. Oddly, he and I hardly ever discussed my case, though he told me he was all for going for a complete 'not guilty' on all the charges. He suggested that there was a strong case to suggest that, in the full measure of reality, the Hornsey 'confessions' were not very admissible because they flowed from my fear of the situation. He became the temporary custodian of the prison journals I was writing for Brian Masters and he advised me that they'd be kept safely for about ten years before any of the highly sensitive and controversial passages could be made public. But I instructed him to hand over all my notes to Brian after the trial was over, or sooner, if possible. Brian formalised an exchange of letters between us and I signed it and that document was the nearest thing to a contract that I ever had. I had written into it a section that gave David Martin my small share of the profits. In financial terms, I was a relative pauper in prison. What little that came in had trickled from what was, to all intents and purposes, begging letters to people outside of prison but I never had regrets in refusing to sell my soul to the devil. The only people to have made money out of my crimes were my critics.

By summertime, my ex-colleagues had ceased to visit me and the novelty of my notoriety had temporarily waned. Janet Leaman, my office manager at the Jobcentre, had been writing to me but had declined to visit. Her letters were supportive of my plight and she reassured me that she was no fair-weather friend. Most of those I knew in the civil service had little to do with my social life anyway and they weren't missed.

On 28 October 1983, David Martin's trial began at the Old Bailey. Haeems and Ivan Lawrence, his defence counsel, had had but a short time to piece together a defensive posture. I thought Dave's choice of solicitor and counsel an odd one because he always insisted that he hated Jews. Eventually, Ivan Lawrence did well for Dave and he was found guilty of only three of the original thirteen charges, though, oddly, the jury found him not guilty of something that he'd actually admitted to in the witness box.

I walked with Dave in the hospital yard at Brixton on the morning of his last appearance at the Old Bailey. We were allowed about twenty minutes' exercise together just after breakfast and before he left for court. I tried to cheer him up as best I could but he was totally fatalistic on the final result, surmising that they'd throw the key away on him. I didn't believe this for a moment and speculated on the breadth of possibilities in sentencing from the pessimistic to the more hopeful. I thought he'd probably be sent to prison for between ten to fifteen years as there were no murders or attempted murders involved. But he said something which surprised me: 'Des, I can't even do another three years.' He was clearly psychologically down on all fronts.

In the end, the great villain of the piece was Judge Kilner-Brown who sentenced Dave to fifteen years, fifteen years and ten years – to run consecutively – making a grand total of forty years! The judge told him that he obviously couldn't serve that time so he recommended that Dave should serve at least twenty-five years. After sentencing and verdicts, Dave was temporarily moved to Wandsworth Prison before being transferred to Parkhurst on the Isle of Wight and I never saw him again.

The duo of Haeems and Lawrence then set about digesting

the mountain of evidence in the case of *Regina* versus Nilsen and both sides had marshalled their experts for the spectacle of the trial. Ralphie Haeems decided that a plea of diminished responsibility was in order and called Dr Patrick Gallwey – who had been engaged as psychiatrist for the defence – to help him prove such a proposition. The court had appointed Dr James MacKeith as their expert and the prosecution had Dr Paul Bowden who was a consultant to the Home Office prison 'health' department. The entire trial would revolve around these three 'experts' – who did not know me at all – arguing about the state of my mind but, come the event, the only thing they revealed was the state of their own differing confusions. It was a trio of State employees of a particular ilk.

Because of my treatment in Brixton, I was in no great mood to co-operate with medics associated in any way with the Crown; I had no faith or confidence in any of them. To me, they were just hired hacks going through the motions helping to maintain the status quo. They had become inured to having seen it all before and had had their feelings of humanity largely anaesthetised by constant exposure to human misery. They received little co-operation from me. It has to be remembered that Dr Bowden produced an initial medical report on me for the trial when everyone assumed that I would be pleading guilty. But he withdrew that one and compiled another one after it had become apparent that a plea of diminished responsibility would be offered instead.

Each of them would try to fit me into his own narrow understanding of me and my situation, though they all agreed that I was not insane. That revelation was the only matter of great importance to me. It was a great, relieving victory.

• • •

On Monday, 24 October 1983, I was crushed inside a security van en route from Brixton Prison to the number 1 court of the

Left: The young Dennis Nilsen came across a large 19th century book in the attic at 47 Academy Road, Fraserburgh, belonging to his grandfather. The page containing this image, depicting the murder of the princes in the Tower of London, were 'well thumbed'. Dennis pondered that his grandfather might have been a fantasist, like himself, enacting out his deepest desires, when he took him out to the wild, desolate dunes, then carried him home asleep *(see page 95). (Alamy)*

Below: The painting, *The Raft of the Medusa*, sexually aroused Dennis Nilsen, specifically the composition of the reclining cadavar being held by the man in the lower left corner *(see page 94). (Public domain)*

Above and right: The World War II pillbox that Dennis Nilsen claimed was where his grandfather would take him and abuse him *(see page 5). (Photographs by and © Peter Paul Hartnett)*

The desolate backdrop of the sand dunes and coastal waters at Philorth beach, Fraserburgh, had an enormous influence on Dennis Nilsen's early development. *(Getty)*

Above: School photograph of Dennis Nilsen, taken around 1954.

Above: The tombstone of Dennis Nilsen's grandparents in Inverallochy cemetery. *(Photograph by and © Peter Paul Hartnett)*

Above: Dennis Nilsen's British Army photograph, taken in 1961. *(Alamy)*

Above: A candid photograph taken at work in an army kitchen during the mid-sixties. *(Alamy)*

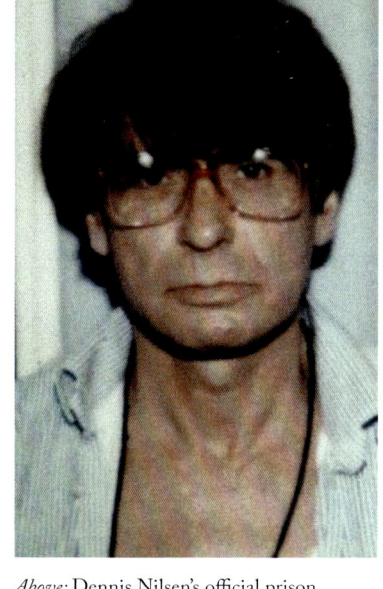

Above: The official photograph of Dennis Nilsen, taken after his arrest in 1983.

Above: Dennis Nilsen's official prison photograph, taken in 1991.

Below: Dennis Nilsen's mother, Betty. She continued to write to her son for many years until he broke off all contact in 2001. *(The Nilsen Archive)*

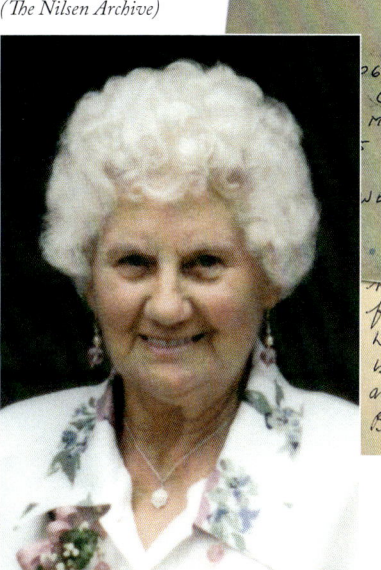

Above: A letter of support and reassurance – sent to her son six months after his conviction – contrary to his opinion of her as being without 'any tenderness' and of being 'emotional ice' *(see page 17).* *(The Nilsen Archive)*

Above: The original, silver-rimmed spectacles that Dennis Nilsen was wearing at the time of his arrest in February 1983. *(The Nilsen Archive)*

Above: Dennis Nilsen's portable radio, used during his time on remand at Brixton Prison in 1983. *(The Nilsen Archive)*

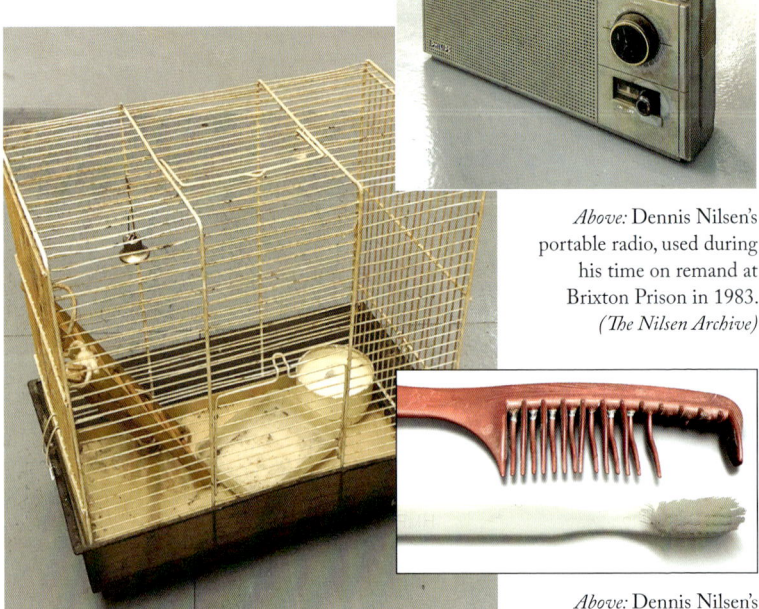

Above: Dennis Nilsen's birdcage, acquired from a pet shop in Wakefield in 1984. It was home to his budgerigars, Hamish, Tweetles and Hamish II. *(The Nilsen Archive)*

Above: Dennis Nilsen's comb and toothbrush, found in his cell after his death in 2018. *(The Nilsen Archive)*

Left: Dennis Nilsen's copy of the first edition of *Killing for Company* by Brian Masters, signed by author and subject *(see page 190)*. *(The Nilsen Archive)*

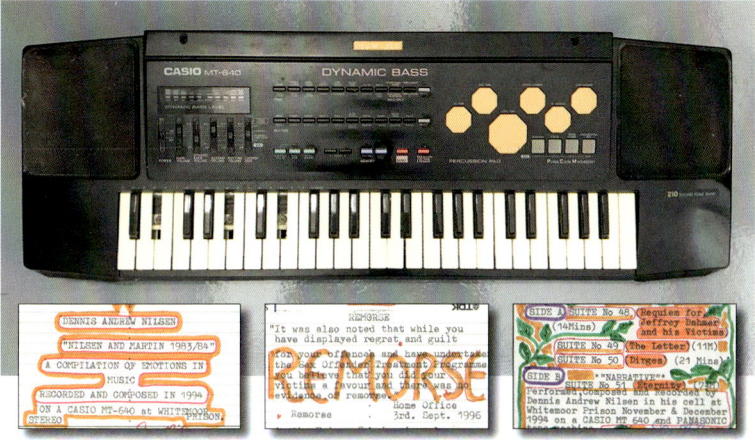

Above: Dennis Nilsen's CASIO MT-640 mini keyboard, purchased and given to him by Brian Masters in 1990. On this instrument, he composed, played and recorded 76 musical compositions over a six-year period. Also pictured, three examples of audio tape artwork *(see page 209)*. *(The Nilsen Archive)*

Left: Dennis Nilsen's first typewriter, given to him by Mike Morley of *Central TV* in 1991. It was the first of four typewriters upon which he typed his autobiography. *(The Nilsen Archive)*

Below: His pencil case. *(The Nilsen Archive)*

Above: Excerpt from the original manuscript page where Dennis Nilsen described the events soon after his arrest in 1983 *(see page 143)*. *(The Nilsen Archive)*

Left: A small selection of the original, typewritten manuscript of Dennis Nilsen's memoirs. *(The Nilsen Archive)*

Above: Bacardi Sunrise, the only oil on canvas that Dennis Nilsen ever painted *(see page 250)*. *(The Nilsen Archive)*

Above right: Dennis Nilsen's original, sketched idea for the painting, and the magazine page from which he cut the figure shown collaged into the painting. *(The Nilsen Archive)*

VIDEO PROJECT 1994   3.

26. Rod ████ was cast to play the Chief Constable and I had given him his one page speech the week before. He has a bee in his bonnet about the police having once been a policeman himself (like me). In this vein he rewrote my material and extended it to three whole pages. Although it was not exactly what I wanted I bowed to his glow of enthusiasm in wanting to deliver his version. The last thing I wanted to do was stifle good creativity therefore I shot it all (the Chief Constable's speech) exactly as he had re written and performed it. It is a fair result worthy of some merit. Rod always gives a good performance considering his very recent and limited exposure to acting.

(margin handwritten note: It came over a rather too long in the end didn't it?)

27. Naturally,given more time,we would all have greatly improved our performances. i.e. We could have done with more takes.

28. On camera it was a straight shoot without cuts for close ups etc. The Zoom lens facility is used slowly from closeup to long shot of the small set.

29. Editing is simply limited to joining the takes together as shot. *(handwritten: it needn't have been. This could have been much better)*

30. It is extremely difficult to avoid the "Talking Heads Syndrome" when trying to put together a 32 minute 'programme' within such restricted time limits and static location.

31. Andy ████ produced the titles on a Machintosh PC and we shot them through the Camera.

32. We will not be recieving an Academy Award for this one but making the effort with what you have is everything in all matters artistic.

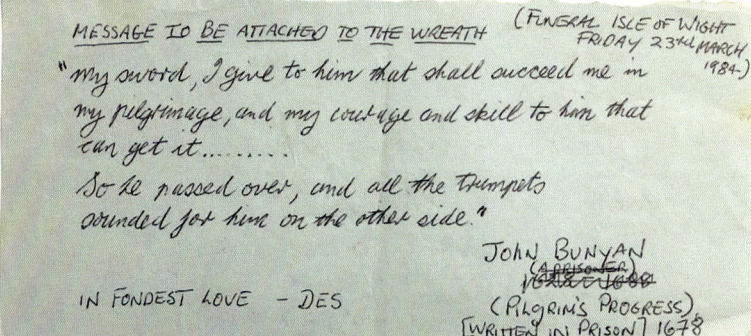

MESSAGE TO BE ATTACHED TO THE WREATH   (FUNERAL ISLE OF WIGHT FRIDAY 23rd MARCH 1984)

"My sword, I give to him that shall succeed me in my pilgrimage, and my courage and skill to him that can get it.........
So he passed over, and all the Trumpets sounded for him on the other side."

JOHN BUNYAN (A PRISONER)
(PILGRIM'S PROGRESS)
[WRITTEN IN PRISON] 1678

IN FONDEST LOVE - DES

THE SUN WANTS ME MURDERED

JAIL MEN HATE NILSEN THE BRAGGER

Loathing for a murderer – from *The Sun*, November 21

Mass killer Nilsen in prison protest

By HARRY ARNOLD

MASS killer Dennis Nilsen has accused *The Sun* of wanting him murdered.

Nilsen . . . hauled to jail for his butchery

Left: The front page of the *The Sun*, April 1984, following Dennis Nilsen's letter to the newspaper, in which he complained about their 'irresponsible behaviour' in reporting a £50,000 bounty on his head. The paper defended his complaint against them in its editorial *(see page 179)*.

Below: Dennis Nilsen's one and only telephone call to a newspaper – to complain about the latest prison restrictions – resulted in this *Daily Mirror* front-page story, in April 1995, featuring his recent penile plethysmograph test *(see page 257)*.

KILLER NILSEN JAIL SEX SHOW

EXCLUSIVE

Wired up for porn tests at Whitemoor

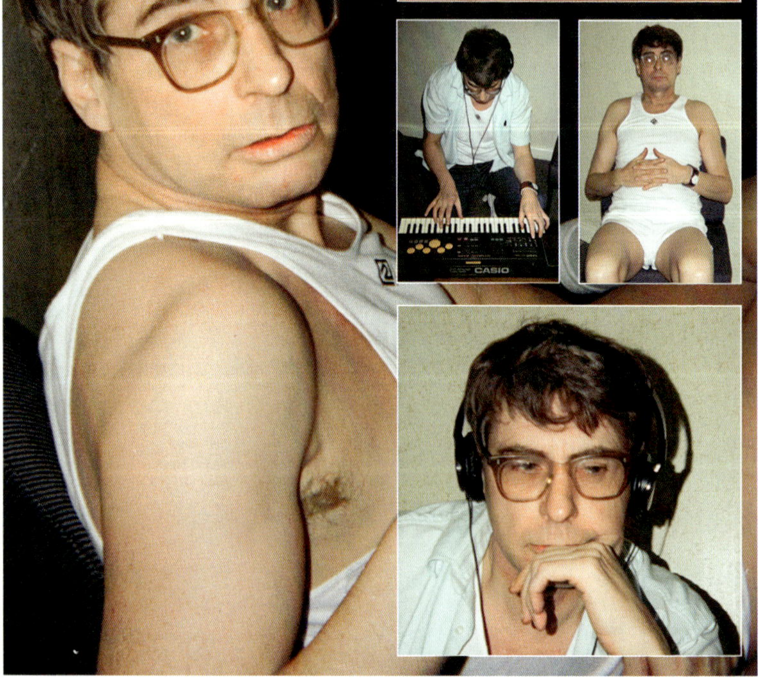

Above: A selection of photographs taken with a disposable camera in the Whitemoor prison chapel lounge on 7 September 1994 *(see page 252)*. (*The Nilsen Archive*)

Central Criminal Court, the Old Bailey. It was the first day whereon I would stand exposed before my peers who would be presented with 'State's evidence' against me, crafted to support the view that I had murdered six men and had attempted to murder two others. Screws ran up the dark tunnel ramp to open the large doors to admit the custody vehicle and the parting of these two huge oak leaves admitted a blaze of sunlight into the dark, inner sanctum.

I descended into the subterranean tunnels beneath the court, handcuffed to my escort, and was deposited in the first cell at the end of the line. This was cell number 3; cells 1 and 2 had been joined together and converted into a kind of communal waiting area.

My cell was a narrow, dingy little Victorian dungeon that contained a tiny, rough, wooden table and stool, each bolted firmly to the wall and floor. The door held the usual single spyhole and high window, which allowed only a dull trace of natural light to break through. Both were covered in years of grime and metal obstructions. Life in those catacombs was lived under the perpetual sepulchral gleam of artificial light where I was kept hidden from view in the vaults.

I sat there, lit up a cigarette and the smoke escaped nowhere in that unventilated situation. I felt the presence of the past very strongly in there. Its bricks were bound together with the mortar of a hundred years of tears and sweat. It was as if the past and the present had become one. I neither dreaded nor feared the future, but was the slave of a wondrous, hollow destiny; stuck in my time; frozen in yesterday; a secret echo from yore.

I was introduced to Robert Black, a kindly old man who was to be my junior defending counsel while Ralph Haeems replenished my dwindling supply of Marlboro cigarettes as the restive mob waited upstairs.

Soon, I was taken to the waiting area where I sat on a long bench, watched by my guards, and I listened to the faint buzz of voices coming from upstairs. The waiting area was long, like a corridor, hollow and sparse with the upper half of the wall clad in white, ceramic tiles and I wondered on all the others who had sat where I now sat, contemplating their fate and waiting for the theatricals to commence.

I was called up the narrow stairs and snapped back into the present. In the set of number 1 court, I rose into a spacious dock and was shown to the defendant's chair. It was high-backed with hard, green leather upholstery and I sat down and panned my enquiring gaze around the infamous hall. A voice called upon the court to rise and the judge entered. He was an old, robed and bewigged man, totally bizarre, in period costume from a bygone age. He planted himself into one of the three red-leathered chairs on the high judgement dais under the ornamental 'sword of justice'. His black-robed usher vanished to the side-lines without having so much as performed a single trick for the audience and the court fell into a hush and waited for the next dramatic motion.

I remembered once seeing an old photograph taken surreptitiously from the public gallery in that number 1 court in 1910. It showed Dr Crippen sitting where I now sat. The place had hardly changed in seventy-three years; a microphone in the witness box and a few other minor refinements. In the early 1900s, they had demolished Newgate Prison and erected the present building on its foundations. They didn't hang people outside the building any more, they just fed them to the vultures of the popular press and cheap media. The place had been built on a dead bedrock of broken bodies and selective aggression and the whole place smelled of pain rather than justice.

I looked at the frail old Mr Justice Croom-Johnson and felt sorry for him declining slowly in the throes of his strange office. The chances were that, in spite of my precarious position and uncertain future inside prison, I would probably live longer than he. My only public utterances in court were to confirm my identity, 'That is correct' (in answer to my name), and the plea of 'Not guilty' to all the charges. Not much of a script.

The court was packed with those seeking entertainment, sensation and a good, marketable story. There were also Mr and Mrs Ockendon, the parents of one of the men I had killed, and they were the only people who really mattered in that courtroom. They were the *real* evidence of my shame and my crimes. I didn't know what they looked like but I knew they were there, trying to fathom how and why I had killed their twenty-three-year-old son.

Allan Green, the prosecuting QC, informed the court that the evidence against me mainly consisted of the extremely long and revealing confession I had made to the police and he would often base his arguments on that tune. Then, with a sudden enthusiasm – and throwing logic out of the window – he would accuse me of being 'a jolly good actor' and, basically, a liar. In other words, the prosecution implied that any statement I made which conformed to their view of me was true, but any statement which ran contrary to their interests was false.

When the three psychiatrists crossed legal swords with Queen's Counsel, they clouded proceedings with a fog of confusion from which no enlightenment resulted. Dr Paul Bowden, Dr Patrick Gallwey and Dr James MacKeith each chose to project a separate version of me. They trumpeted away, valiantly, within the range of their knowledge and within the disciplines of their shaky profession, making it easy for legal counsel to make contending factions look foolish in the contest of legal argument. Each took, from my past, selected bits to strengthen their own case and they discarded that which didn't fit. The truth was less important than winning the case. My state of mind became not so much a matter of science but a matter of speculation in which one guess was as good – or as bad – as another.

I sat like a mute fixture in the dock, powerless, as the rhetoric drifted past. It struck me then, as it did later, that all three men were mistaken in their diagnosis. They were all clearly out of their depth. To understand the workings of any engine – human or otherwise – it is important to understand the functioning and purpose of all its components. And in this, there were significant gaps in their knowledge.

In spite of the appearance of their widely divergent views on my state of mind, there was a surprising degree of unanimity amongst them. There was agreement that I was a man of average intelligence. They agreed that the rituals attending my homicide victims were abnormal and extraordinary. They also agreed that I suffered an 'abnormality of mind', though none of them was too sure how it had come about (or even what to call it). Not to appear fully blank on the subject, they fell back on standard labels of psychiatry, which I'd noted in their original reports: psychopath, anankastic, explosive, schizoid, paranoid, psychotic, sociopathic, dissociative, borderline personality disorder, necrophilia, alcoholic, grandiosity and a partridge in a pear tree. These terms provided no answers but merely restated the question. Understanding must come before treatment.

Over the course of the following ten days, my mind would wander off, momentarily, as I sat in my high-backed chair. I had fleeting glimpses of all my twelve victims seated with me in the space of the dock. They were agog with total misapprehension at the purpose of the proceedings delivered in alien tongues. The ritual of the court was as unreal and distant to them as it was to me. It was a performance of lawyers' tricks that proved nothing and solved nothing. My victims weren't there to haunt me in the dock but to try to detect to what degree society would hold their lives to be significant. The watchers had only names and a staccato of grim, brief, almost impersonal details.

The courtroom twitched nervously to the sweaty gasps of guilt-ridden voyeurs both hating and loving the dirt-filled revelations. How much more would they be startled by the sight of twelve naked, young men, suddenly made manifest in the dock before their eyes? I was the least alone person in that room. The court catalogue had no regard for my companions as having once been real, living men and that memory of them – as persons – would die with all those who knew them.

Stephen Sinclair had been on bail facing a theft charge when I'd met and killed him. If he had not met me at all what would have been the quality of his life now? In court he would have been, himself, just another criminal package to be processed by the State. The culmination of that procedure would have resulted in him being punished for the entire tragedy of his life; prison, then back on the streets, homeless and with a severe drug and psychological problem. But now that he was a murder victim, the pathos of his life had acquired a renewed importance to the State. We had both ended up where we were: he as a preserved specimen in some medical college, and me as a preserved specimen in a penal warehouse because of our own, personal inadequacies. It would not have mattered a lot to the law had our roles been reversed.

The court periodically drew its breath as the ritual proceeded in its formal actions. Descriptions of maggots feeding off putrefying flesh seeming to fill the assembly with the most loathing and disgust. The flower of counsel blushed its bright blooms to catch the gallery and jury in its legal flytrap. It was a theatre of the absurd; a play in seven acts. But I was as mute and silent as my dead victims. For any part that I played, I may as well have not been there. It was a funeral without the corpse; a dream within a dream.

I imagined a Panavision camera on a crane idling round the court moving from this group to that group; from the jury to the public to the judge to the prosecution to the defence and I thought back on the misery I had wrought. The most convincing performance would win the Oscar. Trials are not about truth, just as Shakespeare's *Richard III* is not about history.

The prosecuting counsel always referred to me as 'Mr Nilsen', which showed greater respect and courtesy to me than my own defending counsel, Ivan Lawrence, offered, who, in spitting spasms of veiled disgust, dismissed me as just 'Nilsen'. In the brief contacts I had with Mr Lawrence outside of court, he simply referred to me, directly, as 'you' or, when addressing others, as 'he'. I was merely a legal article to him. There was no rapport, sociability or warmth radiated to me by my counsel. He was professionally brisk, retreating and distant, verging on rudeness on two occasions. I suppose he reserved his 'gentlemanly' conduct for other 'gentlemen'.

The Home Office psychiatrist, Dr Paul Bowden, stated that I was 'a very rare animal indeed' and that I had killed in order to transfer my guilt about being a homosexual on to the more 'respectable' plane of being a murderer. Apart from a tendency of wanting to kill people, he stated that there was nothing seriously wrong with me, mentally. But I wondered how he was able to judge my past state of mind by examining my present state of mind. During Dr Bowden's evidence in the witness box, Ivan Lawrence became exasperated in being unable to tease one sliver of information from him that might have been useful to the defence case. Dr Bowden became the 'Doctor No' of the trial. He just wouldn't budge.

In the early stages of my period on remand in Brixton, I had read an expert medical report, by a top pathologist, on the body of Stephen Sinclair. When I had made a statement to the police, about the time that I killed him, I gave a provisional date of 2 February. When the pathologist made his 'expert' observations on the condition of the two halves of the body, he stated that Sinclair had been dead for about a week, which would tie in neatly with the police 'evidence' that I had, indeed, killed him on the second – a week before the medical examination. However, when I checked back more carefully, while under no immediate pressure to give an exact date, I established that I had, in fact, strangled Stephen Sinclair very late on 26 January and perhaps just into the morning of the twenty-seventh. So, he had actually been dead for *two* weeks.

The 'expert', remember, was saying that he had been dead for *one* week.

If I'd been out of the country when the death had occurred, and was pleading not guilty, then here was a Home Office expert willing to support his 'expert' opinion, on oath in court, which would have been instrumental in convicting me – though innocent – of this murder. This particular pathologist had been a full week out of line in estimating the death of Stephen Sinclair and there can be no doubt about this. I know, because I killed him. One needs to view, with serious scepticism, the validity of Crown expert evidence, furnished for proving the Crown's case by Crown employees. The more those people talked about their 'honour' and 'high ethical codes', the more I felt inclined to lock away the family silver. He who pays the piper always calls the tune.

At 4.25 p.m. on Friday, 4 November 1983, the State, through the agency of the judicial system, made its pronouncement on me. The anonymous jury, having gained its thrills and shocks from this theatre of the absurd, had finally – by a majority of ten to two – agreed with the prosecution and the judge's view of me and my past actions. The media would take up the clarion call of me as being 'evil beyond belief'. The flashbulbs popped and the wolves howled and, in the universal public consciousness, I joined the ranks of the damned alongside Crippen, Heath, Haigh, Brady, Hindley and Sutcliffe.

In the end, Allan Green, the prosecuting QC, had convinced the jury that I was guilty of all charges: six counts of murder and two counts of attempted murder, while Ivan Lawrence's eloquence at the Bar was insufficient to obtain the result of 'not guilty to murder but guilty to manslaughter on the grounds of diminished responsibility'. Before the judge passed sentence, he did not allow me to say anything and solemnly handed down a life sentence with the recommendation that I should serve at least twenty-five years. In his summing up, he did give rise to his own emotions when he hinted to the jury that there were evil men who did evil things. However, as he was passing the mandatory sentence, he did not give the 'you are a wicked, evil man' lecture and, for that, I was grateful.

The inflection that Mr Justice Croom-Johnson was to give on 'evil' was strong in his summing up. He was feeding the jury with a simple concept that they could grasp: 'There are evil people who do evil things' and 'Committing murder is one of them' or 'A mind can be evil without being abnormal' or, to crown it all, 'There must be no excuses for Nilsen if he had moral defects. A nasty nature is not arrested or retarded development of mind.' He had raised the prospect of me having an evil, nasty nature suffused with moral defects. If this was, in fact, the case then there would have been a manifest record of it throughout my past life. But where was the evidence to support this supposition? He was hard put to draw conclusions about anything other than my acts of homicide themselves and my actions of concealment attending them. In this, he simply restated the question at issue: 'Why?'

Of course, privately, he might have harboured the common prejudice and disgust at the fact of my homosexuality as one of my major 'moral defects'. He was only to know what he was given in evidence and was never a party to the full, unfettered story of my life and all its multifarious circumstances. He judged on what he had. Evil, immoral people (in as much as they ever existed) would leave a trail of wickedness over the history of their past lives but no significant evidence of this existed in my case. Damage in me existed inside my secret, psychological, personal evolution.

The previous actions in my life were, prior to my offences, consistently moral ones flowing from good, moral aspirations and intentions. My subsequent offences were acts 'out of character' and not on a continuum of a bad character. The catharsis of arrest and its relief helped me regain my normal profile of morality. Was my full flood of confession the actions of a man of wicked, immoral standards? Would not an evil man have clung to the excusing defence of denial and legal appeals. Detective Chief Inspector Peter Jay stated, at my trial, that he had never known a defendant to be so immediately co-operative in providing evidence against himself and in assisting the police in identifying victims from photographs, right up to my trial. I embraced my guilt; I didn't shy away from it in denial. I even continued to assist police in trying to identify other victims long after my trial was over.

The buzz of the court left me as I departed by the felon's exit, which is always down. Later, Mr Justice Croom-Johnson wrote to the Home Secretary, 'Nilsen has today been convicted, before me, of six counts of murder and two counts of attempted murder and sentenced to life imprisonment on each count. He had, on his own admission, killed another nine or ten people and attempted to kill another five. I recommend that he should serve a minimum of twenty-five years before he is considered for release on licence. I do not think the facts of his case need any further elaboration by me.'

Downstairs, Ivan Lawrence approached and asked me if I had any complaints against the conduct of his performance as my counsel. I told him, 'No.' Either result would have been satisfactory to me for different reasons. If the court had accepted my 'diminished responsibility' plea then this would have reduced the degree of my culpability. On the minus side that would have exposed me to the very real prospect of being locked up in a secure, mental hospital. As the court's verdict turned out to be one of 'murder', I was given the full, unremitting treatment as 'devil incarnate' but spared the human indignity of a mental hospital. In my opinion, Ivan Lawrence's failings in court were just what the doctor ordered and brought me the advantage of the better of the two results; better a 'monster' than an accredited 'lunatic'. In that sense, I was satisfied with his performance. He was an able QC but his mind may have suffered a diminution of accomplishment due to having not had enough time to prepare a fuller plan and due to the overwhelming dark clouds of my perceived 'monstrosity'.

I told Ralph Haeems that I was happy and relieved that the trial was over, though I knew, inside myself, that, for the bereaved, their trials would never be over. Downstairs, I received a quick visit from a young man, named Martin Hunter-Craig, whom I had only ever met on about three casual occasions and his motive in asking to see me seemed to be a mystery.

As I was quickly hustled out to a waiting minivan, I was warned to expect a vengeful mob outside the Old Bailey. We drove out of the tunnel into the flashing glare of photographers jostling for position where a small, but audible, crowd was in full-throated voice with a repertoire of insults. Some people were even hanging on to the side and roof of the small van, though we soon left them behind in their monotonous gloom as we joined the dense, rush hour traffic. We headed west and on to the flyover to the north. One of the screws voiced our destination in one word, 'Scrubs.' Halfway down the Westway a mobile photographer, satisfied that he had enough pictures, left to meet his deadline. He was a pillion passenger on a motorcycle and had been keeping up with us since leaving the court.

6

HMP Wormwood Scrubs | 1983

We soon approached the famously recognisable frontage of Wormwood Scrubs Prison and, after a relatively brief stay in the prison reception area, I was deposited in the hospital wing where a prison governor explained the existence of the 'Rule 43' Segregation Unit. He reminded me that I would be safe from attack by other inmates there, though I couldn't imagine why any prisoner would have any cause to attack me. I told the governor that I had no intention of ever seeking protection and would take my chances with the rest of the imprisoned humanity.

I settled down for the night with a mug of diesel (prison tea) and pondered on the long, tiring course of recent events. I switched on my radio and the late news was full of the trial. It was a time to enjoy my last commercially made cigarettes because now that I was a convicted prisoner there would be no more of them. The hospital wing was blissfully quiet, after the constant noise of shouts and banging at Brixton, and I fell into the sleep of utter exhaustion.

It passed, dreamless, into the sudden activity of prison routine the next morning when I asked one of the orderlies why I was being kept in the hospital. 'Until they decide what to do with you,' he replied. They allowed me to watch some TV and I was amazed at the sight of full colour and movement on the screen after nine months in drab, colourless isolation. The world that I looked at on that TV was not the world I'd known before my first imprisonment on remand. Everything had changed drastically, and I now felt like a ghost looking at an alien world of flesh and blood people. With an endless sentence ahead of me, I felt that, in that moment of truth, I'd been expelled from society for evermore. I would have to adapt my sense of personal, moral and mental survival to the starkness of a totally new situation. All that mattered to me was that I could keep my individuality alive inside the machine.

After a couple of days, I was moved on to C wing awaiting allocation to another prison. In the exercise yard the throng parted like the Red Sea as I walked the crowded circuit on my own. There were a few mutterings from knots of prisoners standing around the margins but nobody did or said anything to me. In the seven months that I was kept at the Scrubs I had no friends and had scant communication with anyone.

The Sunday papers of 6 November were full of 'revelations' of a sensational nature. People from everywhere seemed to be queuing up to sell their stories for hard cash. The first 'true', 'shock-horror', 'exclusive' came sharp into the eyes of four million readers who were to learn of a love affair between myself and my office manageress, no less. I had only ever met Janet Leaman socially, on one or two occasions, when all the office staff had gone to the local pub for a lunchtime drink and, being naturally outraged by the suggestion in the article, she set about suing the paper. She eventually settled for what was described as a 'substantial sum' in damages while the *News of the World* printed a microscopic apology to her in a later edition.

Three days after I'd accepted that brief visit at the Old Bailey from Martin Hunter-Craig, the motive for it became apparent when his two-page 'exclusive' appeared in the *Sunday People*. The reader is reminded that this was someone I had only met about three times in my entire life and I didn't even remember his name until it was pointed out to me. The headline read, 'Hitler Fantasy of the Beast of Cranley Gardens' with the subheading announcing, 'My life with mass murderer Dennis Nilsen' and I quickly realised that, from then on, practically every piece written about me in the popular press would be – on the whole – entirely made up.

Amongst the flurry of requests I'd received from writers and journalists soon after my arrest, one of them was from a journalist called John Lisners who blew his sensationalism over the land through the medium of the *News of the World*. I guessed at the sort of product Lisners would have turned out and I politely declined to assist him. However, he later used my letter to gain access to my mother who (wrongly) took it that I was co-operating with him and, within a couple of weeks of my trial finishing, Lisners had a paperback out on sale that carried the modest title of *House of Horrors*. The entire work was replete with errors of fact and had, about it, the usual sneering, sarcastic tones. It was a hotch potch of second-hand speculation, innuendo and ill-informed opinion, and confirmed to me that Lisners' literary ability was well matched to working on the *News of the World*.

Meanwhile, in another part of the gutter, Douglas Stewart was expounding his profitable version of me for another Sunday amusement sheet. During my trial, the court had had some prior notice of 'revelations' to come from Stewart when, on oath, he had said a few things that were patently untrue. He said that he had no idea the Golden Lion public house in Dean Street was a gay bar. He told the court that I'd introduced myself to him as 'Dennis', something I never did; I preferred to be called 'Des' (my sister, Sylvia, had started to call me Des when I was a boy). And he had stated that on the night he came to 195 Melrose Avenue in 1980, he noticed '195' on the front door (as was clearly apparent on the police photograph taken in 1983). However, that was a brand-new door put on by the renovator of the property and the old door, from my time there, had no number on it. At my trial, Stewart admitted that he'd already sold his story to the *Sunday Mirror* to which Ivan

Lawrence, my defence counsel, added '...and of course, newspapers want details, don't they, not hazy recollections'.

Soon, I was visited by the busy Ralphie Haeems who advised me that there were no grounds for an appeal. I asked him about David Martin but, apparently, Dave was refusing to see him. He was currently being held in the Special Security Block (SSB) in Parkhurst Prison and was broken-hearted on all fronts; he was completely burned up with not a spark of human enterprise left to give. I was insane with love for him but I just couldn't do a thing about it because he was madly in love with Sue Stephens, and he couldn't do a thing about *that*.

As a result of her association with Dave, she was charged with handling stolen goods and I'd heard that she had been remanded in custody. I estimated that Dave would have been horrified at the thought of her languishing on remand in the awful Holloway Prison, so I resolved to help secure her release from custody. It was enough reason for me to know that Dave still loved her, betrayal or not.

The police at Hornsey had earlier said that they wanted to talk to me again about the periods in my life when I would go out, get drunk and not remember where I'd been. They imagined that I might have gone with someone to their flat and killed them while under the amnesia of alcohol. I wrote to them, pointing out the injustice in keeping Sue – this first offender – in custody and told them that if they wanted any further co-operation from me, then they should secure her release by not opposing bail. On his visit I told Ralphie what I'd done and he asked me if I wanted the press informed. I said I did because it would put further pressure on the authorities. I'd never tried to blackmail anyone before but remained unabashed because the 'threat' of Sue Stephens absconding while released on bail was minuscule as far as the State was concerned.

On Sunday, 4 December 1983, a half page story appeared in the *News of the World* written by the much-briefed John Lisners. It was headed, 'Nilsen in Strange Bid to Free Sue'. The story contained not only the main facts of the situation but was padded out with other details, both true and fictitious. But a few days later, Sue Stephens was, indeed, released on bail pending her appeal against the six-month sentence imposed upon her. Her lawyer had made an application to a judge in chambers and it appeared that the police didn't raise any objections. Having aided me with helping Sue Stephens' plight, there was nothing left for Ralphie Haeems to do for me so he walked out of my life, never to be seen again.

Brian Masters was still my only regular visitor and, after the trial, he was hard at work typing the first draft of what was to become the book, *Killing for Company*. One afternoon I was waiting in the prison visitors' hall for Brian to be processed and admitted. The hall was crowded with wives, children and prisoners' friends and parents and a little boy came over to my table with a sticky mess of a Mars Bar in his hand; most of the chocolate being already on his face. He asked: 'Do you want a bit, mister?' His parents were nodding approvingly in my direction and smiling. I smiled back: 'No, but thanks for the offer. My mother taught me never to take sweets from strange kids.' There were odd moments when I managed to gain the benefits of anonymity.

Back on C wing, I was moved – along with all the other prisoners on that wing – to B wing because they wanted the whole of C wing to be dedicated to remand prisoners. At the time, I was employed in a workshop, packing computer video game cassettes into Christmas presentation boxes, as BBC Radio 2 played over the loudspeaker system and two white-coated screws 'supervised'. The convicted long-term 'gangster'-types, awaiting allocation to other prisons, sat in their own group at the other end of the shop fitting sink plugs to small chains.

Exercise happened every workday once the workshops had closed in the afternoon. The odd prisoner, not wanting to be seen talking to me, would mutter under his breath when passing me on the wing landing, 'Watch your back mate.' From the start, the 'gangster' types didn't like me and I didn't have to wait long for the subculture to vent its hostile frustration.

On 21 December, I took my usual walk, alone, around the yard. It was nearly dusk and the air was cold with a slight breeze. I walked over to the side of a small, red-brick building in the yard to stand and roll a cigarette, in some shelter, as knots of other prisoners did likewise. I lit my roll-up and stared out into the yard where the prisoners were still following the circuit in twos and threes. Out of the corner of my eye, I noticed someone moving up to the wall at my immediate left, then, suddenly, I saw a quick movement and felt something like a soft blow to my left cheek. I turned my head and saw the white face of a young man who had dropped something before running over to the far side of the exercise yard. Still standing there, a little puzzled, I noticed blood streaming down my prison jersey and jeans. 'He's cut me,' I thought, but as I couldn't feel any pain I didn't think it was very serious, so I resolved to tend to it when I got back to my cell.

The young man, now frittering about on the far side of the yard, appeared at a loss for what to do and he bolted to the screws, to my right, demanding to be taken off the yard; he appeared to be thrown totally off-balance by my composure and disinterested immobility. The horrified knot of prisoners by the wall had, by this time, dispersed to join the circling walkers as I just stood there smoking. I watched their frightened faces as they passed by me. There was now blood on the tarmac, though it had stopped flowing freely, and the bottom left side of my face was numb.

After some minutes, a few screws appeared from around the corner and I was marched off to the prison hospital where I was invited to lie on a black couch as I told them I was all right and only walking wounded. Wing governor Morrison, a Scot, appeared on the scene and asked me what had happened. I answered that it was a small-time 'gangster' trying to make a name for himself and I told him that I intended to deny him the notoriety he craved by refusing to identify him. 'We know who it is,' said Morrison, adding, 'he's saying he did it in self-defence.' I replied, 'You and I and everybody else know that's a load of rubbish,' and I reiterated that I didn't want anyone prosecuted because that would be playing into his hands. I didn't want this guy bleating around the landings saying that I'd grassed him up resulting in him receiving five years for GBH.

A young, female doctor arrived from Hammersmith Hospital to stitch up the cut and I spent most of the procedure joking with her, until she insisted that I keep my jaw still so that she could get on with the job. She inserted about eleven stitches with a small piece of clear adhesive tape between each one and I thanked her for her efforts and continued the banter. I had a good rapport with her as she spoke with an easy Northern Irish accent and I asked her, 'Does this mean I'll never work in pictures again?'

I was shown to a hospital cell for the night to eat my tea meal and have a smoke before officers from the Thames Valley Police arrived. As I'd once been in the Met, officers from another force had been called in as a safeguard against any defendant accusing them of partisanship. Having told the police that I didn't want to co-operate, reiterating my reasons, they asked me to write and sign a statement to indicate as much, which I did. I didn't want any two-bit razor thug to end up as any kind of martyr and wanted him to know that, even though he was the attacker, I was still in charge of the longer-term situation.

As time passed, the air of distant hostility warmed, somewhat, and one or two prisoners would have a quick, fairly furtive talk with me before moving on. One said, 'If some bastard did that to me [my wound], I would see he went down for a long time.' But at the time I was still tied by a strong, emotional bond to David Martin. I loved him with a deep commitment and I wondered what he would have wanted me to do. He, alone, was still the central focus of my romantic and sexual aspirations and was the only man I could think about in that way; the rest of prison mankind were pure gargoyles when set against him.

Apart from the continuing tedium of mindless workshops and a lot of 'bang-up', the only positive aspects of life in the Scrubs were a film show once a week, a well-stocked library and the occasional Sunday afternoon concert in the large, Anglican church. A lot of it was of the uninspired propaganda of gospel singing but I felt really uplifted to hear a good, classical programme performed by the Academy of St Martin in the Fields conducted by Sir Neville Marriner. On one occasion, in the prison theatre, we were allowed to see an obscure, contemporary, comedy play performed by the prison drama group who were supplemented by 'resting' professional actors from outside. It took a lot of guts for them to perform because the play was punctuated by loud hoots, catcalls and general noisy abuse from the convicted assembly. The whole air of unreality was accentuated by the free and detectable odour of cannabis in the hall. When one of the young female actors came on, there was a clarion call of 'get 'er fucked!' One could well imagine what the guillotine mob must have looked and sounded like in the French Revolution during the 'reign of terror'.

By the early part of 1984, Brian Masters had sent me the first typewritten draft of *Killing for Company*, though a title hadn't been decided upon at that stage. I read through it and made my comments in about three or four exercise books, though halfway through, I gave up and just passed on to Brian what I'd done. I had written much of the material for the book but it was Brian's views and conclusions that prevailed and I resigned myself to accepting that it was not my point of view. Taking all the circumstances into consideration, it was an honest attempt to examine my aberrant, past behaviour and it offered some detailed and organised explanation. I didn't think Brian was too convinced with the ending that I'd furnished him with (the 'I-planned-it-all-along-because-I-enjoyed-killing' conclusion). It was like the Hays film code in America in that it was necessary to see the 'villain' get his just desserts after an unambiguous 'confession' ('it's a fair cop, guv!'). Also, I figured it was what everybody wanted to hear.

The only prisoner at the Scrubs who stayed indelibly in my memory of warm reminiscence was a person called 'Elsie'. 'She' stood out like a one-'woman' cabaret on the wing and was never consistently explicit about what gender she belonged to. She'd been arrested for ripping off some old, hapless sugar daddy and, still attired in the latest Paris spring fashions, had been remanded to Holloway Prison. The sleuths of Scotland Yard and the courts took her for a 'broad' on the game until the truth was revealed by a surprised grope to the pubic regions. Now ensconced in the Scrubs, while working as a cleaner on B wing, she shared a cell with a young skinhead who bonded with her and I was rather touched by this couple; so different in background and personality yet matching together so well. It was an eye-opener of great contrasts; the long, fair-haired, effeminate queen and the cropped-headed, London skinhead, small and well proportioned. I had one or two amiable chats with Elsie but had no romantic or sexual stirrings about her. In prison, all good things were eventually brought to an end and Elsie and her mate were soon separated when they were sent to different prisons.

As February 1984 progressed, I became intolerant of the grinding negation of a prison regime where there was no great quality of life or creative and satisfying expectation. We were, for the most part, kept locked up in our cells with no proper cell association. I'd been in prison for a year now and, being a category A prisoner, I was regularly moved to a different cell. The pressure of resentment against the regime built up inside me and the bubble burst one Sunday afternoon.

After the post-lunch slop out, we were told that the afternoon exercise period was being cancelled due to staff shortages and I remonstrated with the senior officer on duty about them ignoring prison rules. He was in no mood to discuss their decisions and ordered me to get behind my door. 'Yes,' I bade, adding, 'when I've finished slopping out.' He repeated his order, 'I'm telling you to get behind your door. Now!' But I stood my ground and asked, 'What if I don't want to?' He replied, 'Then I'll put you there,' to which I retorted, 'You and whose army?' Well, at this he immediately shouted for assistance and an army arrived in the shape of about half a dozen screws who bundled me into my cell.

By teatime, they wouldn't let me collect my food with the other prisoners and they locked me up during the evening association period. I was very angry and banged on my steel door, getting no response from them at all. Tired and despondent, I eventually settled down, quietly, for the night and by around 8.30 p.m., I was dozing off. Suddenly, I heard my cell door being opened and a voice called out, 'You can slop out now, Nilsen.' I got up and took my chamber pot out to the recess. All the other prisoners had been locked away and the landing was lined with screws. After slopping out, I walked back to my cell door then, suddenly, someone shouted, 'Right, grab him,' and a gaggle of heavy-duty screws jumped on me. They pressed me down to the floor and, securing my limbs, carried me off down the landing still clad in only Y-fronts and blue T-shirt.

The posse put me, face down, on the stone floor of the Punishment Block strip cell and forced me into a 'body belt'; a thick, leather belt secured around my waist with metal handcuffs attached to each side where my wrists were securely imprisoned. The cell was completely empty save for a small, plastic chamber pot and an uncovered hot water pipe that ran the width of the cell under the high Victorian window. There was no glass in the windowpanes and the freezing night air sucked out what little warmth there was. I couldn't even sit on the pipe because it was red hot and the tight restriction of the cuffs forced my elbows backwards, which prevented me from sitting down properly or lying down at all. And so, attired with practically nothing, in the middle of February, I was to spend the next twelve hours in this rather painful and constantly irritating condition.

A few days later, the *Sun* proclaimed, 'Murderer Nilsen Goes

Berserk in Cell' and went on to describe the incident, which was, of course, replete with exaggerations and lies. They even introduced a new angle, claiming, 'Underworld bosses are believed to have put out a £50,000 contract for the murder of Nilsen.' The *Sun*'s informant had also sold the same story to the *Daily Express*, whose version of the tale included the entirely false revelation that 'The Home Office is investigating an underworld plot to murder mass killer...'

Here was a mainline news report in two English newspapers who had 'investigated' nothing but had simply printed a saleable story with absolutely no thought as to whether it was true or not. If it were a case of criticising my criminal actions, then that would have been fair comment but the two stories were effectively advertising – to millions of people, including convicts inside prison – that if someone were to kill me, they would receive £50,000.

After I'd been shown the two news items, I asked the duty governor about them. His reply was, 'Nilsen, you should know about the gutter press by now.' It was certainly news to him that, according to the *Daily Express*, '...governor Ian Dunbar will take steps to put Nilsen away from other prisoners for his own safety.'

If a contract had existed, then it would have been fairly easy for someone to put it into effect; there was ample opportunity to 'get me' in the yard as I still took my daily communal exercise alone, as had been shown by the razor attack of a couple of months earlier. I also mingled with the crowd going to work on the association landing and while going to concerts and the library. Whenever I took a communal shower in a bath house, the place was crowded with dozens of prisoners who could easily have attacked me while I was at my most vulnerable. Once a week, a couple of hundred prisoners packed into the cinema and we watched the weekly movie in complete darkness. Anybody could have stuck a knife in me at any time.

Thirteen March started just like any other day as I wound my weary way down to the teatime bang-up. In my cell, I was gripped by an uneasy feeling. I couldn't apply myself to anything and just laid on my bed while my mind raced, feverishly, over a puzzle of images. At the six o'clock unlock, I ambled down to the ground floor for the evening's period of association and got chatting to a man who mentioned that he'd known David Martin from Dave's previous sentence. That was enough for me, so I joined him at the table and we talked about Dave for the rest of the association period. The time flew by and when I returned to my cell, I just laid on my bed, staring into space pondering, over and over, the joy of that long conversation about Dave, before falling asleep at around nine o'clock.

I was awoken just before 1 a.m. from a bizarre dream involving Dave and I distinctly heard, in a half-whispered voice, 'Des.' I quickly got up because I thought it had come from the other side of my cell door. I snapped on the light and flashed a glance at my watch. 'Can't be a cleaner at this time of night,' I thought. I put my head to the door for a moment and listened. There was no sound of movement. I sat on my bed and switched on the radio, which was tuned to LBC, and a voice erupted from the device, announcing that David Martin had been found dead in his cell at Parkhurst Prison.

I was numbed, transfixed and immobilised. The news soon moved on to something else but I just sat there, dazed and unsure whether or not I'd imagined the words. I waited in disbelief until the next news bulletin came on and repeated the dreaded news. I sat there on my bed until dawn, staring with sightless eyes; the tears running down my cheeks and, once or twice, I'd look up to the door hoping he'd come and speak to me again.

Later, I applied to the governor for permission to travel to the Isle of Wight to attend David's funeral but the application was rejected out of hand. The governor ruled, 'You're not a blood relative and your ties to him are only personal and emotional,' so I resolved to send some flowers and a short message to the funeral. I decided on the stark, contrasting simplicity of a single white rose, representing purity, and a single red rose for burning passion. Irony was not ignored. I chose a quotation from a former prisoner, John Bunyan, who wrote in 1678, 'My sword, I give to him that shall succeed me in my pilgrimage, and my courage and skill to him that can get it... So, he passed over, and all the trumpets sounded for him on the other side.'

Brian Masters kindly volunteered to go to the funeral and deliver them on my behalf and, apart from David's parents, a few relatives and a gaggle of journalists, there was no great presence.

Later that spring, the petty thief who'd slashed my face was looking for a popular justification to cover his own inadequacy. Albert Moffat was a hopeless failure, frustrated and eager to be somebody in the 'gangster' subculture, so it was entirely appropriate that he should consult his organ, the *Sun*, whose headline read, 'Why I Slashed Killer, by Jailbird'. I didn't believe a word of Moffat's story and wrote an essay of denunciation and sent it to Ralph Haeems. In the essay, I also voiced my concerns about the *Sun*'s earlier irresponsible behaviour in, effectively, inviting other prisoners to kill me for the fictitious £50,000 reward. I assumed Haeems had arranged for it to be typed out and given to the *Sun* because, on 25 April 1984, they made it their front page and editorial comment. 'The Sun Wants Me Murdered' was their headline and their 'News Special' ran the full gamut of stock phrases. They had, largely, invented stories purporting to describe my life in prison and had then criticised my supposed 'attitude' to those made-up stories. Forever posing as the great arbitrators of morality decency, justice and good common sense, their editorial piece proclaimed that the idea that they were plotting to murder me was all in my mind and that I was lucky I hadn't been hanged.

They had missed the point completely. My grievance was solely about their made-up stories and the lies about my life, which had been created since my trial, and not about any fair criticism of the offences that I had perpetrated. I didn't think it mattered what crime a man was in prison for but I felt that a newspaper should report fairly on all prisoners whether they be fixed penalty motorist or multiple killer.

I hadn't accused the *Sun* of plotting to murder me. Where I took issue was on the point of spreading the word of a non-existent contract of £50,000 on my life, which could well have incited one of their readers to try to earn the money. Such complete irresponsibility in journalism amounted to actually advertising a 'contract' whose existence hinged on the word of an ex-con, anxious to sell the *Sun* an 'interesting' tale. They would not improve over the decades ahead and their formula, when reporting about me, would remain the same, 'Make it short. Make it simple. Make it up.'

7

HMP Parkhurst | 1984

In 1984, the prison department finally decided to move me to Parkhurst; ironically, on the same week that David Martin's inquest was being held at Newport on the Isle of Wight. On my arrival, I was immediately placed in the Punishment Block for reasons of Good Order and Discipline (GOAD).

In the governor's mind, I was an accumulation of problems, which placed him and his career in a sensitive position. Peter Sutcliffe had been attacked there, having been cut on the face by a 'gangster'. Before that, a notorious murderer had held one of his junior governors hostage, at knife point, in his office. A drugs baron named Sinclair had been found dead – at a remarkably young age – of a 'heart attack' in the Special Security Block. David Martin had been found dead in the SSB less than a year later and, now, I had arrived, awkwardly, in his lap. I don't think he wanted another notorious corpse to have to explain away. To my mind, all sudden deaths in prison were suspicious until the authorities could prove otherwise. Unfortunately, it was the Home Office who did the post-mortems.

Through the long, hot summer of 1984, I became militant towards my continued solitary confinement in the Parkhurst Punishment Block. I was put in the 'strong box' (strip cell) at one stage, and I also had an enforced spell in the strip cell of the hospital, prior to being moved back to the Block. On the hospital landing, I was in the next cell to Graham Young, also known as the St Albans poisoner. One of his jobs in the hospital was to make the tea, which caused me to muse that his access to dangerous substances had not diminished!

By mid-June, I was summoned to appear at the trial of my assailant, Albert Moffat, at Knightsbridge Crown Court in London, and I was shipped back to Wormwood Scrubs. While Moffat had been in the Punishment Block at the Scrubs following the attack, he had met up with another prisoner in there called Paul Heath* and the both of them were agreed that Heath should give evidence at Moffat's trial. Heath was nowhere near the exercise yard on that day in December 1983 and I didn't quite see how anything he might have to say should have any bearing on the case.

On the morning of Monday 18 June, I was moved from the Punishment Block to the Scrubs reception area to dress in my 'civvies' once again but, before we left for court, the senior officer in charge of my escort party noticed that the photo in my category A book didn't tally with the moustache I'd recently grown. A new photo would have to be taken but that posed a slight problem because I was now suited up and ready to go. I was told, 'You'll just have to come back into the prison, dressed like that, for the picture.' By this time, all sorts of people were coming in to start work and there I was, looking every bit the civil servant, striding confidently through the Scrubs followed closely by two uniformed screws. I must have looked like one of the governors on his rounds. Various people even greeted me with, 'Good morning, sir,' as I passed by them. This ritual was even followed by one of the screws from the workshop that I'd once worked in; he didn't recognise me at all in the suit and moustache. At the photography shed, there was a line of prisoners waiting for their official snaps and they just stood silent and agog as I marched to the head of the queue and took my place

* *Not his real name.*

in the hot seat. The authorities got their colour shots for the 'A' book and I was on my way.

I waited below court in a small, locked room until I was called from above. I entered the witness box and the court warden arranged for me to take the oath. He seemed surprised to learn that I wasn't a Christian when I told him that I wished to slightly modify the oath of affirmation, which threw everybody, including the judge, Mr Justice Friend. My version was that 'I promise to tell the truth but will not answer any questions pertaining to the identity of my assailant.' The judge retorted that Moffat had already admitted that he'd attacked me but that he'd done so in self-defence. Then, after a short recess, I gave the facts under cross-examination without mentioning Moffat by name or identifying him as my assailant.

The defending counsel, Mr Matthews QC, concentrated on convincing the jury that, from the notoriety in, and surrounding, my past offences, I was a complete monster and was well capable of anything that his client had accused me of. I, naturally, admitted to my past but it seemed like I was the one on trial for my past offences and not Moffat. I could well have imagined the prejudices forming in the minds of the jury. 'He's a multiple murderer. He cut up and boiled parts of bodies. He's queer and he's not even a Christian.' Paradoxically, though, my notoriety worked to achieve the desired result: the acquittal of Moffat. The jury decided that there was insufficient evidence to convict him and, bearing in mind my much-hyped past, there was a strong element of reasonable doubt in their minds.

When he walked from the court, he fell back into the arms of the *Sun* and, on 22 June, the 'Nilsen Faces Jail Hate Vendetta' 'exclusive' was published. It was the same old story juggled around a little with my eleven stitches having been elevated to eighty-nine.

In December 1988, Moffat would reappear in the *Sunday Mirror*, regaling its readers with 'My Knife Fight with Mass Killer Nilsen' where he expanded the razor incident towards the proportions of the gunfight at the OK Corral.

'Moffat slashed Nilsen across the face and throat, scarring him for life in a violent battle... Nilsen would walk up to you and say "I am Dennis Nilsen. I have killed 15 men."' And I suppose I showed them all the notches on my gun? Come on Albert, tell us about the piercing, shark-like eyes.

'He had these piercing, shark-like eyes and he fixes them on you... I waited for him to come at me with his blade and I pulled out my blade and we tried to kill each other...' You speak for yourself.

'He is a monster...' I wondered when that would come.

'He is very dapper and takes great care with his appearance.' Christ, I'm being short-changed. What's happened to the 'piercing, shark-like eyes' of a few sentences ago? As it was Sunday, Moffat ended his pungent epistle with a religious message, 'I used to see him going to chapel to pray to God but really, I think he must have been praying to the devil.' Cue fade-out, cue organ music and let them titles roll.

8

HMP Wakefield | 1984

On 4 July 1984, I was moved from Parkhurst to Wakefield Prison in Yorkshire. In 1876, they finished off the building of Wakefield Prison while Chief Crazy Horse was finishing off George Armstrong Custer at the Battle of the Little Bighorn. Here, we had two pointless acts where nothing had changed much in basic attitudes, because both prisoners and the Native American Indians continue to get a bad deal.

Wakefield Prison was an old Victorian pile of red brick. It comprised a central hall from which radiated four wings à la Strangeways. It had been modified, along with its perimeter security, to take account of its new status as a maximum-security, dispersal, training prison. After George Blake and train robber Ronnie Biggs slipped over the walls of two London prisons, the Mountbatten enquiry was commissioned to examine the question of security. The result was a hotchpotch of jumbled ideas and it had been proposed that all the 'bad eggs' should be housed in the one, centralised prison. However, this idea was dropped in favour of dispersing them, more thinly, throughout several high security 'dispersal' prisons. Wakefield had been converted into such a prison and, around that time, held the biggest concentration of category A prisoners in England.

Inside Wakefield, there was also a prison within a prison in the shape of the infamous F wing. In the mid-seventies, this was used as the notorious Special Control Unit, which was meant to apply a harsh regime on troublemakers who were considered to be in need of conditioning towards an attitude of meek and docile submission to the authorities. Those prisoners were to be placed on ninety-day solitary, hard punishment programmes and if they didn't perform correctly, the whole ninety-day cycle would begin again. In the history of penology, Wakefield was never to be held in regard as any instrument of rehabilitation, except in the minds of those who ran it, which was why it had been termed a 'screws' prison'.

I was to remain there until late April 1990 – almost six years – and was at odds with the jailers there from the outset. It was insufferable being constantly dictated to by petty officials with no skill or imagination who initiated some pretty bad moves concerning my time inside. On my arrival, their first bad move had been to put me on B2 landing, which was a closed Segregation Unit for prisoners who had sought protection after they had 'ripped off' or 'grassed' other prisoners in order to avoid paying money they owed. I applied to be moved from there but the authorities were not inclined to heed me; I was told I was being kept there so that they could get to know what I was like. It did cause me to wonder how one could 'get to know' someone while they were locked up in a cell for twenty-three hours a day.

So, in order for them to transfer me to the Punishment Block, I disobeyed their orders and was, as planned, transferred to F wing and left there on one kind of punishment or another for three months. I spoke to another prisoner there, though I couldn't see his face as he was on the second floor and behind a window of thick pebble lens glass. I also spoke to him when I was in the 'cage' for exercise, where he could see me but I couldn't see him.

While I was in the strip cell, a solitary prisoner on exercise came to the small, four-inch aperture at my window, knelt down and asked me who I was and where I'd come from. I gave him my details and asked him if he had any smokes, though I could hear one of the screws telling him to get away from my window. He left for a few moments and, upon returning, pushed a matchbox into my hands through the small opening, inside which I found some tobacco, cigarette papers and matches. He was Robert Maudsley who was then the sole resident of a special, sealed isolation unit in F wing. He was to be kept like this for many years and was not allowed physical access to any other prisoner. He had once been sent to Broadmoor for a killing 'on the out' and while there, he'd been involved in the killing of another patient. He had then been sent to Wakefield where he'd been located on one of the 'normal' wings but one night, during the association period, he lured a prisoner to his cell and killed him. Not satisfied with that, he then put the corpse under his bed and repeated the act with another hapless inmate. He was transferred to F wing and when his trial resulted in him receiving a double life sentence, it was decided to keep him away from other prisoners for the foreseeable future.

In time, they'd built this special, self-contained unit for him where he now spent his solitary existence. Because of his propensity to kill other prisoners, he wouldn't have survived very long if returned to a 'normal' wing. The mob would have killed him, not necessarily out of revenge, but to feel secure in the knowledge that a very prevalent threat to all of them had been permanently removed. He had, by his own actions, painted himself into a very tight corner. Whatever he may have done, I remembered Robert Maudsley's kindness to me while I was languishing, smokeless, in that strip cell in Wakefield.

Eventually I was moved to C wing where I was put in a category A cell on the twos (second floor landing) and for the first few weeks, I was a strange, alien specimen to be gawked at but ignored. I was employed in (work)shop 13, the engineer's machine shop, and it was a nice change to meet and work with civilian engineer instructors who treated me with common courtesy and respect. A few of the 'gangsters' approached me out of curiosity, one being another category A man who was situated a couple of cells along from me. His name was Derek Hopkinson, a Geordie, who gave me my first taste of cannabis. He was nice enough to me but was soon shipped out to another prison for 'security' reasons then, eventually, shot dead by police for pointing a starting pistol at them at a siege confrontation.

By Christmas 1984, the unseen prisoner I'd talked with in the Punishment Block came back on to C wing. His name was Jimmy Butler and he'd been awarded two life sentences at his trial for a number of offences committed while he was staying at a parole hostel from a previous sentence. In order to supplement the paltry wage from working in the prison workshops, one depended on private cash sent in from outside of prison and, as Jimmy had no such source, he was – as so many were – left to live by his wits and skills to earn extra cash from within the thriving prison black market economy. One of his earning skills was in making delicately crafted picture frames from matchsticks and selling them to other cons.

Cash, in the form of coins only (excluding pound coins) was the official medium of exchange at Wakefield. The unofficial medium was cannabis, tobacco and just about every commodity from the prison canteen (shop) where a good businessman could live very comfortably, especially if he was a drugs or tobacco baron.

Each wing had at least one bookie with whom one could risk one's pittance on the horses. As there was a large kitchen for prisoners' use on the ground floor, there was also a thriving wing baker who made and sold cakes and fine pastries. Other catering businesses sold a variety of hot foods ranging from fry-ups to curries. The wing tailors would, for a small fee, alter and adapt items of prison-issue clothing to give one a more presentable appearance. One could also make use of the special laundry facilities and have items starched and carefully pressed for a modest 10p per item. These were only some of the many services that were available on

C wing at Wakefield at that time. The screws turned a blind eye to these activities so long as the general wing atmosphere remained at peace.

Jimmy's best earning potential, as he well knew, came from his own body. He was blonde, slim, smooth, with an infectious smile, and was youthful in appearance and, in a climate bereft of such luxuries, he was bound to attract sexual interest. He was also a proud, angry, frustrated and volatile young man and totally unsuitable as a serious partner for a relationship based on mutually-bonding love. I was drawn to him, sexually, from the moment I first saw him.

By the time I'd arrived at Wakefield, Jimmy had become 'sugar daddy-ly' involved with a prisoner of substantial means; an older man by the name of Bill Rudd* who had been doing business resulting in cheques being passed from his bank account to the contacts of serving prisoners. Having been caught out, Bill was swiftly moved to another prison and the cons on his cheque list (including Jimmy) were moved to the Punishment Block for reasons of GOAD, which was where I'd first met him.

Upon his return to C wing, Jimmy was 'sugar daddy-less' and this void was immediately filled by the 'Approacher'. He was a small, fifty-five-year-old, frog-eyed man with a taste for small boys (or as another prisoner best described him, 'a gross tamperer of the highest order'). When they were desperate for ready cash, many of the younger prisoners would get it from the Approacher in exchange for small, painless services. The lad, in the man's cell, would drop his pants while the Approacher would masturbate himself with one hand and stroke the young buttocks with his other hand. Well, in time, he approached Jimmy and offered to give him his entire week's wages in return for this 'friendship' and with Jimmy being in one of his short, 'free' phases, he agreed. Jimmy still maintained his independence within those liaisons and hated to be tied down in total dependency to his partner. He disliked what he was doing and

* *Not his real name.*

knowing the sexual power he had over the Approacher, he would inject calculated moments of humiliation on his hapless 'spouse'.

Jimmy's motor was anger, not love, and he was a loner who tended to flit about at his own convenience. He was clearly of a mind to target me as someone who would be interesting to know and I often found him hovering in my vicinity, sending out the kind of signals which I was wont to respond to in time.

By January 1985, I had received an advance copy of Brian Masters' book, *Killing for Company*. I didn't care much for the title, which struck me as having a bit of the music hall flavour about it and remember commenting at the time, 'Why didn't they go the whole way and call it *Carry on Killing*?' The prison library at Wakefield bought a copy of *KfC* (euphemistically referred to by some cons as 'Kentucky Fried Chicken') and when I asked about it, one of the librarians told me that the current waiting list was recorded at forty-four applicants. Sometime later, I saw the prison library copy and it was clear that interest had been concentrated on two chapters: 'Victims' and 'Disposal', as those pages were well-thumbed and worn. These were the popular ingredients which the mass of people wanted to read and what the 'punters' were paying for and, to my mind, said more about the tastes of the reader than it said about me. The cutting up of dead bodies had always been an area of high excitement inside the mythology of the public consciousness. In this, *KfC* did what the Sunday 'dreadfuls' and true crime magazines never dared to do: be explicit.

On its release, one MP said that *Killing for Company* was obscene and should be banned and I wondered what particular passage in the book had excited him so. People weren't concerned with the minutiae of how the dinner was cooked because they wished only to savour and enjoy the sight, smell and nourishing taste of it. They were certainly able to gorge themselves to satisfaction on *KfC*.

With all its flaws, it was still the only serious study on my aberrant actions and Brian did his best, within the structures of his own, honest ambitions. He had no experience of many essential traits of my developing existence and one needed to get the feel of my childhood in a remote 'alien' Scottish community. Such people that dwelled therein must have appeared odd to a cultured outsider from the English capital city and he, equally odd, to them.

Brian demonstrated a squeamishness at his involvement in his opening lines in his Preface: 'This has been, in many ways, a disturbing book to write, and some will no doubt find it an unpleasant one to read.' If any writer found it disturbing to write about a subject, surely, he shouldn't do it. Writing should not be disturbing but enjoyable. To open any publication with 'some will no doubt find it an unpleasant one to read' is a shameless advertisement of the horrors to come and that was precisely the stimulant signal the sensation seekers were looking for.

Towards the end of the book, I saw how I had become a concept; an object of grotesque unknowability: 'Nilsen has done monstrous things, and the responsible attitude would be to study his personality, probingly in the hope of finding out why. Not for his sake, to give him a chance of redemption, but for ours, to deepen our knowledge and improve the chances of detecting such an aberrant personality before it does harm and causes grief. If the death penalty were still in force, it would now be idiotic to kill Nilsen, for that would be to destroy the only evidence worth exploring.' The attitude expressed in that passage could well have tumbled from the lips of Josef Mengele who saw nothing wrong in using subhumans to advance our knowledge.

I remembered commenting to Brian, in a letter, that *KfC* was really a monster story cloaked in learned technique. I said it without the slightest bitterness because writing books was all about 'showbusiness' and the professional had to strive for a saleable commodity.

He later sent me some of the reviews and he was to ride, assuredly, on the strong, swift rapids of critical acclaim. The only review not published about *KfC* was the one by the subject of the study: me. In the week of its release, there was saturation media coverage on the 'House of Horrors Monster' and it went on to win the Crime Writers Association Gold Dagger prize for non-fiction.

Meanwhile, back in Wakefield Prison, Jimmy Butler was beginning to extend to me more and more invitations to his cell. He wanted to be associated with me but I advanced tentatively in case the passing whim of his curiosity blew over. One afternoon, the Approacher was sitting in Jimmy's cell, like a silent and obedient dog, making me feel a little awkward in this ménage à trois. The Approacher didn't like me because I was a growing threat to his sexual and domestic stability and I could feel the tension in the cell. I took Jimmy to one side and told him that my presence was obviously causing friction between him and his friend and suggested that it might be better if I stopped coming around to his cell for a while. Jimmy refused to hear of any such thing and simply said, 'If he doesn't like it, he can fuck off.' When Jimmy was roused to anger, he was a blunt and fiery Yorkshireman all the way, hailing from Huddersfield.

The Approacher could sense that his relationship was under threat and he took desperate, but stupid, measures, which were doomed to backfire on him. He went into the wing office and produced a note, which he told had been passed to him while he was at work in the prison workshop. Apparently, the note was along the following lines: 'Keep away from Jimmy Butler or I'll get you. [Signed] Denis Nielson [sic].' The prison official took a good look at it and noticed that, as well as being misspelled, it appeared to be in the Approacher's own handwriting. He also recalled that there had been other, similar, threatening notes produced by him in the past concerning other people he didn't like. I was bemused rather than angry because there was a tragic pathos (and a personal identification) at watching the man clinging hopelessly and desperately to the central pillar of his life. Had it not been for my rising libido, I would've been well advised to give Jimmy Butler a big miss. After a further series of rows between Jimmy and the Approacher, the break became complete and I was present at the humiliating tirade of abuse that Jimmy flung at him.

. . .

Having sent David Martin's parents a belated letter of condolence over the loss of their beloved son, they responded favourably and, following an exchange of letters, Joan and Ralph Martin came to Wakefield to visit me. I found them to be both warm and responsive people and when I met Joan, I kissed her as one would be expected to hug and kiss a mother; something which I was never encouraged to do with my own, natural mother. Ralph had a firm, honest handshake. I felt guilt and great sadness at their bereavement. Their tragedy was greater because Dave was their only child. I felt that if I'd only tried harder to be with him and had had the tenacity to send more letters to him, then I might have persuaded him to hang on to life. He needed to be constantly assured that he mattered. He needed the kind of love and understanding that he wasn't likely to get in a small, specialised unit of 'tough guys' who were never going to show those kinds of 'weaknesses'. Dave needed to be indulged like a child because emotionally, in many ways, that's what he was.

During one of Joan and Ralph's two visits, they gave me a small, commemorative card of the entry in the book of remembrance made at Dave's funeral. They also left me a portrait photograph of him. It was an enlargement of a smaller snap and had been hand-coloured. I would have liked to have seen more of the Martins but, at the same time, I didn't feel it right to expect them to visit me on any regular basis because they were both now retired, living on a small income, and the return fare for two from Kings Cross, London, to Wakefield, Yorkshire, was not an insubstantial sum. We exchanged greetings cards for a few years and then the contact petered out.

I did get a card from Ralph in 1991, telling me briefly that Joan had died of cancer the year before, but he included no new address on the Christmas card. My two meetings with them nestled warm in my memory and my contribution to Brian Masters' book was dedicated to David Ralph Martin and it is so inscribed therein.

Brian was still my only regular visitor and he continued to see me on about five or six occasions a year. It was he who had sent me the means to buy a small vacuum flask, a battery-driven record player and a budgie with cage. For the latter, the rule at Wakefield was that one was only allowed to keep a cock bird and, in early August 1984, I dispatched the postal order and letter to the local, approved pet shop (run by one of the screws' wives) applying for a cock bird of any colour. Soon, a cage and my new ornithological ally arrived. He was a small, quiet, yellow and green effort whom I named 'Hamish'. I later discovered 'he' was in fact a 'she' but the name had, by then, stuck and it didn't seem right to change it. She became the most affectionate little companion I ever had in prison.

Over the following five years, I was employed as an engineering machinist and was to gain quite some expertise on most of the machines and lathes, etc. Engineering was not my line of work but I did my job and tried to think about more creative things. I had applied to transfer to full-time education but this was always rejected. However, a professor (Maurice Beresford) and a lecturer would come in from outside and voluntarily take an evening class on Thursdays during term time and I attended and enjoyed these enormously. They helped to keep my brain alive during the bleak, non-creative years and were the high spots of my educational and cultural life at Wakefield. I asked Jimmy how he'd managed to get on to education so easily. 'Des,' he replied, 'if you were young and good looking like me, you'd have no trouble getting on!'

Although I became his partner in all things domestic and sexual, Jimmy still didn't want to be seen with me in the exercise yard. In fact, very few prisoners felt comfortable about being publicly seen in my company. The commercialisation of the Nilsen 'myth' had come on a pace with a wax effigy of me being placed in the chamber of horrors in London's Madame Tussauds' exhibition. They had acquired my clothes held in the prison property store: a grey, herringbone tweed jacket, a couple of light blue shirts, a couple of sober ties, socks, black trousers and a pair of brown (zip up the side) boots. Brian wanted to donate them to Tussauds but I insisted that they paid me £500 for them. I would not allow those ghouls to have the only clothing that I had – off my back – free of charge.

Jimmy had recently read *Killing for Company* and had been so traumatised by the experience that he was a little distant and withdrawn for a few days. It certainly must have been a bit unnerving to reflect on the 'dangers' of continuing a sexual relationship with a literary exposed grotesque. He made no comment whatsoever about it except for the disturbingly ambiguous sentence, 'This is bad news, Des... This is bad news.'

In constructing some measure of stability and economic viability into our partnership, Jimmy and I started a business making and selling curry over the weekends. I would concentrate on the production and he would handle the ordering of supplies and the financial side. I was, after all, a trained chef and could produce saleable goods. We built up a regular clientele and were able to make about £9 a week, on top of our workshop wages, to spend in the canteen. The authorities would, again, turn a blind eye so long as it didn't pose any threat to the stability of the wing. But as time progressed, Jimmy became bored with the business and neglected to do his job (he was still on education and the novelty of that was wearing a bit thin as well). He had a good brain and I appreciated that he was more intelligent than I but it was the motivation to apply his potential that was lacking. By late summer, he had tired with the curry business altogether and it had to fold – much against my will.

He loved a row and, as he said one day many years later to a newspaper, it was the making up afterwards that he craved. Well, we had our fair share of rows and quite a few reunions. After he punched me on the mouth one time, I just looked at him and said, 'Now what?' He was shaking all over and suddenly burst into tears, throwing his arms around me. I held him close and loved him and, although he may have been a bastard, he was *my* bastard.

By November 1985, our estrangements had become lengthier and I was increasingly numbed by Jimmy's cold indifference towards being the one to make the reconciliation. One Sunday, I was standing outside my cell and I noticed him coming along the other side of the landing, carrying his dinner and a mug of coffee. As he passed opposite me, he said something uncomplimentary and, with no response from me, threw his coffee at me and his chicken dinner over the rail. By this time, Jimmy was shouting threats and abuse at me but I just stood there looking at him, feeling the very warm coffee on my jeans while a couple of landing screws came over and ushered him back to his cell. During the after lunch bang-up, he was taken down to the Punishment Block and, to my grief-stricken amazement, I never saw him again. The governor had him shipped up to Frankland Prison and he completed his sentence at that strange northern nick.

With Jimmy gone, I lapsed into a depressed, dispirited isolation. An article in the *Sunday Mirror*, on 15 December, added to my feelings of dejection. The headline read, 'Obscene: Outrage at Gay Killer "Comedy"'. Apparently, a play had been featuring at the Duke's Head theatre in Richmond, Surrey. It was described as a black comedy and was performed by an actor who played me. Nobody would have heard of this tiny production in a quiet corner of suburban Home Counties England until a reporter stirred it up in order to make a tension-filled story. He had contacted Stephen Sinclair's adoptive parents, told them of the play and then solicited their 'outraged' reaction.

During the summer, I had reapplied to go on education and,

again, had been rejected. In a kind of desperation, I completed and submitted an Open University application form and was informed that there would be a place for me. I'd opted for Social Science as a subject of study and, in committing myself to this, had hoped to escape from the baleful influences of prison routine.

In this mood for change, I made a serious attempt at a reconciliation with my mother. The rest of the family had abandoned me, lock, stock and barrel, and I asked Brian Masters to ask her if I effected a temporary transfer to a local prison in Aberdeenshire, would she visit me? Having privately told Brian that she would, I made the official application for a temporary transfer. The Home Office reply documentation arrived with the comment that a transfer to Peterhead Prison (a maximum-security prison not far from Strichen and Fraserburgh) was not possible but they would consider Aberdeen Prison. Then the reply finished with the bombshell that, in enquiring, they had found no evidence that there was anyone in the North East of Scotland who wished to visit me and, therefore, the application was, effectively, turned down.

My mother was playing her usual game. Her public persona was of the caring mother standing by her homicidal, deranged son, radiating an aura of shocked surprise at how it had all occurred but her private face was one of guilt-ridden fear of ever having to meet me, face-to-face, in order to confront all the lies of her past. I wrote her a stiff letter pointing out her hypocrisy and berating her for her two faces. Thereafter, I informed her that I was breaking off contact and would not be seeking further to help bolster up the charade of a relationship which, in effect, didn't exist except in the mind of her public image.

In the run up to Christmas 1985, I wrote to Jimmy at Frankland telling him how much I'd regretted what had happened and I sent a seasonal greetings card. He responded in an all-forgiving way and I pledged to continue corresponding with him for as long as he wanted me to. In effect, we had kissed and made up but the prison department were unbowed in their attitude and wouldn't move Jimmy back, though we exchanged letters on a regular basis right up until he was released in the spring of 1989.

Before we'd broken up at Wakefield, I'd put him in touch with a girl who had been writing regularly to me there. Suzie Westford* hailed from Reading and was a lively individual with a creative, punky appearance and, after only a couple of letters, Jimmy had built up the notion in his head that they should get married. Oh, what a tangled web we all weave. They had expanded this theme with their plans and my cautionary words of advice were met with hostile resentment by Jimmy.

The dull, expressionless routine of Wakefield shuffled in the new year of 1986 and I had still not had any contacts regarding the Open University. Eventually, in February, a bundle of 'units' were dumped in my lap and I was invited to start. I missed the first day entirely when I'd been charged with some obscure offence and I found myself, as usual, taking one of my regular trips to the Punishment Block. A screw had, one morning, provoked me with his loud announcements along the landing, in the obvious earshot of everyone, 'I see Nilsen's down for the Open University. What's he doing, gardening and necrophilia?' I verbally retaliated, which resulted in my being punished. It was clear to me that any long-term commitment to study for a degree would, and could, be disrupted at the malicious whim of uneducated turnkeys who openly resented that money was being spent on this 'monster'.

My attempts at the Open University floundered permanently after only three months. It was chaos in the education department and everyone on OU was crammed into a cluttered classroom-cum-storeroom. There was a black and white TV set with video around which we huddled and watched our weekly OU programmes. In another part of the room there were a couple of cassette tape machines upon which some students had recorded radio broadcasts that they

---

* *Not her real name.*

would then listen to. We had no access to any other documentaries, news, current affairs, art, drama or any such other TV material at all. I asked if I could borrow one of the cassette recorders in order to listen to the issued OU tapes in my cell but I was told I'd have to give up my battery record player for such an 'exchange'. I wasn't prepared to do this because my classical music LPs were the tranquillising mainstay of my peace and emotional life during the long hours of being locked up in my cell. The final straw came in April when I was moved to a cell on the threes (third floor), which had, on my outside wall, a booster speaker for the landing TV. Every evening and all weekend this unbelievable noise pumped directly into my cell through the wall and when I asked for a cell move all I got was, 'Nilsen, you'll go where you're put!' I'd lost the will to live and the great machine of the Open University book closed with a bang.

The days and nights were very much of a sameness, made bearable only by my hearing links with BBC Radio 3 and 4. The Proms season was always an expected treat worth waiting for, where life threw up a candle in the darkest, wildest nights, and I still had Hamish's optimistic chirps on my shoulder as she delighted in preening my hair.

Earlier in the year, I'd written to the Home Office asking them to clarify the official view on homosexual relationships inside prisons and had passed the text of their reply on to *Gay Times* magazine, as it was a ruling which was likely to affect all gay men inside prison. They dripped snippets of this very controversial subject out to the popular papers and the *Sun* blew a full, trumpet fanfare right across the top of one of their pages, 'Mass Killer Nilsen Asks for Gay Sex in Cells' and 'The Cheek of Nilsen'. Other papers headlined, 'Nilsen's Plea for Gay Sex in Jail' (what other sex is there in jail?) and 'Nilsen's Query On Jail Sex'. The *Gay Times*' full-page piece laid down the usual background before launching into the nitty-gritty, quoting the various paragraphs under Prison Rule 47. In summary, the Home Office opinion amounted to nothing less than, 'men engaging in any sexual acts anywhere in prison would be punished'. *Gay Times* then went on to comment on the Home Office's reply.

Elsewhere in the press was the paperback launch of *Killing for Company* and, to coincide with it, a major article by Brian Masters was published in the *Observer* surrounding the unfortunate Carl Stottor, whom I had been found guilty of trying to kill. The whole substance of the article expounded Carl Stottor's obsession with the psychological notion that he was indelibly traumatised and that his life had been totally ruined by my subduing him by partial strangulation and, later, by partial drowning. I made no defence for the fear and pain that my actions caused him at the time and for that, I bore full responsibility. However, I did believe that he conveniently heaped all the acute, psychological problems of his troubled life squarely on to me. Brian's narrative told how I had 'ignored his pitiful pleas for mercy' but if I'd done this, then he wouldn't have been around to tell his tale.

Carl stated to Brian in the article, 'Is Nilsen my murderer or my saviour? I don't know how I should feel about him. There have been times when I wish he had left me for dead.' Brian then fell into the 'victimhood culture' of blaming all the complex tragedy and damaged personality of Carl's life (long before I ever met him) on to the peg of convenience, invited by the arrival of an interesting 'monster' on the scene, by saying, 'In a quite dreadful way, Carl Stottor is still Nilsen's victim.'

I received several letters from Carl (always presented in the most intimate of endearments…almost like love letters) and I did my best, under my circumstances, to help him resolve his problems. In fact, this was mentioned by Brian, 'He [Stottor] has even thought he might like to visit Nilsen in prison, as a kind of cathartic exercise, and with this in mind, is in correspondence with him.' At Carl's request, I applied to the Home Office for him to visit me but I heard no more about it. It was also proposed that Brian accompany him on the visit so that he wouldn't have had to face me alone.

Later, Carl Stottor re-emerged in print in the *Sun*, with a headline proclaiming, 'Evil Nilsen Writes to Man He Nearly Killed'. The whole article gave the impression of me pestering him to come and visit me; the truth being that it was his idea. It concluded, 'he was shocked when Nilsen, 43, invited him to visit him in prison... Carl will not be visiting Nilsen... "He still frightens me, and I want to push him into my past and get on with my life."' After the *Sun* story, he wrote to me again but I didn't reply.

My repeated visits to the Punishment Block took, from me, all notion of respect for my crude captors, with all the kindnesses that I received coming from prisoners. While I was exercising in the wire cage, one of the screws on the other side of the wire was giving me a lecture. 'You can't beat the system, Nilsen. Look where you find yourself now.' At that moment, Simmons, the number 1 governor, approached the Block for his routine rounds as the screw straightened himself up, stood to attention and said, 'Good morning, Sir.' The governor nodded 'good morning' to the screw then glanced at me and gave a very curt 'Morning, Nilsen', to which I replied, 'Morning, Simmons' (omitting the 'Mr'). The colour drained from his face as he moved on and I turned to the screw, who was clearly agitated by this insult to his master. 'You see,' I said, 'in many ways I am a lot freer than you are. You've got to spend your life kissing his arse but I can fuck him off any time I want to.'

On another occasion, I found myself in the Punishment Block again on some charge or other, was found guilty and given an umpteenth award of solitary confinement with loss of all privileges. As I was going into the shower, one of the screws named Pickford* was speaking to me as if I were an animal. I walked up to him, eye-balled him and, without laying a finger on him, said, 'Who do you think you're talking to?' At this, he started calling for help, while another screw jumped me from behind. All the other screws arrived and piled in, each grabbing some flesh and applying pressure, with

---

* *Not his real name.*

one of them actually throttling me. They twisted my limbs and wrists in individually placed holds and lifted me off the ground like that. The pain was excruciating as they pinned me to the concrete floor and proceeded to rip off my clothes; literally tearing upwards at the material. I could feel the cotton of my shirt, vest and underpants cutting into my skin until the garments just shredded. I felt a sharp pain as the material cut deep between my buttocks, then felt my neck vertebrae crack or click slightly, as my head was forced back and held, while the laughter echoed to the loud clang of the door. I lay on the floor, naked, numbed in joints, bleeding and with aching muscles.

After this attack, my right hand was numb for over a week and it was several weeks before I had the full, controlled use of it back. There were bloody lash marks on the front of my body and the area of my groin where the strips of shredding material had cut into my flesh. In order to justify all this, they threw a charge sheet into the strip cell, accusing me of assaulting Pickford. Following the lengthy adjudication, in which I defended myself with absolute honesty and integrity, I was sent out of the room while the panel considered their verdict. On returning, they had found the charge proved and I was asked if I had anything to say in mitigation. I said that, because I hadn't committed any assault, there was nothing to mitigate. Then I was told something very strange: 'You have to learn that you can't buck the system', and was awarded forty-two days' loss of all privileges and solitary confinement. That remark was very significant in that had they really believed the assault charge was true, they would have said something along the lines of: 'We can't have people like you going around assaulting prison officers' but my crime, in their eyes, was 'bucking the system' as revealed in the denouncement.

I returned to C wing just before Christmas 1987 but, in the first few days, I was snatched after breakfast and found myself on a journey to London. Some weeks earlier, I'd applied to go to

Wormwood Scrubs for accumulated visits and this would facilitate easier access to Brian Masters and Suzie Westford. For security reasons, category A prisoners were not told when they would be moved.

$$\bullet \ \bullet \ \bullet$$

It was to be the first time that I'd been outside of Wakefield in four years. All I took was my radio and a couple of books. A neighbour on the wing, Alec Gunn, always looked after Hamish when I was away on punishment and, for this visit, he'd put her with his cock bird, Billy; the two birds seemed to get on well enough short of copulation.

The van arrived in North London and I was able to see the familiar passage of the North Circular Road skirting north of my old police patch of Willesden Green. At a service station along the route, the screws fixed themselves up with something to eat and drink, ignoring the creature handcuffed in the van. Then they became lost in the one-way traffic system. After Hanger Lane, I told the principal officer in charge that he was going the wrong way but he was not disposed to taking advice from anyone who knew the area better than he did.

The Scrubs looked like the same dilapidated ruin that it did in 1984. I was housed on B wing, the lifers' wing, and I noticed the cigarette packet that I'd left in the exercise yard had aged a bit.

The purpose of my visit was largely nullified because Brian Masters was off to India to live in a Maharana's Palace in Rajasthan where he was researching his new book on this area of his interest. I sent a visiting order to Joan and Ralph Martin but received no acknowledgement, which led me to believe that they'd moved. I did, however, manage to get a couple of visits from Suzie so, in this regard, my journey to London wasn't altogether wasted.

As the Scrubs had an excellent library, I was able to enjoy their wide and interesting selection. There was also a games association area with a TV, proper, organised film shows – with a big screen on Saturday mornings – and a canteen system where I could purchase anything from my private cash, except tobacco. My cell was left unlocked all day and the atmosphere was more relaxed than at Wakefield, where I was free to associate with the other cons on the wing, though most of them avoided me for reasons primarily associated with them being seen with a known gay.

Two cells down from me was housed one of the Birmingham Six. Billy Power and his other co-appellants were gathered in London for their appeal hearing (which had failed). I had already read the Chris Mullin book, *Error of Judgement*, which catalogued most of the official discrepancies in the case, and I'd been fully aware and informed about this case because it had been highlighted in the left-wing press for years. Adding to my conviction that they were not guilty, was my personal experience of police behaviour. I passed a Sunday paper to Billy, which contained some material concerning his failed appeal, telling him that the result was disgraceful and that it had come as no surprise to me. After handing him the paper, I walked out because I could see that he needed to be alone in the trauma of his latest, temporary defeat.

There was another cause célèbre on D wing in the form of Winston Silcott who'd been convicted of murdering PC Blakelock during the Broadwater Farm disturbances in Tottenham, London, in 1985. The prosecution never presented any evidence against him and resorted to verbalising a statement, which he denied making. Of all the thousands of pictures taken of the 'riot' that day, there was no evidence that he was even involved. A gang of rioters had descended on PC Blakelock who had been stabbed to death with about forty wounds. The police and racist public opinion demanded that someone go down for this ghastly offence and, it seemed, Winston Silcott was selected. Racism offends against the dignity of our common humanity as does firm and controlling belief in superstition and magic. Whenever I was confronted by racist views I would stop the conversation and challenge those views with countering rebuke. This didn't win me many allies but it stated my position and gave the man making the 'casual race put-down' pause to think about what he had just said. It is frankly stupid to judge any person by the cosmetic reality of skin colour.

After my month at the Scrubs was up, I wondered why I hadn't moved back to Wakey and the answer arrived in a press article that made me, and my fellow prisoners, smile. It was by an 'ace' reporter from the *Daily Mirror* who seemed to have made a good living from reporting 'scoops' on me. This was his January 1988 offering in which he didn't seem to realise I wasn't in Wakefield, at all, but a few miles away from his London office. His headline read, 'The Fiend Princess Won't See on Visit to Jail'. Apparently, I was being banned from meeting Princess Anne during her visit to Wakefield Prison. When I was down in the Block there, I'd wondered why they'd been whitewashing the walls of the exercise cage.

· · ·

After HRH had been and gone, I was shipped back to Wakefield. I was still rejected for education and continued the useless grind as an appendage of a noisy, oily machine. I settled back into the wing and lived out my routine existence as best I could. I found solace from the lack of a lover in books and classical music and with the aid of a couple of cannabis joints where I could be 'live' at the Royal Albert Hall for a Radio 3 concert. Hamish would twitter more loudly as the fumes got to her and she was inclined to do little dances in front of the mirror on top of her cage during these highs. She seemed to like the music as well as the smoke.

Due to the generosity of fellow prisoners, more and more cannabis was coming my way. I wasn't a regular user but I'd often indulge over a weekend and it provided a relief from the pure tedium of prison routine. In that relaxed state, I was better able to focus on things, generally, and on the past in particular.

In the autumn, I received a letter from a journalist called Tim Barlass who informed me that he would be working for a new national daily tabloid called *The Post*, which would be different from other tabloids in that it would feature more serious news. I gave him the benefit of my doubts and wrote him a letter in reply. On 11 November 1988, he published a two page 'exclusive' in the *The Post* with a sensational, three-inch headline, 'My Jail Hell' and supported the story with a photo of me, which had been taken a month after I'd left the army, in September 1972. In the piece, sub-headed 'Life of a Loner', they printed most of my letter, which caused much embarrassment to my jailers.

The other tabloids seemed to be a bit put out by *The Post*'s exclusive and, that same month, the *Sunday Mirror* made an offer to Brian Masters, which, it transpired, he couldn't refuse. He was commissioned to interview me for yet another 'exclusive', and, on his next visit to see me, he asked for permission to show the *Sunday Mirror* some of my recent prison letters to him. The huge headline on their front page proclaimed, 'Nilsen: Mass Killer Talks'. I sometimes wondered if Brian ever actually listened to *anything* I said to him; he had me incorrectly described as 'a rule 43 inmate… Nilsen's single cell is on an isolation wing "for his own protection"' and the article even mixed up David Martin with Jimmy Butler! At the bottom of the page they had the gall to write, 'The *Sunday Mirror* has not paid Nilsen or any of his relatives any money', implying that I may have asked for a fee, something I had never, ever done.

The following week, another *Sunday Mirror* 'exclusive' read, 'My Knife Fight with Mass Killer Nilsen' by, wait for it…Albert Moffat. 'I slashed his face…I'd do it again…he deserved to die.' Oddly, they didn't say whether they'd paid Moffat for his story.

By this time, I was 'enjoying' another short spell in the Block on punishment only, this time, they'd removed *all* privileges, including smoking. While languishing in solitary confinement, I managed to find a copy of a newspaper where I saw, advertised, a mini keyboard sale. There was a Casio going for £199 (with dynamic bass), so I tore out the ad and kept it. As Brian was always telling me to occupy my time creatively, I sent it to him with the strong hint that he might see his way to buying it for me and he responded positively and promised to buy it for my birthday in eleven months' time.

In the spring of 1989, Jimmy Butler was due for release from Frankland Prison. He was going out to an empty world with no roots, no money and no real prospects for the future, and seemed certain to follow a cycle of homelessness, unemployment, burglary and back to prison. It had been the pattern of his whole life and I sought to remedy this in my small way. I gave him permission to use my letters in any way he sought fit in order to get some money to set himself up in the world outside (a permanent address, some basic furnishings, household items, clothes; a stable base from which to seek employment). But a week before his release, the prison authorities confiscated all my letters to him, even though they'd passed the censor at both ends. The Home Office, it appeared, had now ventured into commissioning acts of public theft.

The next official move was to ban all letters from Jimmy Butler and to ban him from ever visiting me (as a security risk). The odd letter slipped through (probably by mistake) but with this continuing signal of discouragement, my contact with him soon dried up for ever. He stayed with Suzie Westford for a short time, before moving on to Brighton, but not before he took my advice and contacted the newspapers. After having phoned the *Daily Mirror*, Jimmy was picked up in a car and whisked off to a hotel where he was milked of all his pertinent knowledge of me, in return for a small fee. The ensuing article was published in the *Sunday Mirror* on 2 April 1989 and was titled, 'House of Horrors Murderer Dennis Nilsen's 18 Months of Gay Love Behind Bars with Jailbird Jimmy'. The piece was not all accurate but it was as good as one could get, under the tabloid circumstances, and was more positive than I could have hoped.

Back at Wakefield, I became involved with a new arrival on C wing called Stephen Gadd*, a man in his late forties who had been convicted of being sexually involved with consenting, underaged schoolboys in their mid-teens (the homosexual age of consent at that time was twenty-one). Stephen and I hit it off almost immediately because he made no secret of the fact that he was gay. We began to see a lot of each other and a kind of bond of dependency grew in me, and so I embarked on my last romantic attachment ever and 1990 would herald in its nemesis.

Stephen Gadd had a craving to seduce people. It was a part of his personality; to impress adult figures and gain favour. I think he was still, subconsciously, trying to impress Mother and everyone in authority became a kind of parental figure in an endless chain from teacher upwards. Like many of a paedophilia orientation, he couldn't connect with the adult, emotional world and became fixated with diversions like maths, computers, mechanical things and concepts in the non-human abstract. Although he was homely and very sociable on the surface, there was no depth to his emotional attachments. His libido could only become excited at the prospect of dominating his partner. His stimulants, therefore, were non-threatening types, hence the sexual and emotional attraction to boys and those who exhibited juvenile traits. In many ways, like me, he was trapped back there in his stunted, emotional past in a confusion of distorted self-images and fantasies.

He wanted me for everything on a friendship level and the intensity of my sexual attraction to him simmered along while he sought his carnal pleasures elsewhere. Of course, I became jealous of these clandestine liaisons and we had many rows but always made up afterwards.

His mother kept him well supplied with 'toys'; he was never

* *Not his real name.*

short of all the luxuries necessary for a decent, material life in prison and his cell was luxurious by comparable standards. He also had a Yamaha Stationmaster keyboard – one of the best – and made chocolate eclairs in the wing kitchen for sale. He had a steady group of customers and was forever wheeling and dealing; it was as if he was establishing a lair to attract likely 'prey', i.e., vulnerable partners. He felt no guilt for his offences and, with reference to them, would say, 'I'll be more careful next time.' He simply had not the slightest notion of any wrongdoing on his part and, as far as he was concerned, the boys were agreeable to sex and that was that.

Stephen started in the education centre on computers and, in the ensuing autumn months, the two of us were founder members of the Wakefield Drama Group. Stephen had a good ability to be able to play, on his keyboard, any music he could hear. I, on the other hand, could play no musical instrument at all but two months in advance of my birthday, Brian sent me in the Casio MT-640 keyboard as promised. Almost immediately, I conceived a plan for a musical collaboration with Stephen for the production of a 'rock opera' where I would write the lyrics and he, the music. Over September and October 1989, I wrote about twenty-five songs and passed them on to Stephen for them to be battered into musical shape. I waited and waited but nothing happened. 'Give me more time,' he would say before, eventually, admitting defeat. Try as he might, no ideas would come and, as far as creativity was concerned, he was completely barren and the project was shelved indefinitely!

By the start of the new decade, my frustration with Stephen was rapidly reaching a crisis and, after yet another period of estrangement, I set about him with my fists, in the recess before bang-up. The next day, we were both in front of the governor on adjudication and given a £3 fine with the admonishment that any repeat fights would result in a period of detention in the Block. As we returned to the wing, the duty principal officer quipped, 'It's not an adjudication you two need, it's a marriage guidance counsellor.' Thereafter, an uneasy peace ensued between us.

For some weeks, I'd been trying to gain access to the recording equipment in the education centre, with a view to making a musical tape for the Koestler Awards. Arthur Koestler had left money to set up a competitive scheme to encourage the arts amongst prisoners, though his good intentions had been somewhat muddied by the dead hand of the prison department and its cumbersome system of organisation. I had kept on at an education screw to be allowed to make the recording but he continued to prevaricate, raising one feeble excuse after another. One evening, I cornered him and offered to sacrifice my Thursday evening session at Professor Beresford's class to do the recording and, to my amazement, he gave his consent.

So the next Thursday evening, I arrived with my Casio keyboard under my arm and he showed me into a small cubbyhole where they kept the videos and the recording equipment. In it, there were two prisoners watching *Carry on Cabby* on the TV in there. 'You can do it there so long as you don't disturb anyone,' he quipped as he handed me a C15 cassette, which would record only seven and a half minutes each side. Try as I might, I simply couldn't prevail against the adverse conditions with all the distractions and, the next day, I put in an official application to the governor for a proper facility to make the Koestler recording. Nothing happened for a few weeks but, leaving nothing to chance, I asked Suzie Westford to send me two high quality C90 or C60 recording tapes and, eventually, I was afforded the facility of one hour in an empty classroom – supervised by a teacher – to make the recording.

With only twelve hours total playing experience on the keyboard, I composed a piece of music there and then. 'Suite No. 1', with all its crude imperfections, was my first salute to the effort of trying. I titled it 'Masters' in appreciation of the fact that there would have been no music at all but for the kind agency of Brian Masters. I asked Stephen to run off a copy, which I gave to the education screw as my Koestler entry and the original was handed out to Brian. He tried to be diplomatic in his comments but he could see it for what it was. I didn't know it at the time but that was to be my last artistic effort of any kind at Wakefield.

Eventually, I discovered that Stephen was also having a full-blown sexual relationship with someone else so, after another heated exchange, what there had been was now over. Later, on one of the landings, the other guy rushed down the stairs and set upon me with his fists and I ended up concussed and waking up to a melee of screws around me. After that, a principal officer and two screws came to my cell, told me to pack my kit and prepare to move out to another prison where I was only allowed to take Hamish, her cage and a small cardboard box with a few essentials. 'The rest of your kit will be sent on,' they promised and within five minutes I was on my way to reception.

I walked into that early May sunshine of 1990, carrying most of my worldly goods in a cardboard box, after a sojourn of six years in the largest category A dispersal prison in Britain. A screw carried Hamish in her cage and she twittered uncertainly at this new, sudden, outdoor environment. I was handcuffed to another screw and told that I was going to Full Sutton Prison, about eleven miles south-east of York. It wouldn't be a very long journey but, by the time we arrived, I had already put, from my mind, the very existence of Wakefield.

9

HMP Full Sutton | 1990

Full Sutton had started up as a World War II airfield, after which its disused runways were used as a motor racing track where, in the early fifties, up and coming drivers such as Jim Clark had spent weekends racing. The land had been sequestered for the building of a new maximum-security prison, which had opened in 1987 at a cost of £50 million.

Its interiors were narrow and claustrophobic and there were many dark recesses, stairwells and odd rooms located in quiet – almost hidden – places, like the basement of some inner-city, tower block complex. It was impossible to police and impossible for any meaningful surveillance. The corridors in the cell areas were about five feet wide and one felt deprived of private breathing space. The cells themselves were much smaller than the Victorian variety and appeared more so with the addition of a sink and a lavatory in each. I was located on C wing where small groups of 'gangsters' ruled and, as I didn't fit in with the attitudes and rules of the pack, I was not welcomed and the few that were initially friendly were soon warned off by these hidden bullies.

Soon, I began to receive anonymous notes pushed under my cell door. 'Nilsen get off the wing or be killed,' was typical. When I walked into the TV room, the few men in there would walk out. One evening, a group entered and as some took up the empty chairs

212

another two tried to cover the door and window with a blanket. I guessed the situation they were planning and got up and left the scene. The next day, the wing governor called me into his office and warned me that they'd received some anonymous threats to my life and he reminded me that I could apply for protection under Rule 43. I told him, 'Here I am and here I intend to stay. I'm not running,' and, with that, I returned to my cell.

A few nights later, I was reading a book on my bed when two, hooded men put in an appearance at my doorway. Never one to tarry, I swung off the bed, grabbed a battery from the table and hurled it at them, which smashed into the door beside one of their heads. The shock of my actions caused the one with the jug of boiling sugar water to misaim and he tipped it far short of its target, before they turned and fled in frightened confusion. I poked my head out of the door and could see a screw looking down from the glass-panelled office at the end of the landing but he registered no reaction, as if it were quite normal to see two hooded prisoners running about the landing. The following day, there were more notes pushed under my door – this time in red ink – and, by this time, nobody spoke to me at all. Thereafter, whenever I left my cell, I took to carrying around an R20 battery concealed in my right fist. If I was going to be 'jumped', then the first in line would sustain a broken jaw. During an evening in the TV room, I heard a commotion outside in the corridor and, when I looked, I could see smoke coming from my cell door. The seat of the fire was on top of my bed and in extinguishing it, the screw had sprayed all my property – including my keyboard.

The governor finally lost his professional bottle, called me into his office and informed me of his decision to place me in the Segregation Unit for reasons of Good Order and Discipline (GOAD) and I was left to languish there, in relative solitary confinement, for the entire summer of 1990. Almost a full year later (up to date as ever) the *News of the World* would report this 'latest news' as 'Murderer Nilsen in Cell Attack', as 'revealed' by 'a freed ex-cellmate'.

In stark contrast to those who ran the Punishment Block at Wakefield, the screws in the Full Sutton Block were quite polite and civilised. While I was incarcerated there, I was not subjected to any undue restriction, apart from what was compatible with the Segregation Unit routine. The library lady visited once a week and I was allowed a bath or a shower nearly every day. I was nominally designated as 'doing self-study in my cell' and was paid an allowance of about £4 a week with which I purchased tobacco. I was allowed to exercise with other prisoners in the same predicament as myself and our little team of GOAD prisoners spent our hour's exercise sunbathing in the secondary exercise yard.

Next to ours was the hospital yard and our periods on exercise often coincided. They wheeled one young man out in his wheelchair whom I had known briefly at Wakefield and I was struck by a sight: they'd cut off one of his legs below the knee due to circulation or infection problems. That sight brought, sharply, home to me the reality of the destruction of the many young lives my binges had destroyed. There, in the peaceful tranquillity of that lazy, hot summer's day, was the evidence of the reality of my past and, when I returned to my cell, I was violently sick. Periodically, sudden reminders of my past would leap out at me and my self-containment would be caught off guard. They didn't lessen with the passage of time and have remained one of the hazards of having a dark past.

In the high summer, Hornsey Police paid me a visit, wishing me to assist them in the identification of two people they thought might fit the puzzle of my unknown victims. A photograph of a New Zealand student named Smith was produced and I was told he was reputed to have disappeared during my homicidal tenure. I didn't recognise him. Of the second victim, I was given only a name, 'Holmes', and told that he was fourteen years old in 1978 and had vanished around December that year. The police believed he may have been my first victim; the 'Irish youth' whom I had met in the Cricklewood Arms on 30 December. I viewed this idea as a distinct possibility but, as there was no photograph for me to make a positive ID, they returned to Hornsey never to be seen again.

I was later interviewed by one of the prison officials who informed me that they had started a new concept called a Vulnerable Prisoners Unit (VPU) and had located it on A wing. They suggested that I might be relocated there. I reiterated my belief that it was just another name for a 'Rule 43 Segregation Unit', for prisoners who had asked for protection, and I explained that I didn't want to go on it as I'd never asked for protection. I was told that, unless I agreed, I'd have to remain in solitary confinement, in the Block, indefinitely. Therefore, not intending to become a martyr to a stubborn, relatively unimportant principle, I reluctantly agreed to a trial period on the VPU.

It contained all manner of folks, forced to seek common refuge by the nature of their offences or other vulnerabilities, including ex-policemen, ex-prison officers, ex-lawyers, super-grasses and those with bad debts from the main wings. We were a potpourri of all things bright and not so beautiful. The inaccurate collective name for everyone on a VPU was 'nonce', which once referred only to prisoners who had offended against children but the term had been expanded, as a prejudice, to encompass everyone on a VPU. The residents of the A wing VPU were, initially, a bit wary of me but at least they weren't hostile and I made a few surface acquaintances in the short time I was there. Some of them were frightened of me (judged by the nature of my offences) and I sought to relieve them of those fears.

The prison kitchen workers (none of whom resided on the VPU) refused to wash up the dirty food trays from the 'nonce' wing and carried on a guerrilla war against the VPU by doing disgusting things to our food, ranging from human excrement in the custard to razor blades or shards of glass in the pies and stews. The governor on the VPU didn't allow cell association on the insulting grounds that, 'If we left you perverts alone for a minute unsupervised, you'd be at it!' as one screw delicately put it. We were given the worst jobs, no education facilities and no access to the outdoor sports field (on account that it would upset the 'gangsters'). But, strangely, we were mixed with the main prison for the purpose of visits in the visitors' hall.

In October, a couple of screws associated with the church visited my cell one lunchtime and, with an awkward and wan expression, said, 'I'm sorry, it's about your grandmother.' 'She's dead,' I interrupted, assuming this was what he was implying. She was, after all, into her ninety-sixth year. They had intercepted a holiday postcard from Brian Masters informing me of the sad news in a couple of brisk one-liners. The date of the funeral had been given as that very day. I propped the postcard up on my table and laid myself on top of the bed, staring at it. It was a grand, colourful scene of Venice; the city floating on a technicolour blue sea. How far removed it was from the drab, grey life of dear departed Granny Whyte. I often wondered what had kept her going all those years. What reserves of hidden, inner strength did she have to fall back on? She always seemed to be in a hurry, never daring to stop for one instant and reflect on the tragedy of her life and situation.

Granny Whyte's reaction to my arrest and offences was inevitable: 'He must be mad.' Mind you, she would have formed that opinion in response to the news of my homosexuality alone. My differences from the predictable path of the family were always so great that now they had an easy 'logical' explanation for them. Fate had also dogged them with a strain of insanity within the family; I had no idea that her sister, Christian Anne, had lived and died in a mental institution.

Granny's death saw the double standards of my mother in full swing. She had sent a wreath to the funeral inscribed, 'From Dennis' to maintain the illusion of propriety. As she was being interred, with all due religious pomp and feeling, I was being informed of her death, second hand, from a postcard from Venice. No member of the family thought to write and tell me. Likewise, I hadn't even been told of the death of my older 'brother', Olav, the year before and, to this very day, I have received no communication from any member of my family on that subject. I respected their wishes not to have anything to do with me or my situation but what rankled was my mother's perpetuation of the lie of some kind of forgiving, family normality in the face of common adversity.

Having no full-time employment, I was pleased to be involved in a creative project, which was tailor-made for my talents. Someone in authority had conceived the idea that we put on a concert that Christmas under the auspices of an officer called Jennie. We held a meeting where ideas were discussed and I was given the job as writer and director and, with that, we advertised on the wing noticeboard for talents and acts. Meanwhile, I exiled myself in my cell for a few days to produce a programme, including the scripts for about seven comedy sketches, to slot between the acts. I reckoned we had enough material for a three-hour show and Jennie ran off four photocopies of all the sketches titled *Not the Greatest Show on Earth*.

At the first rehearsal, most of the cast didn't bother to turn up and I was disappointed with the lack of commitment from the others as they started to fall by the wayside, one by one. It was now well into November and the performance was scheduled to occur just before Christmas. We were running out of time, fast.

One of the committee members told me he was in contact with a reporter at the *Sunday Mirror* and that she was going to visit him at Full Sutton. He intimated that he could 'make a few quid' with a story about me and I told him that once the concert was out of the way, I'd write something and give it to him to do with as he pleased. But, in early December, we were all confronted with an 'exclusive' in the *Sunday Mirror* headlined something along the line of, 'Perverts' Panto in Monster Jail'. The journalist had even quoted from the script in the article.

I was incandescent with rage and the post-mortem began that very instant when an emergency committee meeting was called in the stage manager's cell. He was emphatic that a screw must have contacted the press and was joined by a chorus of agreement from the assembled committee, with only one dissenting voice: mine. Many of the participating prisoners were angry at having had their names splashed all over the *Sunday Mirror* with the connection that they were located on the 'nonce' wing, which many had kept secret from associates and correspondents outside. My own rage was in how it had damaged the production.

My brief period on the VPU had been a salutary experience in ignorance, greed, envy and 'selling out for personal gain'. Then, just as the thaw began in March 1991, I was told to pack my kit and I was on the move again. My boxes of possessions, Hamish in her cage and I were bundled into the back of a secure minivan with slender bars on the smoked glass windows and we headed south. My destination: Parkhurst.

10

HMPs Parkhurst and Albany | 1991

We stopped for lunch at Leicester Prison, a dilapidated local ruin, and I was dumped in a large communal holding cell where food duly arrived. There was much coming and going of prisoners in the reception area – to and from the local court – awaiting disposal and allocation. As I sat there eating my fodder, I was joined by three young prisoners, who had obviously just returned from court with small sentences, and I presumed they'd been kept in this holding cell with me pending their movement to an appropriate category prison. We made the usual sociable exchange of cigarettes and, as they were under the misapprehension that I, too, had just returned from a court appearance, I was asked, 'How long did you get?' I replied, unabashed, 'I got twenty-five minimum, the bastards.' 'What?' asked the wide-eyed youngster, 'Twenty-five months? If I got that, I'd fucking top myself.' At that point, a screw entered and my three temporary companions left with him and strode confidently on to their low security bus and off into their future. The organisation and security were so lax that I could have gone with them and travelled some miles before anyone would have realised their mistake. Their bus would have been easier to escape from than my single-prisoner, high-security van with a five-screw escort.

We departed down the motorway for the Solent ferry and the Isle of Wight and arrived at Parkhurst in the early evening. At reception, I was kept waiting for quite some time before being told I was going on the wing and that I couldn't take my keyboard. At this, the alarm bells in my head began to ring (at Parkhurst, one wasn't allowed keyboards down the Punishment Block).

Sure enough, I was ensconced in the Block where a screw told me that the delay at reception had been so that the feeling of the prisoners could be gauged at the prospect of me going on to a normal location on the wing. The reaction had been significantly hostile by a vociferous minority who had tried to persuade the authorities that I should be sent elsewhere. So, I settled down for the night in the ancient dungeons of Parkhurst Prison Block, which hadn't changed a bit in the past six years.

I later received a visit from Brian who told me that he'd been approached by Lord Longford*, who had expressed a desire to visit me. Brian advised against it and I think he was hinting at the 'trouble' which might come my way through the noble lord's high profile with the tabloids. But I didn't like being advised whom I should or shouldn't see and, subsequently, exchanged pleasant letters with Frank Longford and he visited me for many years to come.

· · ·

Inside a couple of short weeks, I was moved to Albany, the prison next door. In advance of the move, I was told that I'd be going on normal location but it was only when I was actually on E wing that I discovered it was another blasted Vulnerable Prisoner Unit (VPU).

At Albany, the landings consisted of three spurs branching off from a narrow area surrounding a barred stairwell. They were piled four high with gates subdividing everything; there were no less than five gates from inside my cell to the wing exit, for example! Each spur contained eight cells that were small and claustrophobic and were the smallest in existence, at seven feet by six feet, with no integral

---

* Campaigning Labour peer, well known for his work in prison reform.

sanitation. I had to slop out my bucket of urine and excrement in the traditional way and live with the stench in the intervening period. No cell association was allowed and evening association in the small association area was by rotation, i.e., a different landing on different nights.

A lot of the time was spent banged-up in those pigeon box cells and the general atmosphere was infused with stifling control and cramped conditions. The association area simply comprised a large and a small TV room and a small hall containing a ping-pong table. It was the most ill-equipped and depressing location I had ever been in, barring Brixton. I was only in the place ten minutes when I had a strong desire to be out of it and was at war with the prevailing official attitudes from the very start.

The visiting area for VPU prisoners was a small, wooden portacabin, just inside the gate. There was no easy access to the canteen and our visitors had to carry our refreshments from the main visiting area on a tray, out into the open, across the yard – in all weathers – and up to the portacabin. Through this, we were made to feel apart and subnormal and it was there that I met Frank Longford for the first time. There he stood, as one could well have imagined him, a living salute to the embalmer's art. He looked antiquated and I wondered how the hell his organs still functioned, especially when he told me he'd been a heavy drinker all his life. He informed me that he was writing a book called *Prisoner or Patient* and said he'd be making a reference to me in it to which I quipped that I hoped I'd be mentioned under the 'prisoner' heading. I soon found that, before I made a joke, I had to warn him in advance or he was bound not to get it. If he had any creative failings, it was that he didn't seem to have a conscious sense of humour and he had Van Gogh's ear for music.

Early on, I had applied to attend full-time education but this was refused out of hand as I'd been allocated to work in the wood mill. With the authority's intransigence, it was inevitable that the disagreement would culminate in me frequently being placed on punishment in the Block, for which I received no measure of empathy for my aspirations in front of the number 1 governor, Ray Mitchell.

The cell windows in the Segregation Unit had not been cleaned since the prison had first opened and were sealed with years of grime, which allowed little natural light to enter. Outside, the windows were covered by a metal grille to prevent prisoners from passing things from cell-to-cell. There was no bed; just a mattress on a raised slab on the floor. Calls of nature had to be accomplished in a bucket in the corner of the cell with few slop-outs allowed and I was given up to one hour's exercise in a small, concrete and wire cage.

That summer of 1991, I was in a cell next door to a Nigerian drugs smuggler who was being transferred to another prison the next day. This guy made my mouth water as he talked about the refreshing and exotic tastes of Nigerian seafood dishes. He seemed fascinated by me and my tales of David Martin and we talked through the wall long into the night. I told him that one of the great things I admired about Dave was that he was a 'doer', constantly trying to escape. Early the next morning he departed under heavy escort to continue his sentence in a different prison. Then, a few hours later, on the lunchtime local radio news, I learned that the van in which he was travelling had stopped to refuel whereupon he'd seized the opportunity of an open door to slip his cuffs and make a run for it. With great athletic skill and force of resolution, he jumped a low wall and relieved a surprised customer of her red sports car (she had also stopped to refuel). Our intrepid Nigerian was soon roaring down the Queen's highway – free as a bird – as a gaggle of fat, unfit screws were no match to counter his fleet-of-foot agility. I was inwardly gratified to see the great power of the monolithic State temporarily humbled by the sparks of human initiative, enterprise and creative individuality.

Elsewhere, the side effects of communicating with Frank

Longford were beginning to reveal themselves in the shape of tabloid stories. On Friday, 26 April 1991, the *Daily Star* claimed 'Loony Killer Insults Gulf War Heroes'. Their story began, '...in a letter to Lord Longford...' and proceeded to twist my words into their own interpretation, as per formula.

A few weeks later, the *Sun* told its readers that the 'Potty Peer Is Frisked in Jail', citing a visit he'd paid to me. On that visit, I thought I'd bring a bit of humour into everyone's life (while I was in the Block) and, upon entering the visiting portacabin to see him, I called out, loud enough for everyone to hear, 'Frank, have you brought the drugs?' Prison governors have absolutely no sense of humour and most of my humorous banter also went right over m'lord's head. Another time, he asked me, before the visit ended, 'Is there anything I can do for you before I go?' After thinking for a moment, I said, 'Yes, can you sing "My Way" for me, Frank?'

It must have been slightly unsettling for Lord Longford not to have been given the due deference required of his position in society by me. He was no snob but was, perhaps, frustrated that his Christian message wasn't getting through to me, as it had done with Myra Hindley. I stand as Frank's supreme failure on that count, though I made no strenuous effort to convert him to Humanism.

Meanwhile, the *News of the World* was still marketing 'topical' news, this time on the recent fate of 23 Cranley Gardens. 'Mass Murderer's Home for Sale', 'Grisly Secret of a "Des Res"'. The 'exclusive' meandered along its predictable course, ending with, 'The unusual thing neighbours noticed about the quiet civil servant was that he kept the windows open in all weathers to get rid of the stench from the corpses.' Yes, I kept the windows open during the summer. Doesn't everybody? The only time, in the winter, that I kept the front bedroom window open was in the two weeks after I had killed Stephen Sinclair and up to the time of my arrest (though I closed it when I returned home in the evening). The reason was to retard the decomposition of Sinclair's body. This form of refrigeration was effective in as much as it threw the Home Office pathologist out in his estimation of the time of death by a whole week. To the left of the news piece was a photo of my bath and gas cooker from my flat. The caption read, 'Nilsen Boiled up the Corpses in a Pan' and there was my large saucepan atop the cooking rings in the picture. That, and a picture of the front of the house, brought memories flooding back, stark and real. One of the surprising things about my stay in Cranley Gardens was that, in addition to all my other deeds, I half strangled at least another two men into unconsciousness there before they were used as sexual props to my drunken fantasies. To date, they have never come forward. The only other survivors from those attacks were Paul Nobbs, Carl Stottor and the Japanese guy. The first two were washed in the bath as part of the ritual; the 'son of the Orient' kicked me in the stomach and made good his escape.

I was soon back on the wing from my spell in the Block and back to the detested wood mill and the routine incidents in the life of simple prison folk: stabbings, fights, gang warfare, drugs, arson, bullying, false witness and general mayhem. And sometimes the prisoners were responsible for a lot of it!

But it wasn't long before I was in front of the governor yet again. As I was walking past the Block on the way to the VPU's exercise yard during our half an hour's exercise, I heard the plaintive voice of an old ex-Broadmoor resident whom I'd met briefly at Wakefield. Back there, he'd asked for Rule 43 protection after being subjected to many threats and bullying. They kept thieving his vegan rations and putting human excrement on his bed and I remember he'd asked my advice on what to do about it. He knew who the main culprit was and I said, 'Well, get behind this bully in the dinner queue. Take your steel tray and hit him as hard as you can with it on the side of his head. He'll go into hospital and you'll go down the Block on fifty-six days' punishment. Now, when you come back on the wing, the bullies will stay well clear of you, saying, "Don't mess with him or he'll put a steel tray over your bonce." It's as simple as that.' But the poor dear was not prepared to stand up for himself. He applied for protection and I never saw him again – until that morning at Albany. There he was again, incarcerated in the Block, no doubt because of some petty omission or remark associated with his mental illness. He was certainly an easy target for the screws to pick on; what used to get up their noses was that he was Indian with an upper-class accent, having been educated at an English public school.

I'd stopped by the wire, briefly, to offer what reassurance I could, in the misery of his solitary confinement, when, suddenly, I could hear some loud shouting and bawling behind me. I turned around to be confronted by a principal officer (PO). He was shouting at both me and the two screws standing some short distance away at the exercise yard gate, so I enquired of him, 'Are you calling to a dog or are you attempting to communicate with me?' at which he renewed his shouting with some vigour, 'Get away from that wire now!' and to the two hapless screws, 'You're supposed to be watching them. Get a grip.' I passed on my way into the yard and walked around the circuit with some cons who asked what the row had been all about and I explained the situation, pointing over towards the PO. But when he saw me pointing at him this incensed his further fury and he came over to the wire. 'Why haven't you got the guts to speak about me to my face?' he ranted. I quickly replied: 'Well, if that's what you want, I will. I was just telling these guys what a wanker you are.' His face grew redder and he stormed off muttering, angrily, to himself. I was charged with using insulting language to the PO and warned for adjudication the next day when I pleaded not guilty. The PO had slightly coloured his evidence to give it more serious gravity, saying that I'd called him 'a *fucking* wanker', but I argued that I was merely obeying an order; he'd solicited my thoughts and opinion and I had given them to him, honestly. I added that there was never any intention to give insult until he'd requested it. Sure enough, I was found guilty and fined a week's wages, though I thought he might have let me have that one 'on the house' as it was my fiftieth charge.

Meanwhile, Brian Masters had provided stories to the *Sunday Telegraph*, 'The Killer Comes into his Own', the *Daily Mirror*, 'Coming Soon: The Movie of Nilsen Fiend' and, by the middle of May, he was back in the frame in the *Sunday Telegraph*, this time roping in Frank Longford with him in 'Conversation Between the Author and Lord Longford on the Nature of Redemption'.

The broad line of Frank's argument seemed to suggest that I was capable of redemption, though Brian seemed not so sure, and the conversation players batted their ideas of me back and forth with no particular direction or conclusion.

In one passage, Masters plumbed for the personal view that I was insane, 'You cannot butter a slice of toast while, a few inches away, there simmers the head of somebody you have known, eat the toast and still be sane.' I didn't know where he'd got that domestic information from but that situation was far distant from the truth. On the three occasions when I subjected heads to moist heat on top of the stove – and boiled some of the flesh from two other bodies – I certainly didn't mix this grim work with my own personal, nutritional arrangements. During those procedures, I drank a lot and the food I consumed would come from the Barracuda fish restaurant or Kentucky Fried Chicken in Muswell Hill. I ate those meals in the living room, well away from the stove. It was hard enough not to be sick in the knowledge of what lay next door and I certainly made no toast.

Frank posed the question, 'What ought to be done with Nilsen, then?' Brian was in no doubt that, 'I think he ought to be studied and treated, as much for our sake as for his. There ought to be some continuing attempt to make him better understand the inadmissibility of his acts, as apparently Myra now does.' To compare my attitude to my offences adversely with the 'positive' attitude of Myra Hindley was, to me, insulting in the extreme. On her arrest, Hindley denied the charges. On my arrest, I furnished the police with the full evidence against myself and gave information which the police would never have discovered by themselves. I was also a willing collaborator in my own prosecution while Hindley didn't offer any assistance whatsoever. She stayed in denial for about twenty years, still firmly denying responsibility for some murders, and deciding to 'come clean' only many years later, when she could see some light at the end of the penal tunnel. When I was informed of my whole life tariff, I felt that it was as just as I could hope to expect. There would be no remission for my victims, nor their relatives.

In August, Brian asked me to write something on Jeffrey Dahmer who was currently awaiting trial on charges of multiple murder in Milwaukee, USA. I knew little about Dahmer but endeavoured to give a speculative profile of his 'fantasy syndrome'. His case and pending trial were topical in the press at this time; in fact, while I had been exercising in the Punishment Block yard, a 'gangster' in the next cage had alluded, humorously, to it saying, 'Would you keep my brain in the fridge and eat it with some tomato ketchup?' I retorted sharply, 'I don't think there's enough in your head for a small sandwich.' In November 1991, a feature appeared in *Vanity Fair* magazine under the heading, 'Dahmer's Inferno' by Brian Masters and they had used my letter in a full-page transcription. The body of the article was Masters' comparison between me and Dahmer and was a rehash of how I was treated in *Killing for Company*.

By this time, to my delight, I had been allowed on full-time education. They had, again, failed to break my resistance in the Block and had decided to do something positively constructive for a change. Maybe Frank Longford had also been giving them earache at head office. There was a measure of creative delight in my new post in education. I was especially taken with the history class of Mrs Royles who, I thought, was an effective communicator and had a genuine, enthusiastic interest in her subject, which was also one of my favourites. I also had an engrossing interest in the classes held by Martin Davies (the head of education) and the art classes run by his wife, Penny. In the succeeding month, I researched and wrote some history pieces for Mrs Royles with the main historical subject being in the interwar years and World War II itself. I wrote mini-biographical essays on the rise of fascism in Italy, Il Duce, the rise of Hitler in Germany, Reich III and four cardinal aspects of World War II, from a British perspective. These were: Dunkirk and the Fall of France, The Battle of Britain, Pearl Harbor and D-Day 1944.

I also managed to turn out a creaky composition, which I'd recorded in a back room on a dilapidated tape recorder of monophonic reproduction. It was bloody awful with the odd spark of musical expression but, despite this, it became known as my *Suite No. 2*.

By late November, Brian was back on the box with a film made for the BBC 2 *Bookmark* series. It was a tale of how a writer (Brian) came to write a book about a multiple murderer (me) and Mrs Royles had taped the film and allowed me to watch it. I thought it flat and unimaginative and offered little by the way of pertinent information. Its main selling point seemed to be extracts from a colour film that I'd made in 1975 or 1976 with my former flatmate, Twinkle. It contained the outtakes on something I'd made and discarded in a funeral pyre in my back garden in Melrose Avenue. I had obviously overlooked this can of clips, which were not to be used in the main film, and I'd allowed Masters to exploit them to publicise his book.

In early 1992, Brian was featured in yet another article – this time the *Sunday Express* – called, 'Nilsen Since Conviction'. It comprised a narrative of one of his visits to me at Albany and was, largely, positive. He did, however, manage to raise an oblique whimper in defence of the tabloids, 'He refers to the "myth" of Nilsen the Monster as some confection of the tabloid press, as if he had not, in fact, squeezed the life from up to 15 people and mutilated their bodies.' Brian, of course, knew that there were twelve victims and not fifteen.

As well as starting on education, I had also joined the Albany drama class. The drama director was Barry Bigby, one of the few Albany screws I had any rapport with, and he also played in a local Newport drama group. He certainly knew his stuff and would have worked well on the professional stage, on film or on TV. He took the plunge and, in the run up to Christmas, resolved to put on a production in the new year. But, as copyright was always a difficulty with these things, I volunteered to write an hour-long comedy and, in the new year, I presented the typewritten draft for comments, which he (and members of the group) thought was very funny. What more could one ask of a comedy? Well, after the governor's initial support seemed to have evaporated, Barry suggested we changed it to a radio play instead, so I said I'd adapt the script accordingly. 'No,' he insisted, adding that it would be OK in its presently scripted form! It was a spoof on Herman Melville's *Moby Dick*, which I'd alternatively titled *The Moby Dick Show* or *Thar She Blows* and was a camp romp into the humorous imagination. Although we managed to get most of the play down on tape, the drama group was finally closed down by management in the early summer of 1992.

• • •

At the highest levels of command, it was decided that Albany Prison should be taken out of the maximum-security dispersal system and relegated to the role of a category B prison, therefore, all category A prisoners would need to be moved to other prisons and we were all called into the wing office to state our preferences for transfer. I'd heard of a new prison called Whitemoor and, while it was the devil I didn't know, I felt it couldn't be any worse than Wakefield, Full Sutton, Parkhurst, Wormwood Scrubs or Albany. For security reasons, I was given no firm date for the move, only that it would be sometime that year (1992). In any event, I would be relieved to get away from the pit of Albany.

Well ahead of my move, the head of education, Martin Davies, had solicited donations of pictures to be put on local public exhibition to be auctioned off to raise money for a charity, which would help finance the building of a library annex to a local school. More than willing to help, I donated a folio of about six pictures I'd drawn, which could help bring in much needed funds. The organisers used my name to gain the maximum publicity for the event – by way of various tabloid headlines – and then, before it opened, removed my pictures from the exhibition. The reason they gave was that other artists had apparently refused to have their work exhibited alongside that of a monster of such diabolical hue and had threatened to withdraw their work if my monstrous pictures were not removed.

Around this time, I acquired my second budgie. An acquaintance of mine called me round to his cell. For a couple of ounces of tobacco, he'd purchased a companion for his budgie but was living to regret the decision. He said, 'Des, it's always fighting with my bird. It's a complete nutter. If I can't get rid of it, I'll have to wring its neck or put it out of the window.' This response horrified me and I took a closer look at it. Every feather on its body began to tremble in abject fear when I approached it. 'Who did you get this one off?' I asked him. 'Peter Garner,' he replied. 'Case explained,' said I. Peter Garner* was always getting things sent in for the sole purpose of selling them. He was a great consumer of debt and had a reputation for treating his birds badly, hence the trembling. Rather than see the bird destroyed, I agreed to take it and said I'd see how it got on with my bird, Hamish, over the weekend. I then became the keeper of one dark green cock budgie whom I named Tweetles. I put him with my light green hen and they formed an immediate bond based on the clear understanding that it was the hen who was in charge. In

---

* *Not his real name.*

a few months, the traumas of his past were forgotten to the extent that he no longer trembled when a human came near him.

Even trapped in a prison tower block, I could still keep in contact with the sights and sounds of the wild birds outside. During one afternoon's bang-up, I noticed a black-headed gull was trapped by one of its legs and was hanging, struggling desperately in pain, from a coil of razor wire. I pressed my bell and called a screw, pointing out what had happened, and requested he call the works screws to get it down. Within fifteen minutes one duly arrived on the scene and looked up at the gull hanging there and, in response to my questions from the window, said there was nothing he could do. 'Why don't you get a fucking ladder?' I intoned. 'We can't do that,' he said, 'we're too busy.' With that, he departed and it was the last I saw of him. 'Too busy,' I said to myself, 'too busy having another fucking tea break.'

The gull's snow-white feathers were flecked by the bright red of its own blood and a pool of it had begun to form on the flat roof underneath. I just stood there and watched, grief stricken, with a feeling of helplessness as tears began to form in my eyes. It was dying the worst way: very slowly and through great pain. I continued to watch over it, willing it to know that there was someone with it, giving it spiritual support. Then, within the space of fifteen minutes, a wonder came to light. The bird's leg untangled from the wire and it fell the foot or so on to the flat roof. Getting painfully up on to its good leg – the damaged one hanging limp and useless – the dear creature flew off. And it survived because, after that, I often saw it flying around the yard, its good leg tucked up underneath and its damaged one hanging down. Nature is very cruel and dispassionate but, in its multifarious circumstances, it can be compassionate. It was a victory over adversity and no less glorious because it occurred, virtually unseen, to one of the humbler creations of nature.

By this time, I had crudely composed and recorded another three musical suites in the little room at the end of the education department. On another occasion, I'd managed to get hold of a video camera, loaned to me by the psychology department and, although I'd never used one before, I put it through its paces with a few test shoots. Me and another guy were fooling around with it to see what its picture quality was like in the classroom. I jovially pointed it at a third man and, to my complete shock and surprise, he took some kind of traumatic, psychological 'turn', went very pale and said he felt sick. It was the sight and act of the camera pointing at him and the incident was left unexplained.

Come the July, we were all sacked from education in line with the planned cuts and the general restructuring of the department. I guessed that a lot of the teaching effort would now be directed towards the new concept of Sex Offender Treatment Programmes (SOTP) where they had earlier operated a pilot exercise along those lines in one of the classrooms (I wasn't invited to participate). So there we all were, out on our ears, with no financial support but for the pittance of an unemployment allowance of a couple of quid a week; hardly enough for a half ounce of Old Holborn tobacco. On the bright side, they'd started to move us category A men out to new prisons and I was hopeful that my time would come soon.

It was a long, hot summer in 1992 and I was able to improve on my suntan by lying on the grass during the weekend exercise and association periods in the open air. I was just about the only prisoner fully stripped down to my white Y-fronts while many prisoners sat around wearing woolly jumpers and some, even, overcoats on those sweltering summer days with temperatures in the eighties. It was as if the removal of clothing would, somehow, expose their vulnerability. I loved the warm weather and the embracing warmth of glorious sunshine. There were borders of pretty flowers around the yard and the humming of bees and insects. The sun was one of my oldest friends and it always gave me a warm welcome, being one of the firm consistencies of my life.

Over those months, I had the strings from the past tugged by various news items thrown at me via the radio at breakfast time. These were sad bulletins on the fate of some characters from my prison past. News came of the death of one guy I'd known at Wakefield who had been instrumental in outing and hounding a Hepatitis B sufferer on C wing. The bully was eventually removed and placed in isolation somewhere while the Hepatitis sufferer was ostracised by nearly everyone on the wing. He was a couple of doors down from me and I spoke to him quite often, though I had no intention of mixing my bodily fluids with his. Despite this, I never felt I was in any risk whatsoever of catching that virus from him.

Hepatitis B is not easy to catch. After my arrest in 1983, the police discovered that my last victim, Stephen Sinclair, was a carrier. The powers that be immediately ordered that I – and all the police who had been near his body – be tested and screened for the virus. They took blood tests and the results, in all our cases, came back negative. Now, to demonstrate how difficult it is to catch, you have to remember the following: I was up to my elbows in Sinclair's fluids, as I extracted his viscera, after having cut off his head and cut him in half. Well, I was never going to achieve this degree of intimacy with the Hepatitis sufferer at Wakefield, therefore, I guessed that the risk of contamination would be negligible. I played a few games of snooker with him so that he'd have someone to play with (though I hated snooker) and mysterious, threatening notes would go up around the wing spreading alarm and hysteria on the subject of contamination. They even had a bath marked 'infected prisoners only' which nobody would use, save for me and my unfortunate neighbour.

Graham Young, the St Albans poisoner, was also to be found dead 'of a heart attack' in his cell in the hospital in Parkhurst, next door. There was a rumour going around that the true state of affairs was that Young had hoarded some of his medicine and taken an overdose.

In early autumn, I received a letter from a Polish American

psychologist who operated at five correctional facilities in the State of Connecticut, USA, and he expressed a keen interest in visiting me in connection with his studies and appreciations of the 'mechanisms' surrounding multiple homicide. I agreed to see him and submitted his particulars to the Home Office so that he could be afforded category A prisoner visiting status. In the meantime, I typed out a ninety-page 'sexual history' I titled, *Orientation in Me: Trick of the Light* to aid him in his deliberations. A month later, I wrote another autobiographical paper that I called, *After the Feast*, which ended its revelation of events in my life, up to the summer of 1988 at Wakefield Prison (those two would later become parts 1 and 2 of this autobiography). In the event, the Home Office refused him permission to visit me and so parts 1 and 2 were relegated to a cardboard box under the bed in my cell.

A few weeks later, I received a letter from Mark Gresswell who worked at Birmingham University and researched at Broadmoor. He was writing a study of the addictive compulsion mechanisms associated with serial homicide. Well, official doors were opened for Mark without further ado and he duly arrived for a first session. We commenced, going over my life, but the sessions were abruptly terminated with my move to Whitemoor in late September.

A month before that move brought the first link in the chain that became the Central TV interview scandal, which, like most deceptions, began innocently enough. Brian Masters relayed a request to me from someone he vaguely described as being 'from Channel Four, I think', asking for my consent to be interviewed, on camera, for a TV documentary on my case. I agreed but voiced my opinion that the Home Office would never allow such an interview to take place. He told me that the TV people were already dealing with that and they would get the necessary permission, adding that they'd be in touch with me by letter. He carried the 'good news' to the potential makers, with a request that they should write to me, formally, to clarify the details.

The letter soon arrived on Central TV official headed notepaper, asking me to participate in the interview for the documentary. I began to exchange letters with Mike Morley, the producer, all of which passed through the official censor, so the prison authorities could have been in no doubt as to what was being proposed and required. Then a date was fixed for a preliminary meeting to be followed by a filming session a week later.

At that preliminary meeting Mike Morley, the interviewer and a profiling psychologist, Paul Britton, informed me, to my great surprise, that they'd be shooting the very next day. Come the event, I was introduced to the two cameramen and the videotaped interview unfolded over two hours in the morning and two hours in the afternoon in the Board of Visitors boardroom. The day before, I had loaned Paul Britton Part 1 of my autobiography to give him additional information with which to help him frame his questions (it took me eight months to get it back), then, after the interview, the TV quartet departed and Morley said he would keep me informed of developments.

By 30 September 1992, I was on the Isle of Wight ferry heading for my new location of Whitemoor Prison, recently opened by Norma Major, the then prime minister's wife. Within the space of a few hours, my Albany past felt well and truly over as I, two budgies and five screws sped across the flatlands of North East Cambridgeshire.

11

HMP Whitemoor | 1992

Whitemoor Prison had been constructed on part of an old railway marshalling yard a couple of miles outside the town of March in Cambridgeshire. En route to the prison, I remember driving through the shabby, run-down town, which, after a few hundred years, was in need of some spark of enterprise and human initiative. That much-needed investment had come in the dubious shape of Whitemoor Prison and, by 1991, the first prisoners had begun to arrive even as the workmen were still finishing off the interiors.

Having, by now, learned from the mistakes of Frankland and Full Sutton prisons, the architects had reverted to the old Victorian layout of the wing accommodation. Instead of narrow, dark passageways and the labyrinth of unpoliceable nooks and crannies, they had opted for galleries where all the cells opened on to a common hall area, which could be easily observed from either end of the landings.

Each wing was divided into three spurs, cross-like, with the fourth stem of the cross comprising the wing offices. This stem joined on to a 200-yard-long corridor forming a kind of backbone that connected all the wings and adjunctive services like gymnasium, chapel and the education centre. At the far end of the prison was an Astroturf football field while at the opposite end, and all on its own, was a prison within a prison, namely the 'inescapable' Special Security Unit (SSU).

The number 1 governor was Andrew Barclay and I never set eyes on him in all the time he was there until he left in July 1994. The only firm policy which prevailed involved appeasing one half of the prison at the expense of the other half. Let me explain the set up: A and B wings (including the Segregation Unit, a separate unit altogether) were designated the VPU (Vulnerable Prisoners Unit) while C and D were described as 'main' locations. Prisoners on the main were referred to as 'gangsters' and had exclusive use of the education centre, including the video equipment and all the facilities in the computer room. They also had structured classes. However, all of this had gone to waste because a sizable portion of the 'gangsters' on education did nothing more than sit around watching videos, reading tabloid newspapers and smoking dope. Management just wanted them off the wings. The education department for the VPU purloined the prisoners' rest rooms on A and B wings and designated them 'classrooms'. There were no structured classes as such, just a policy of 'open learning'.

Management had allocated me to full-time education and I asked to study history, creative writing, video and film studies, screen writing, creating a newspaper or magazine, drama, music, art and all related activities, but I found they had a severely limited range of subjects and courses and I had to choose from a greatly restricted list. Initially, the authorities believed that I'd be useful in helping the department look good in the numbers game by passing several GCSEs (without much tuition) but when they discovered that I would not be an exam-passing machine, to make them look good, they went right off me. Thereafter, I was openly encouraged to come off full-time education and, for the most part, I was frozen out.

Things were relatively free and easy on the VPU and the screws stuck to their fixed, mechanical routines. There was an air of the inner city about the place, with all the attending graces: minor taxing, bullying, hooch brewing, some cell thieving and drugs. It was the same on the main, only the scale and intensity was greater; where you'd get a 'dig' (punch) on the VPU, you would be knifed on the main. It stood to reason, then, that life on the main was far more pressurised than it was on the VPU and there were quite a few transfers. Some men had just had enough of the turbulent stress of life over there while others left because of debts to the drugs barons. Also, sex offenders who were hiding out on the main were transferred to the VPU once the 'gangsters' had discovered what they were in for. The VPU also became a dumping ground for incurable or unmanageable rejects from Broadmoor and Rampton special secure hospitals and governors from other dispersal prisons up and down the country seemed to empty their Punishment Blocks, rounding up their troublesome prisoners and dumping them all on the lap of Whitemoor.

It was a crazy place in those early days and it seemed that Barclay and his management team had confused 'liberalism' with 'anarchy'; one had to do something really bad in order to get nicked. There were a lot of loud people around and life was exceedingly noisy with many prisoners shouting to each other from their windows late into the night. Some men didn't work but lived off the proceeds of drugs or private cash sent in from outside. A radio could be stolen from a cell and be offered for sale on the adjoining wing within the hour – with no questions asked. Everything was available for trade and nearly everything had a commodity value.

There was no shortage of cannabis on the wings and I was a regular user during weekends. I paid for it with tobacco or phonecards, though some cons had a habit far in excess of what they could afford, resulting in trouble! The bigger barons had minders and enforcers while some of the harder barons did their own enforcement.

Offenders against children lived in a measure of personal fear because there was also a 'gangster' element very much alive on the VPU. Intimidation was a very discreet affair; one-to-one, or, more often than not, two-to-one. The weaker members of the community attracted attention as natural victims for regular exploitation and, such was their fear of the implied threat, they never complained to the screws. Grassing resulted in more pain and further ostracisation. Staff weren't overly concerned with this, in fact, most of the time they just didn't want to get involved.

A year earlier, in 1991, a young graphic designer had begun a correspondence with me, as we had a deal of mutual interests. His name was Mark Austin and he ran his own business in Chelsea Harbour in London, commuting there every day from Bedfordshire. He was a married man with a little girl and another baby on the way. Our friendship developed to such a degree that we agreed that it would be mutually beneficial to have regular visits and Mark was to be my best friend and supporter in all things creative. I spoke to Brian Masters of my intention to have closer ties with Mark but he warned me against it, saying that a contact had informed him that Mark was probably a plant working for the *Daily Mail*, who were fishing for a story. Brian had already spoken against me seeing Frank Longford and I became suspicious of his motives and felt that he resented losing his 'monopoly' access to me. I told Brian that I intended to see Mark, in spite of what I believed were his unfounded suspicions, and didn't assess Mark as being of the type of character which Masters was suggesting. Unlike Mark and Frank Longford, Brian didn't radiate much warmth in my direction and I always guessed that, in the exercise of his 'duty' in visiting me, he was suffering in silence and putting on a brave face.

Nineteen ninety-two folded and 1993 opened with a bang. Mike Morley from Central TV wrote and said they were having difficulties with the Home Office concerning the transmission of his documentary *Murder in Mind*, which included the interview they'd filmed with me at Albany Prison. These 'difficulties' would soon explode on to the front burners of national news and the decision to try to stop the documentary airing was taken by the home secretary, Kenneth Clark.

I was handed a cutting from the *Today* newspaper headlined, 'Ban on Silence of the Lambs TV Talk with Killer Nilsen'. The piece told how 'television bosses were yesterday banned by a judge from showing journalists...interview with serial killer...dismembering bodies...the Home Office· changed its mind...was not policy to allow interviews with category A killers to be shown...'

This came at me like a sudden sock in the teeth and was the first intimation I had that the Home Office were claiming authorship and copyright on my words. I had agreed to the interview in the express belief that they were recording for a publicly transmitted broadcast. Permission had obviously been given because the Home Office had allowed it to be made in the full knowledge of what I believed to be the case. All my correspondence with Central TV had been monitored by the usual censorship procedures in prison and I had no agreement or correspondence with the Home Office to give any interview.

When one smells a rat, one has to poke around with a sharp stick to discover the source of the smell and, in the first instance, Mike Morley broke off all communication with me but the press reports continued to flow.

The *Sun* ran with a confused narrative, stating, 'Killer Nilsen Wants to be a Telly Star' in which, 'Nilsen...revelled in his chilling television performance' and claimed to have obtained all this from Lord Longford. The article finished on the note that the Home Office '...is expected to sue [Central TV] over copyright and breach of contract'.

The more serious newspapers were at it too. The *Independent* told, accurately, how 'Nilsen TV Producer "Deceived" Prison' by their crime correspondent, Terry Kirby. The plot was, indeed, beginning to thicken with a fog of criminal deception. It went on, 'A television producer tricked his way into a top security prison to film an interview with...Nilsen, the High Court was told yesterday.'

The subject remained controversial news for some days and all sorts of irrelevant opinions were solicited on the matter – except for mine. By this time, it was clear to me that all the involved factions had been avidly deceiving each other, united only in the common goal of getting the interview, for their own diverse purposes, by deceiving me.

In the end, the Home Office failed in its attempt to ban the broadcast and immediately lodged an appeal, which was also rejected, and the programme went out as scheduled. The brief, three-minute clip, selected from the four hours of tape, was not representative of the interview as a whole and was picked for its sensationalism, pure and simple.

I solicited an explanation from the Home Office through the Request & Complaint procedure but none was forthcoming, so I engaged the services of a local solicitor to make further enquiries. But all that they were able to uncover was an admission that the two cameramen were indeed senior detectives (who they named).

When the home secretary, Ken Clark, was interviewed on BBC Radio 4 during the controversy, he avoided the main details of the issue and concentrated his attack on me and his public duty to prevent 'murderers like Nilsen from happily describing their crimes in full view of victims', etc. Anyone would have thought that the interview had been my idea.

Terry Kirby of the *Independent* was made aware of the true facts through the agency of Mark Austin, armed with a copy of my statement and all the correspondence I'd had with Central TV. Kirby, at first, seemed keen to run with it as a legitimate news story but then began to hum and haw, finally admitting his bosses had placed an embargo on the revelations. So much for the independence of the *Independent*.

Following transmission of the programme, the issue dried up and vanished into the thin air of British hypocrisy. I gave my full statement on the Central TV interview to the local Cambridgeshire police for action but all they did was to send it to John Stevens (the then deputy chief constable of the Cambridgeshire Constabulary) who ruled that there was no criminal offence. I then wrote to the Police Complaints Authority who advised me to address my complaint to the Cambridgeshire Constabulary, thereby neatly closing the establishment circle.

Only one good thing came out of the Central TV interview fiasco and it was that Mike Morley sent me a manual typewriter that he'd found lying around in a cupboard at the office. They no longer used them – being into word processing PCs by then – and I was thankful for this kind gift.

After my recent exposure on television, a flood of unrelated press articles about me appeared. The *Sun* reiterated the lie that I had given my victims drugged drinks and that I had killed for revenge after being jilted by David Gallichan. In February 1993, the *Daily Sport* 'revealed' that grass refused to grow in the back garden at 195 Melrose Avenue (I wondered if they'd tried planting seeds?). The *Daily Telegraph* interviewed Carl Stottor in an article titled, 'A Very Brief Acquaintance with Evil' with a new picture of Carl hanging about a street corner and looking as pretty as ever. The *Guardian* solicited the views of characters like Brian Masters, Colin Wilson, Chris Bishop and a crime story writer from *True Crime*, Brian Marriner, under the headline, 'The Serial Killer as Celebrity – Journey into Iniquity' that treaded the well-worn, tedious path of ignorant theories and 'educated' speculation.

During that summer of 1993, we on the VPU, for the first and only time, were given five days' access to the education centre for the purposes of an annual summer school. There were various activities, including drama, and I opted for video production though, come the event, there were only three men on it – including the instructor, Martin Franks. However, in the few short sessions, me, a guy who called himself Billy Bananas and the instructor were able to produce a ten-minute piece titled *The Invigilator*, a kind of bizarre comedy/horror. It was shot by Billy Bananas under my direction while Martin and I acted the parts of tutor and student respectively. Management were not happy with the result and, apart from them and we cast, no one else was allowed to view it.

Cons from the main, who attended the education centre, had started a free prison newspaper called the *Insider* and it began to appear on the landings. It seemed to be the mad uncle of *VIZ* magazine and expressed all the prejudices of the 'gangsters'. One of the teachers persuaded me to send in some pieces and I consented to write a couple of regular columns; one under the pen name, 'The Pink Panther' and a video review section under the name of reviewer, 'Cynthia Gizzard'. It was a creative time.

As my musical compositions on the mini keyboard expanded, Mark sent me in a small portable sound mixer so that I could attempt to play and record a full symphony but it was immediately impounded because it wasn't on the list of privileges. Security checked with the education department who vindictively replied, 'There would be no educational application in allowing Nilsen to have a portable sound mixer.' They'd already told me that I couldn't study music, as it was something they didn't do, so the mixer lay in the property store until 1996 when it was handed back out to Mark, still in its original packaging, unused.

Around this time, the papers were full of the mystery of a serial killer who was frequenting gay watering holes in London and seducing potential victims before going back to their flats for a bit of bondage. They got more than they'd bargained for because, after he'd tied them up, he amused himself with them before strangling them to death. The police eventually picked up and charged Colin Ireland with the five murders who, even after his arrest and conviction, still avidly maintained that he was not queer. He came to Whitemoor soon after his trial and was lodged on B wing where I met him a couple of times at the lifers' group meetings. He seemed to be a reasonable enough guy to me and could certainly express himself. Sometime later, he was suspected of having a hit list of 'perverts' he was going to 'do' on B wing and, whether he had one or not, he was moved to the Block on GOAD and, thereafter, out to another prison.

Earlier in the year, the convicted ex-member of a murderous paedophile gang, Leslie Bailey, had arrived on A wing. He'd only been there a matter of minutes when a few cons gave him a couple of 'digs' and he was promptly transferred to the other VPU wing (B) before most of us were aware that he'd even arrived in the prison. I spoke out against the sort of attitude which prompted the attack, pointing out that it was a case of 'the pot calling the kettle black'. We were all in the same boat and there was no reasonable right for one set of sex offenders to sit in judgement over another. Leslie Bailey was no better protected on B wing and, one night in October, two psychos entered Bailey's cell. As one returned to the landing to stand watch, the other strangled him to death. The few days that followed were taken up with mass police interviews of everyone on B wing and some on A wing, including me. One guy falsely confessed to the killing but later changed his mind when the police asked him to explain the semen in Leslie Bailey's anus. In his tiny mind, he'd thought that the yob 'gangsters' would consider him a hero if they thought he'd killed a child killer. I, however, thought it a strange community where some people would be proud to be a murderer and horrified at being thought a homosexual.

Eventually, the police got two suspects in the frame and, with the help of a prisoner prepared to give evidence for the prosecution, they were whisked off to the Block and a long wait for trial. The two ex-B wing prisoners, Michael Cain and John Brookes, were convicted of Bailey's murder and sentenced to life imprisonment. There were many on B wing who swore that they'd got the wrong men and that the real murderers had got off scot free. But as we weren't party to all the supposed evidence, it was difficult to judge. Bailey's death did nothing to redress the wrong of the murders of young Barry Lewis, Mark Tildesley or Jason Swift – Bailey's victims.

It was just another pointless killing to satisfy one lust or another; the lust of inadequate sexuality and the lust for revenge. Perverts all.

Come the start of the new evening class term, I decided to sign up to the drama group, which was run by a civilian drama instructor, Chris Newell and two other prisoners – her confidants. They wanted to put on a full-scale production and, as her two confidants loved rugby, they chose to do a rugby comedy *Up 'n' Under* by John Godber. There were clearly no women available to take the part of the female PT instructor, so it was decided to make 'her' a gay, camp man and they looked to me to play the part, which I was only too happy to accept. With this character change, the play was funnier than was ever conceived by John Godber. However, with only a few weeks to go before the final performance over Christmas, a vital member of the cast dropped out, so it was decided that Chris would play the female PTI and I would take the part of the man who'd dropped out. And, in that short space of time, we managed to put on a performance in front of a prisoner audience, which was a moderate success, made funnier by the fact that a lot of us didn't really know what we were doing. The cons enjoyed it and that was all that mattered.

Fresh from my first real thespian 'victory', I walked straight into the pit of despondency. On Christmas Day, 1993, I went to the TV room down the landing and watched the Clint Eastwood western *Unforgiven*. When I returned to my cell, I was shocked to discover my budgie, Hamish, lying in an inch and a half of water in my wash basin. I picked her up but my attempts to revive her were to no avail. Immediately, thoughts raced through my fevered mind that someone must have purposely killed her but, luckily, I was under the calming influence of a joint and was able to rationalise what had probably happened. There were small droplets of water all over the floor. Hamish was always flying at the mirror above the sink and, in doing so, I figured she may have fallen in. It was obvious that she hadn't drowned because of the slight depth of water and the droplets on the floor gave witness to the fact that she must have been flapping furiously to take off when she must have had a heart attack under the strain. By budgie standards she was an old bird; well over nine. Tweetles looked very disconsolate and lost sitting up there on his own, his partner no more.

I wrapped Hamish in some white tissues, put her in a white plastic carrier bag and asked one of the screws if he would bury her in his garden, which he agreed to do. Earlier, I'd been in the middle of composing a piece about the performer's fear of going on stage (*Suite No. 32*) but I changed the mood, halfway through the piece, with the emotional grief I felt for my dear friend; that little green bird who had been my companion for so long. Tiny bird – big heart. The loss of a loved one is a very sad and private thing and all the creatures of creation have to face that great day of sublime equality.

A few days later, two screws arrived to do a cell security check. One asked, 'Why don't you take down the budgie's window perch?' I told him that her ghost still needed something to sit on. It was more my wish to cling to a small part of my normality; the safe, reassuring little cycles of my domestic routine. We shared cages and her 'spirit' was still there (and will always remain). Mine was a crowded cell; so many spirits.

In the new year, Mark sent me in another hen, the image of Hamish (whom I also named Hamish) and Tweetles took to her straight away.

• • •

In the nineties, the Home Office was becoming a sinister, overtly political agency of the Tory party and government. It heralded a period of the most draconian diminution of the rights of the citizen in favour of new, unjust powers to the agencies of the State. New concepts appeared in the form of 'criminal trespass' and 'the erosion of a citizen's right to silence when confronted by the power of the police'. New 'moral' slogans were equally illogical: 'Return to Victorian Values' and the plain, stupid 'Prison Works'. Prime minister, John Major, and his new henchman at the Home Office, Michael Howard, would be playing hard to the public galleries with the sort of opinions expressed in the *Sun* editorials. They would be tough on crime and criminals without, for one moment, ever addressing the causes of crime. Harsh sentences and harsh treatment inside prison was the only language they understood and, consequently, sentences became longer, new criminal offences were created and prisons became fuller.

By April 1994, there was much leaking of 'secret' memos from the Home Office laying the ground for things to come. There was a piece in the *Sunday Telegraph* announcing that a list of selected prisoners had been drawn up by the home secretary, Michael Howard, to send to the prime minister, assuring him and the public that these men, as a matter of political policy, would spend the rest of their natural lives inside prison (as retribution and deterrence). It came as no surprise to me that they speculated that my name was on that list. Fred West, who had just been arrested, now had a very clear idea of what lay in store for him. The only woman on the list was Myra Hindley who was being kept in prison well after her 'sell by date' for purely political reasons. I wasn't going to be pleading for release in my own case because the pain my actions had caused would only terminate with the deaths of the sufferers, so it was only just that the same should apply to me. I did, however, take issue with the processes which allowed a politician to set life sentence tariffs in individual cases. That should have been a matter for a free and independent judiciary.

Judge Stephen Tumin, her majesty's inspector of prisons, visited the prison in early 1994 and a list of prison appointees, selected to see him, was drawn up by the management. After I gave them a great deal of earache, they relented and allowed me to be present. I found the judge to be sympathetic and positive in his outlook and

I realised that I'd previously misjudged him. I had believed that all those officials were 'place men', intent on supporting the status quo, but he displayed all the independence and impartiality of one of the better members of the judiciary. He was also an artistically cultured man.

He asked us our questions in turn and I chose to highlight the unfairness of the two differential regimes of the main and the VPU, and I quantified, with actual examples, to illustrate the inequality. I didn't hog his time because there were others eager to make their own, important points. Then one loony explained to the bemused judge that screws crept into his cell when he was asleep and played with his feet! Tumin drew in a deep breath and said, 'Yes, next question?' before moving, diplomatically, on. We all parted amicably, feeling that something positive had been achieved, but I guessed he didn't make any recommendation to encourage the 'anti-nonce' policies at Whitemoor, though he did suggest that more should be done to fulfil the special needs of life-serving prisoners.

By this time, I was midway through the Sex Offender Treatment Programme (SOTP), which I'd begun attending some months earlier. The opening, official shot was that the course was not a cure for perceived sexual aberrations in the prisoner but a cognitive guide to the significant links in the cycle of the offending chain so that risk areas could be identified and avoided. There was nothing revealed to me on that course which I hadn't already worked out for myself, years before. It was, however, educative in that it allowed me to have the shared experience of past traumas with other prisoners. As prisoners were obliged to relate their past experiences – including their early childhoods – there were frequent occasions when some totally broke down, with a complete absence of back-up support or trauma counselling. An embarrassed silence would follow these breakdowns and the void of personal pain hung, unresolved, in the deafening air of general, official inadequacy.

The confidentiality of personal testimony was never guaranteed and stories of personal, offending details were soon circulating, along with all the other gossip, around the prison landings. The SOTP stood, in a specific way, as a 'productive' exercise in intelligence-gathering about the prisoner's past. Telling all was viewed as 'co-operating in addressing past offending behaviour' while refusing to explain some areas of the past was deemed to be 'not co-operating in addressing past offending behaviour' or being 'in denial'.

Strong solicitations were made on the prisoner to 'come clean' and 'admit' to actions which they'd been suspected of but had never been charged with and prisoners were often marked down for not co-operating in these controversial areas of speculation. Of course, no solicitor was ever present during these new 'confessions' and the information revealed would be passed on to the proper authorities (i.e., the police). The SOTP had become an instrument for 'clearing up' unsolved crimes on police files and I could see the danger in a vulnerable prisoner trying to ingratiate himself in the eyes of the prison authorities, being subtly pressurised into making false admissions. Prisoners were told, in no uncertain terms, that their date of release would depend on their full co-operation with all official policies and the reporting system would not be kind to those who resisted. Time and again, in answer to the question 'Why are you doing the course?' the reply was, 'I've been told that I must do it.' Therefore, only in this context could the courses be said to be voluntary.

After I'd completed my course, the official view of my perceived level of risk and dangerousness did not alter. Therefore, I concluded that the course did me no good at all and I refuted their idea that no man could progress without his full co-operation with all their theory-based policies and non-scientific official attitudes.

I still managed to cram in the odd composition and keyboard recording at weekends (a most absorbing pastime) and I gave the spontaneous pieces my full, unfettered attention and concentration. It was like a damn good ride, though mentally exhausting.

In May 1994, a resurgence of tabloid fantasies concerning me reared, unexpectedly, upwards in the form of the *News of the World*'s 'Gay Killer Camps it up in Jail... It's Dennis the Mincing Menace'. It was a completely fabricated story from start to finish and had me mincing up to new arrivals saying, 'We haven't met yet; my name's Dennis.' (Shouldn't that read, 'Oh hello Honky Tonks, how are you?') We all had a good chuckle about it except the wing idiot, who said that I'd cheated the readership by refusing to look anything like the description of me in the paper. The tabloids seemed to have temporarily abandoned the 'piercing, shark-like eyes' persona in favour of the camp, mincing, effeminate image of pathos à la Kenneth Williams/Charles Hawtrey variety.

Two months later, the number 1 governor, Andrew Barclay, was replaced by Robert Brodie Clark from Woodhill Prison. There was a great deal wrong with the way Whitemoor was being managed at the time and a number of fairly urgent priorities were waiting to be dealt with but the premier problem that Brodie Clark decided to eradicate was his favourite: smoking. He proposed a ban in all the visiting areas, including the small, legal visits room, justifying this measure on health grounds. He conducted a consultation exercise with the cons – who disagreed with his proposals – then ignored it and imposed the ban anyway. A few weeks later, a gaggle of doubtfuls joined Brodie Clark's management team in the form of Nick Leader, Ron 'Jumping Jack Flash' Jagger and, as deputy governor, a man called Haley who I had regretted to encounter at Wakefield. This team spelled bad news for the cons.

In the mid-summertime, Mark Austin had sent me in a canvas, palette, brushes, linseed oil and a selection of oil paints, and requested that I paint a picture for him, something which I was more than pleased to carry out. I had, in my last weeks at school, painted a self-conscious oil painting, which was a very feeble enterprise indeed, and I hadn't touched oils since. With the materials that Mark had generously provided, I executed *Bacardi Sunrise* in two brief sessions.

It was no planned contrivance but flowed entirely from the sober, subconscious instinct of an artist working on autopilot, free from the constraints of logic or reason.

In the centre of the picture, dominating the scene, is my bloody handprint, which is self-explanatory. The figure in the foreground is wrapped up in himself, self-contained and separated from his surroundings in a red, enveloping placenta, fully developed but, somehow, still trapped in an embryonic form. He is still not free from the body of the mother and is still psychologically undernourished and attached. Under the clear, blue sky with burning 'fried egg' sun, expressing all the benevolent nourishment upon our life, we see a landscape of two extremes. On the left, he sits in the arid, parched desert of his life, separate from the lush greenery which lies under the pink triangle of homosexuality. He belongs in the valley paradise (shown on the right) but is shut out by the circumstances of his life. For gays, the conventional homophobic desert dries up their aspirations and they are expelled from all the great possibilities of achieving that step to acceptance and gaining entry to the green and pleasant land. They are often despised and rejected. The title, *Bacardi Sunrise*, relates to the awakening, the next morning, in the recognition of the ruinous reality of a life destroyed by the events of the night before. His fantasies were a hopeless attempt to escape to the garden but it was merely a drink-induced, destructive illusion. The sun, the next morning, shines down with equal benevolence or harshness on both plant and man. It performs, but never judges. It is always there. Perhaps all men have a *Bacardi Sunrise* hidden, deep inside, waiting for the right conditions to be born and live.

I handed out the picture to Mark, with the paint still not quite dry, and was pleased to see that he liked it. He later attempted to hand in more painting materials but, to our great surprise and disappointment, they suddenly imposed a ban on this activity with a new Brodie Clark regulation. So I only painted the one oil painting. Given the chance and the oils, I could have embarked on a continuous flow of works in another of my creative binges. In the event, I diverted this energy into music and the recording of more compositions.

Towards the autumn, Mark sent in a disposable camera so that recent shots might be taken of me as I had no decent photos of myself to send out to friends outside prison. The disposable camera duly arrived but I wasn't allowed to have it, nor was it allowed on the wing. The procedure was that a screw would take the pictures in the chapel lounge and the camera could then be handed out to Mark, on a later visit, for developing and printing. On Wednesday, 7 September 1994, just after 4 p.m., my personal officer, Dougie Clapp, picked up the camera from reception and, together with my precious Casio keyboard, we decamped to the chapel lounge. Under my direction, Dougie quickly shot about twenty-four pictures as I adopted as many different poses as I could devise in such a short space of time. Afterwards, I was returned to the wing and the disposable camera was returned to reception and then handed out to Mark on his next visit. Before the authorities allowed this, I had to give a written undertaking that I wouldn't publish any of these photos. This undertaking, although binding on me, was not binding on Mark, who owed no allegiance to petty prison regulations. He owned the camera and the film and I had already waived any copyright to it.

A mere fifty hours after the photos were taken, the elephant turd hit the turbofan in a completely unrelated incident. Six prisoners in the SSU (the 'fortress' deemed impregnable) made a spirited effort to escape. Two of them got as far as the surrounding countryside where they were picked up in the middle of the night after being detected by a helicopter with a heat-seeking camera. In the morning, in the heat of national news, everyone was blaming everybody else with nobody accepting responsibility – especially the home secretary, Michael Howard. In order to avoid awkward questions, he commissioned an ex-inspector of constabulary, Sir John Woodcock, to lead an enquiry into the matter, which would later surface as the Woodcock report. The felony was later compounded with the discovery of a couple of pounds of Semtex explosive in the property of one of the IRA terrorist prisoners in the SSU. It had, apparently, been in the prison for some time and had travelled about with the prisoner. A couple of handguns with ammunition were amongst the other things also found to be in the possession of these 'high security' prisoners.

We were all treated to Governor Brodie Clark, in public statements to the media, talking down the gross incompetence of prison management and talking up 'the brave, alert professionalism of prison staff'. When HMS Whitemoor was steered on to the rocks, we heard no talk about its captain or senior officers going down with the ship and, it transpired, it was the cargo that was entirely responsible for the disaster! The escapees were all moved out to other prisons while we remaining prisoners – not in the least way involved in the escape – were left to feel the wrath and vengeance of a home secretary who was sorely aggrieved at being made to look a fool.

A none-too-bright prisoner told me that a tabloid journalist had been sniffing around trying to tie in my name with the escape. Although A wing was the nearest wing to the SSU, neither I, nor anyone else, had any connection with it or with the prisoners inside it. Well, in order to keep this journalist's snout happy, I told him to say that I was in on the escape from the very beginning and actually planned it. I said, 'I actually got as far as sitting on the outside wall, but then I remembered that I'd forgotten my handbag and, when I returned to my cell to fetch it, the fun was all over and I missed my chance again.' He replied that he didn't believe a word of it and that I was 'a bullshitter'. Search as we all did, there was nothing in subsequent tabloids.

On 16 December 1994, I was given a letter by Brodie Clark from the Home Office stating, for the first time, that the powers that be – at the top – had decided that I would never be released. Apparently, in 1989, someone in government had prevailed upon my trial judge to 'reconsider' the twenty-five-year minimum sentence he'd given me. The then lord chief justice had decreed that the recommendation was too short but gave no explanation and the meek and obliging Mr Justice Croom-Johnson got the message emanating from his superiors on high and admitted that he'd been wrong in making such a short minimum period. Here, we had a judge who had sat through a trial, was acquainted – at first hand – with all the evidence and was now saying that he was 'mistaken'. If he'd admitted his judgement was wrong in November 1983, then how much more could he have been wrong in 1989 as he teetered on the brink of advancing dotage. What, in effect, had happened between 1983 and 1989 to make him change his mind? One might speculate on a point of shifting political ambitions because the final arbiter was the home secretary (who was strictly a political animal).

It was significant that in Michael Howard's list of natural lifers, there were no terrorist murderers (speaking volumes for the extent of political interference). Psychological inadequacy (as in my case) was not acceptable to the State while cold, cognitive malice and hateful deliberation (as in terrorism) was.

The lifers' group had been set up the previous September and it took a few months to settle down into a forum for constructive debate on lifers' issues. Many positive suggestions flowed from the lifers themselves but although management usually agreed in principle they were rarely prepared to act on them and it became a growing forum for accumulative frustrations. In the coming months, frustration caused our first two group chairmen to resign their elected positions: Danny Jones for A wing and Russell Bishop for B wing. I was then elected the new joint chairman of the VPU lifers' group for A wing with John Duffy being the chairman for B wing. Our members consisted of cons from many different races, nationalities, sexual orientations and religions (the term 'sexual orientations' was limited to legal orientations and we would not be supporting or condoning paedophilia or rape, etc.). We then settled in for a series of meetings as regularly as management would allow.

As the sun set on 1994, I took an LSD tab and fell into an eight-hour kaleidoscope of the imagination, projected in the brightest colours and the highest sensations, as my brain shorted out into multi-track hyperdrive. I fast forwarded through a third of a day in what seemed like ten minutes where memories of a lifetime rattled past in a re-edited jumble of fevered tranquillity; so fast and yet in ultra-slow motion. I had never seen brighter colours in this peak of experience and I was there, born and died many times. It was all hallucination but potently real in its time, place and thought. In the replayed mirage of my life, I was abducted and murdered as a small boy by Ian Brady, gassed and tampered with by John Christie, I was captured, tortured and raped by John Wayne Gacy, made a sex slave of Jeffrey Dahmer and caught by Jack the Ripper. I was sedated and sexually molested by my grandfather.

I am man and boy, girl and woman, all together; one forever-changing adaptable being. I am a dog, a cat, a bird and an angel. Demons don't intrude, nor do any feelings of disgust, as I hover on a wondrous high; a wide-eyed observer; putty in a universal hand. I am crucified on the cross of my existence and I don't feel a thing. I am unnailed and lowered into the arms of a great, fat woman.

The sunset is brilliant in blood red, orange, yellow and bright purple. The sand is warm and golden and the air sings with a soporific hum. Choirs are singing from the mirror in my cell and the pictures on my wall become animated as their characters come to life. I drift through the gap under the door and dolly around the empty landings like seeking smoke. Searchlights stream their beams from the high skylights. The screw in the office continues to read his newspaper, oblivious to my presence; unaware of my invisible spirit.

I am four or five years old and sat on my grandfather's knee and he is feeding me copious spoons of 'cough mixture'. My head nods and I begin to drift into tired sleep as he carries me off for a bit of 'harmless' tampering. I am standing, looking down at the naked, unconscious youth being carried in my arms. Limp arms and legs hanging down. It is poetry in motion.

The man in the mirror loves me – no one else – and I cradle my own boyhood in my own, adult arms. I carry my life, its joys and all my contorted garbage around with me, moving forward but staying in place, locked into the solid fix of some immovable rock strata in the mountain of hopelessness. I hover like an unseen camera over my naked body on the bed for anything from one minute to one hour and am unable to perceive one blink throughout.

In the corner of my cell, David Martin is looping a bootlace through the holes in the ceiling ventilation grille. He has torn a vest into strips which he is knotting together. I am paralysed; unable to move or speak. I shut my eyes, refusing to watch his death, and blank it out. When I open them, I can see my grandfather taking him down. Dave's body is clad in a light blue, prison T-shirt and white briefs. The old man handles the limp body with practised confidence as he supports its weight and cuts the ligature with a penknife, magically appearing in his hand. Dave's naked thighs hang straight. The lump of his semi erection points the front of his briefs.

His death throes have issued a dual climax to his life in a weird juxtaposition of having to 'go' in order to cum. The T-shirt rides up, as he is taken down, exposing his midriff and belly button. As the ligature is loosened, a great gust of air escapes from his lungs, which the extreme stricture has, hitherto, trapped. Rushing up from relaxed vocal cords, he gives a last sigh of confirming, resigned contentment, as if that essence of him – that spirit – has finally been released from its mortal captivity.

So passively vacant and 'surprised' lays David Martin, snug in the arms of a familiar stranger holding him, finally, secure and 'safe'. Grandfather buzzes with that great, peak power of total possession. The power and the passive are united as one; complementary and in total perfection. I feel the absolute trust by the unresisting flesh in his arms. Omnipotence demands absolute, unconditional surrender.

• • •

I'd been having difficulty with the quality of the sound recordings I was making and, in January 1995, I only managed to compose one suite. Later, when I attempted to hand it out to Mark Austin on a visit, I discovered that Nick Leader had ordered that I should no longer be allowed to send any of my musical recordings out of prison. Back on the wing, Leader refused to see me on the matter, in spite of promising to do so in front of both myself and Mark in the visitors' hall, and a duty senior officer told me that it was simply on instructions from head office. So, in frustrated response, I decided to publicise my grievance.

The gloves were well and truly off and, with Mark's help, I phoned Jeff Edwards at the *Daily Mirror*, where he functioned as their chief crime correspondent, and I gave him a story. This was the first time in my life that I had direct contact with a reporter – with the sole purpose of providing a story about me – and I told him that I would require no fee.

In April, a series of three, front-page articles appeared in the *Daily Mirror,* which outraged prison management. They were particularly miffed by my revelations of the sex video tests, which I'd recently been subjected to. I was isolated in a small room near the wing entrance with a large TV screen in front of me. A wired clip was placed around my penis and another clip attached to my left finger to monitor and record my level of sexual arousal and, for about ninety minutes, I was then shown a sequence of colour stills of naked boys and girls. Later in the test, I was shown a live action video of a man and woman having sex before gravitating to acts of male violence against the woman, which, finally, culminated in rape and murder. The amateur actors were just not believable for any real-life scenario and were often pathetic and even laughable. Later on, the psychologist revealed, to my utter astonishment, that I was mostly aroused at pictures of mature, naked females (such a blow to the self-esteem of a life-long queer).

As the spring turned towards the summer, we, in the drama group, were revving up for a performance of an Ayckbourn play, *Ten Times Table* with me playing the role of Marxist schoolteacher, Eric Collins. We put on three performances at the end of May; two of them to members of the public. During the second performance, a heavy door fell on my head and, at the last one, I sprained and bruised my right shoulder in the realistic fight sequence. Yes, there's no business like show business. Mark attended the final show in the prison chapel and, afterwards, we decamped in a side office for tea and biscuits where I introduced him to the rest of the cast. It was the last complete production we would do. The audiences were pleased but my expected call from Paramount Pictures never came.

The following Friday, I was sacked from the education department and ordered to report to the Tailors Two workshop from Monday. They knew I would work anywhere but the tailors! One of my earliest memories was of me sitting on the floor in my grandfather's bedroom at 47 Academy Road, Fraserburgh. I remember I had this wooden handled awl in my hand. It was a small, sharp screwdriver-type tool but with a sharp point at the end. As I played with it, I accidentally stabbed it into the back of my left hand and there was blood everywhere (the scar is still there today). I was scared and remembered the noise of granny's Singer, pedal-action, sewing machine in the living room, whirring noisily on and on as she was oblivious to my insecure plight. Eventually, granny came to minister to my wound but this was my first experience of blood and I learned to associate the sewing machine with all the loud shouting and quarrelling that remained in my young memory as disjointed symbols. I still can't stand the noise of sewing machines, in fact, I feel sick at the very thought and sound of them.

And so, to force me to work in the tailor's shop, there began a series of 'nickings' which were to continue throughout the summer, involving at least eight appearances on adjudication. I was on permanent fines, debarred from using the canteen and on one occasion, I was given seven days' solitary confinement in the Block. It was the old game of trying to bend me to the official will, just for the sake of it. Eventually, by the autumn of 1995, wing management finally grew bored with nicking me and offered me work in the contract services workshop, which they should have done in the first place!

By now, I was into my fiftieth year and had found that the attitude of my jailers hadn't changed much in all my time in prison thus far. The screws were queuing up to nick a notorious name for the prestige of having it on their nicking sheets. 'Nicking you could be the high point of my career,' announced one pathetic screw. Little things pleased little minds and it was open season against homosexual multiple murderers.

In my cell I continued with my music and produced some of my most satisfying compositions. I was maturing with age and practice but, after fourteen years in prison, I still had no access to visual arts or quality entertainment (TV, films, documentaries, etc.), though thankfully, I still kept contact with the outside world through BBC Radio 4. But then, in 1996, one of the first new policies to come on stream was the concept of 'volumetric control', which severely limited the amount of personal property a prisoner could hold in his cell. We were allowed two cardboard boxes within which all our kit – including clothing – had to fit. Anything in excess would be removed to long-term storage or had to be handed out of prison. The only exception was that we could also retain one additional outsized item and I was ordered to choose between my keyboard and my typewriter. I chose my typewriter and the resulting creative void, in not being allowed to play or compose any further music, left me to be reliant on Prozac for a spell.

Back in January 1994, crime fiction writer, Ruth Rendell, had written to me to request a contribution to an anthology of the murderous mind which she was compiling. I obliged her with a twenty-page essay I'd written a year earlier, articulating some of the factors that led me to end up killing. It was titled *The Psychograph* and had been entered into an essay-writing competition run by the Prison Reform Trust. I believed that exploring the 'mechanism' of homicide would be a major contribution to understanding serial homicide. The Prison Reform Trust, rating it of little merit, sent it back but Ruth published it (in shortened form) as the last item in her anthology that year (1996) under the title, *The Reason Why*. She also included an extract from *Killing for Company*, which was entirely my own writing, though she credited it to Brian Masters.

Author, Kate Kray, wrote to me in June to assist in her next book, which was to contain a chapter about me. She was the ex-wife of the late Ronnie Kray who had died in Broadmoor Hospital a year earlier. Along with her introductory letter, she had also included a copy of her first book entitled *Lifers*. In reading some of these stories, I was surprised by a complete disregard for the victims, in a barrage of self-justifications, with no direct address of personal culpability. There was even a note of heroic triumphalism in Harry Roberts' testimony where he hinted at a certain pride at his status in the criminal hierarchy 'for killing three coppers'. The text trumpeted the song often sang at football matches

'Harry Roberts is our friend, is our friend, is our friend,
Harry Roberts is our friend. He kills coppers!'

Had old Harry Roberts learned nothing from his long years inside? Did he not even feel tepid regret or compassion for the orphans and wives left to struggle on through life without husbands and fathers in the prime of all of their lives, murdered by Roberts and his confederates? We had the spectacle of the Krays proudly proclaiming, many years after their murders, that they had no regrets for ridding the world of 'scum' like Cornell and McVitie. There was nothing heroic in my deeds and there was nothing heroic in shooting an unarmed man in the head or having your mates holding a man down while you went to work on him with a knife. Those were all our acts and they flowed, not from strength, confidence and potency but from crass inadequacy and weakness. They were acts to be ashamed of, not to be proud of.

I was alarmed some years ago when news reached me that at a fringe meeting of the now defunct Confederation of Conservatives, some of them were drunkenly toasting me for 'clearing the streets of so many unemployed parasites'. Even at first hand, I was once greeted by a newly-arrived prisoner on the wing who wanted to shake my hand 'for killing all these fuckin' queers'. I sent him on his way with an unexpected flea in his ear.

If Kate Kray was looking for another 'working class' criminal 'hero', then she'd have to look elsewhere. Some coppers and some criminals may well have been 'bastards' but that was no reason to murder them. If you did, you merely become a 'bastard' like them – only more so.

Later that same year, a third author made contact. I received a letter from Perth in Western Australia from former ITN newsreader, Gordon Honeycombe, professing that he wanted to tell my story. I wrote back to say that I had already written two parts of an autobiography and I suggested to him that I complete it before he came over from Australia to visit me, when we could then discuss the matter further. That settled, I set about writing a further two parts: *Long Way Down and Rising* (Part 3), which covered my life from 1988 to the end of 1992 and *Whitemoor: A Volume of Extremes* (Part 4), which brought my life up to the end of 1995. I named all four parts *History of a Drowning Boy*, which was the account of my life up to around that point. When he arrived in the UK, Gordon met with Mark Austin, who kept safe all of my writings, letters and other belongings and Mark loaned him a mass of these documents by way of preparatory work.

In order for me to be confident in handing out all four parts of my autobiography, Mark arranged for a solicitor, Arthur Stanton*, to visit me. Letters were exchanged between me and Stanton and, during our later visit, he told me there was no legal impediment to me in handing out the manuscript and he took the completed draft.

Things changed rapidly. Despite his earlier assurances, Stanton refused to yield the manuscript to Gordon or Mark and he even contacted the prison governor to inform him what he had in his possession. He also assured the Home Office that he wouldn't let it out of his safe until the 'legal position' could be clarified. I wrote a formal Request & Complaint form asking what interest the Home Office had in the manuscript and, some weeks later, received an official reply stating that they had no interest in it. They iterated that his holding of it for me constituted no violation of Standing Order 5 (Stanton's specified reason). Satisfied, I sent off a copy of this reply to Stanton demanding that he release the manuscript.

He changed tactics. This time, he stated that he wouldn't release it until his substantial legal bill was paid (a sum quite beyond my purse and meagre prison wage). Gordon Honeycombe refused to foot the bill on the grounds that there was no guarantee that Stanton would relinquish it, even if he was paid, so Stanton held on to my four parts of *History of a Drowning Boy* for another eighteen months. Eventually, Mark stepped in and paid his bill and, following a complaint to the Law Society, Mark won his case and was refunded a significant amount. Stanton returned the full copy of the manuscript to Mark and sent the original back to me at Whitemoor, which I openly handed back out to Mark when he next visited me. There was never any question of me 'smuggling it out' (as had been suggested in the media).

Gordon, by refusing to play any more, had voted himself out of

* *Not his real name.*

the running but not before he was given the only spare copy of Part 1 of the autobiography. He said that he would produce from it (and other sources) one of the best books ever written about a serial killer but I could see that the project, if unchecked, would leap into the Brian Masters mould of un-autobiography and I, therefore, rejected both the contract and the notion of yet another biography.

The draft manuscript was out of the prison but the problem of finding an editor remained unresolved, so I offered the task of editing the manuscript to cult author of gay fiction, Paul Hartnett, with whom I had been corresponding. He accepted and Mark passed on the full original draft (Parts 1-4) to him for the task. All that was now needed was a quiet period of reflection while Paul went about the task of editing. What could be simpler?

• • •

As my birthday approached, in November 1997, Paul had sent me a book: the works of gay artists Pierre and Gilles containing a collection of their work from 1976–96. The book also appeared in the prison library list under the heading 'Art History' (not in the 'Sex' or 'Erotica' section) and there was no age restriction for its sale. Imagine, then, my surprise, which turned to anger, when I was informed by prison reception that I couldn't have it because it was considered 'offensive' and 'indecent'. Over the next two years, I submitted – and had rejected – several Request & Complaint forms, I attended many meetings with wing governors, I contacted the Whitemoor Citizens Advice Bureau, I wrote to the Cambridgeshire Constabulary, I sent a complaint to area prison office (higher than the local prison office), I engaged the services of solicitors, AS Law of Liverpool (who took up my complaint with Holly McLaren, head of residential at Whitemoor) and still they kept this perfectly legal book from me.

Soon after, in a 'routine' search of my cell, the Dedicated Search

Team (DST) removed all six of my gay magazines that depicted nothing but pictures of individual, naked men and I was handed a receipt noting the 'indecent' nature of the contents. Then, following another visit from the DST, during which they removed quantities of documents and letters, I was presented with an official letter on 6 July 1998:

'In light of information that you are seeking to have your autobiography published, HM Prison Whitemoor has sought guidance from headquarters. We are advised that any activity which relates to the publication of a book for profit (whether the prisoner himself is profiting or not) should be interpreted as a business activity. As such, it is banned under Standing Order 5 para 34 (10) and same for the specific exceptions noted there. We are therefore instructed to prevent any correspondence going to or from you which may assist in the publication. You will be informed if any of your correspondence is stopped and your mail will not be delayed by this process.'

But just a few weeks later, the full controversy of my autobiography hit the public right in the eye when I was shown a story in the *Sunday Mirror* with the headline screaming out at me like a bolt from the blue, 'Ex-teacher Who Wants £30,000 for Killer's Sick Memoirs'. Paul Hartnett, it seemed, had tried to sell details of my book to the Sunday tabloids. He had no permission from me to sell or market any part of the book – or any serial rights or any other venture, save but to edit it. If he could solicit interest in the project with any publisher, then well and good but that was the limit of his official involvement. It would be a gross understatement to say that I was disappointed in his part in the article, which was wrong in principle and premature; the time to blow any publicity trumpet would have been when the project was complete. Perhaps, in this case, the article mingled truth and fiction because Paul said that he had been entrapped into giving the interview. The piece berated Paul, me and the project throughout and even solicited a comment from Carl Stottor, one of my surviving victims, as if to justify their tirade. I was willing to give Paul the benefit of any doubts I had concerning his slip of integrity and I convinced myself that he'd only exercised a lack of good judgement, free of active malice. As a friend, he needed to be supported, rather than condemned out of hand.

Several months later, the entire DST gang descended on the wing after 10 p.m. one night, with lights going on, heavy combat boots on the metal stairs, loud voices and barking dogs. They were on a provisional trawl to discover caches of pre-Christmas hooch that might be concealed in prisoners' cells. Some prisoners were aroused from a drowsy, medicated sleep and made to stand in their underpants on the landing while the DST made a cursory ten second inspection of their cells. My door was opened at 11 p.m. and Officer Trowell* stood framed in the steel aperture. 'Nilsen, step outside,' was all he said. I got up from my bed and slowly moved towards the door but he blocked it and refused to let me pass. I asked him to step aside but he stood his ground. As I attempted to squeeze past him he shouted, 'Staff!' and pulled me to the ground whereupon his colleagues joined in, supervised by one of the gang's managers.

I was pinned to the floor and handcuffed and, in this doubled-up position, carted off, still in my underwear, to the Punishment Block. Much painful pressure was applied to the joints of my limbs during this transportation but I no longer cried out in pain because, through the years, I'd become used to it. I was kept, for a couple of days, in a cell furnished only with a cardboard table and chair and some bedding, before being curtly presented with a charge sheet issued by Trowell, alleging an assault by me upon him. The entire DST team on duty that night, including their managers, collaborated

* *Not his real name.*

in this charge and, pending adjudication in the Punishment Block, one of the Block screws came to my door and 'assured' me that if I pleaded guilty, I'd get just the loss of a week's pay and the whole matter would soon blow over and be forgotten. I told him that my position was to tell the truth and that would be a 'not guilty' plea. But following a lengthy process of investigation, in which I was totally honest, the governor dismissed the case.

Concurrent with all this local harassment, the *Daily Mirror* ran a piece to the effect that I'd been found by screws, drunk and legless in my cell, adding that I'd been frogmarched to the Block. It was a typical, popular newspaper fabrication and, for the first time in my life, I lodged an official complaint with the Press Complaints Commission. I had not done so hitherto, after a long catalogue of such stories, simply because I believed that the Commission was just a tool of the press industry.

Piers Morgan, as the paper's editor, replied to the complaint saying that his 'anonymous' sources were reliable, adding, 'I would ask the Commission to consider the veracity and legitimacy of a complaint about an allegation of drunkenness by a man convicted of brutally murdering several young men, having cut up their bodies and stuffed the dismembered remains into the drainage system. The *Mirror* stands by this article.'

I asked the prison service to answer (in writing) the following questions: Had I ever been found drunk in prison? Had I ever been suspected of being drunk in prison? Had I ever been associated with brewing hooch in prison? Had I ever been suspected of brewing or assisting in the brewing or of consuming hooch in prison? The official answer to all these questions was 'no' – making a nonsense of the *Daily Mirror*'s story – and I sent this to the Commission.

After all this, they chose to reject my complaint because of the conflicting scenario between my truthful facts and the *Daily Mirror*'s fabricated concoctions. The experience confirmed to me that the Commission was, indeed, a creature of the press and it exercised no independent integrity as an adjudicator. Thereafter, I made no further appeals to the Commission, no matter how bad their 'news' stories got. I couldn't help but smile when, six years later, Piers Morgan, as editor of the *Daily Mirror*, was dismissed by the company's board and immediately escorted from the premises by security staff.

On 13 July 1999, I received my annual report from the category A Review Team at the Directorate of High Security Prisons. This was the document by which I was 'judged fit or otherwise' to be downgraded to category B (which came with a less severe regime) or remain category A. Part of the report said:

> 'The review team recognised that you fully accept responsibility for your offences and have made some progress in addressing your offending behaviour. However, in the interest of public protection, the progress you have made to date had to be viewed against the gravity of the offences and that there remained areas of risk which needed further work. The Review Team were not satisfied that such evidence was currently available and concluded that you must at present continue to be regarded as highly dangerous, particularly to men, and should therefore remain in Category 'A'.'

The review team didn't so much review me, from year-to-year, as merely rubber stamp the received prejudice – which focused wholly on my distant past – with little understanding of my motivations (at the time) surrounding those acts. Therefore, I wasn't surprised that my 1999 'review' was a carbon copy of the previous year's. When I was a boy in the 1950s there was a machine on the promenade above Fraserburgh beach where you put one penny in its slot and it would automatically deliver a hard ball of bubblegum. As the years passed, this antiquated machine remained in place and the process remained immovably constant; penny in, bubblegum out. My category A review has a great deal in common with that old bubble gum machine: I put my representations in and the negative and purposeful conclusions came out.

They did, however, add something new to the 1999 report, as an additional feature, to prove my continuing failure to address my offending behaviour:

'Reports indicate that while you admit to your guilt and have undertaken offending behaviour work, you continue to attempt to get your autobiography published so you can tell the reasons why you committed the murders, and this throws in doubt your insight and shows little or no consideration for your victims' families.'

The writing of *History of a Drowning Boy* was not written to give reasons, excuses or justifications for my past offences, it is a narrative about my whole life. Much more lurid details of my offences could be found in other 'legitimate' publications already in the public domain. Was my own view and opinion of myself to be censored out of contemporary deliberations? The Home Office, for one, thought it should be. They would say that it was perfectly legitimate for writers, producers and newspapers to perform this function in keeping with the great British traditions of freedom of expression and public information (regardless of the trauma *that* may cause victims or their families) but, at the same time, ruling that the subject himself should stay mute and outside this process. It was my critics who made money from my crimes, not I; some had built a whole career on them.

When news of the Home Office ban on my autobiography reached Brian Masters, he rained forth his valediction on BBC Radio 4. In the interview, both Masters and the interviewer – with harmonious, mutual and rash self-satisfaction – egged one another on towards a common goal, with the interviewer providing an added sneer of concurrence. Masters suggested to the interviewer that my autobiography couldn't be written by me but had to be filtered through the interpretation of someone else, otherwise it would be skewed and unbalanced. He said it needed a third party to see what was significant and what should be discarded, explaining that, of the notes I wrote for him in 1983 for his book, he had discarded about 90 per cent as much of it was nothing to do with my crimes. I presumed that he'd either binned his unused material or locked it away so that someone else wouldn't – or couldn't – test the veracity of his work and its interpretations. What *he* believed was significant may not have been the same as what *others* might have believed.

The press was full of wild stories claiming that large sums had been demanded and offered by publishers for *History of a Drowning Boy*. One speculation screamed '£100,000' in its headlines. Others, suggesting I had smuggled the manuscript out of prison, appeared with regular frequency but none dared to mar the flow of these fictional confections by ever contacting me for a statement. The truth was more prosaic: no one was interested in publishing this 'hot potato' and no money had been mentioned, nor asked for, and I had always made it clear that I required no author's fee.

. . .

By July 2000, I was called to assist the complainant in a libel trial. *Lord Longford's Prison Diaries* had just been published and one of the prisoners mentioned therein had taken exception to what the earl had written about him. I was no censor of views, no matter how wrong-headed or objectionable they might have appeared to me and, despite my letters to that effect, *Lord Longford's Prison Diaries* was withdrawn from sale, which was a shame.

Frank was helpful in writing to ministers at the Home Office and bringing important and pertinent questions before the House of Lords. He was a solitary voice in the upper house, supporting my right to freedom of expression when other literary peers like Archer, Rendell and (P D) James kept a low profile. I was grateful to him for his stand on this but because of Frank's unremitting stance against homosexuality, a corrosive element entered our relationship and it gradually petered out in the total absence of common ground. I decided to write to him requesting that he no longer visited me. I also felt guilty about the obvious stress to his health at having to travel all the way to Whitemoor by public transport and the indignities of the rough search procedures meted out by a maximum-security prison. I opened with:

'Dear Frank,

In your faith, Easter Monday symbolises "new life" and a raising from the dead…'

I then explained – at length – how my homosexuality, and his intolerance of it, had forced me to think hard about our friendship. Finally, my letter concluded:

'I do not hate you, Frank. I do not even dislike you. You are an old man who, if you lived in China, would be subject to traditional reverence because of your great age. Great wisdom is supposed to come with age. I guess it must be left to the voices of posterity to judge what measure of wisdom now resides in you in your ninety-fifth year of life and political activity.

Perhaps you and Pope John Paul will share the same bus on the road to moral oblivion… who knows? Neither of you is any holier than the meanest pansy trying to scrape a living prostituting himself on the streets of Bangkok (if God has no sense of humour he has nothing). More in sadness than in anger, I would not wish for you to continue visiting me here in prison. We have, between us, some irreconcilable differences of action in our approach to our fellow men.

I grow and learn from the traumas of my past. You, parrot-fixed dogmas. I do not view my Humanism as a dogma but as a working hypothesis. I learn and I grow (and I change). You do what you must, and may your God forgive you. As for me... I will do the creative, 'living thing' until I fall off my twig.

Yours,

Des Nilsen.'

It was hard to assess how he received this letter other than to conclude that he didn't reply and that I never saw him again. I was saddened to learn of his death sixteen months later. There was no malice in him; he was an espouser of 'unfashionable' people and causes, for which he was branded 'a potty peer' by the tabloids. Near the end of each visit, Frank would say that he'd pray for me in the fond hope that, one day, I might see the light of Church teachings. He seemed to refuse to accept that there could be any light other than his own and so, in this regard, I was one of his failures. In my beliefs, I had always entertained the possibility that I might be wrong but Frank accepted no such doctrinal uncertainties; he believed as a matter of blind faith. As he disappeared into the ether of non-existence, he clung doggedly to the belief that his dogmatic sun revolved around the earth and such things are apt to unhinge a man's powers of independent rational judgement.

Out of the blue, one morning, I received the following official note:

'To J. Bamber, J. Duffy, D. Nilsen.

A member of staff from Lifer Unit (HQ) is bringing a senior member of the Japanese prison service to visit Whitemoor. The Japanese Ministry of Defence is reviewing their sentencing policy. Mr Ryuji Tatsuya has expressed his wish to meet 2 or 3 lifers who are serving a Whole of Life sentence. I would therefore like to invite all three of you to an informal meeting on the 25th October at approximately 2pm. I am informed there will be no language difficulty.

F. Apps, Lifer Manager'

Come the event, John Duffy and I met Mr Ryuji Tatsuya, the governor of Japan's Yokohama Prison, and he asked a number of searching questions pertinent to British 'whole life tariff' prisoners such as ourselves (Jeremy Bamber had to cancel due to having a social visit at the allotted time). He told us about how he ran his prison, intimating that, in Japan, people expected prisons to be places of punishment rather than venues for rehabilitation. I was a bit shocked when he said there was no association amongst prisoners as that was viewed to be a recipe for trouble in prison. Japanese prisoners spent eight hours each day working and, even at work, they weren't allowed to talk to one another.

The emphasis was on a controlled, restricted, regimented regime of work where prisoners were paid £12 a month, with access to the prison canteen (to make private purchases) only once a month. There were 1200 men in Mr Tatsuya's prison, each of whom was allowed one letter and one visit a month. It was made clear to both John Duffy and I that our crimes, if committed in Japan, would most assuredly have resulted in the death penalty for us and it was suggested by others (not Mr Tatsuya) that sudden death, in our case, might have been a merciful kindness when compared with an endless life of living death inside the cold mechanics of a Japanese prison. I didn't agree, arguing that imprisonment was, fundamentally, a state of mind and it was how the mind handled a long, indeterminate prison sentence that ultimately dictated the quality of one's life. I added that whenever I felt 'put upon' I could reflect on the fact that my victims had no choice at all in having any kind of life.

Mr Tatsuya was pleasant enough on the surface and quietly spoken and he seemed surprised when I shook his hand when we were introduced. I couldn't imagine a Japanese prisoner daring to shake his prison governor's hand. Mr Tatsuya was a young man with lushly-black, shining hair, olive skin, small and slim of stature and wearing spectacles; quite gorgeous really (the Japanese…don'tcha love 'em?).

In my dreams, I still saw images from the past. They didn't daunt or oppress me but, by their periodic frequency, their potency still haunted me. They seemed real and unreal at the same time. Sometimes I thought that, somehow, I must have imagined them.

The soundtrack whispers over and over again, David, David, David… He is standing in a bright, white light near the barred gate at the end of the landing. The great light comes from around and within him. I move, treacle-slow, towards him with a massive effort but hidden hands strive to hold me back. Nevertheless, I make slow, forward progress. Now I stand before him and reach out. We are both naked and as youthful as we were then, in 1983. There is a bolt of joy within me when he, too, reaches out. Then there is that electric charge of union as our hands clasp. We pull one another in and embrace. I feel the soft warmth of his body against mine and we consummate eternity as our mouths become one in the endless kiss. Next, I am carrying him in my arms up some wide, endless staircase…up, up towards clearer crystal air…

…and there the dream ends. In another dream, Jimmy Butler and I stood, naked, embracing in a cell at Wakefield Prison in 1985, my erection pressed up against him; his against me. We were, for that long languid moment, one entity.

The last time I hugged anyone was when I hugged Jimmy Butler at Wakefield Prison in 1985, fifteen years previously. That was how far I had moved from the warmth of people. During my years of imprisonment, close on 1000 prisoners (both men and women) had died violent deaths in prison. Where was the official concern for *those* victims and their relatives? Politicians batted an eyelid, but they were crocodile tears and, afterwards, they implemented harsher, longer, more controlling penalties.

• • •

Quite unexpectedly, I received an anonymous letter from a person purporting to be a friend of my mother, adding that my mother was unable to write herself because she'd recently had an eye operation. The letter also stated that some good friends of my mother had put up the money for her to visit me in prison and that she (the letter writer) would like to accompany my mother on that visit, which confirmed to me that she was probably a journalist. I wrote to my mother (via the letter writer) suggesting that a respectable interlude of correspondence might apply between us before she was cleared to visit me. In a further two letters, I asked my mother to address the doubt and the mystery of my true paternity, upon which she became both defensive and combative. Despite my request, the letter writer didn't send me my mother's address, therefore, I was never able to apply to the Home Office for visiting status for her (the police have to visit the applicant and submit a report). None of this seemed to sink in with either of them and, therein, the visiting enterprise collapsed into acrimony from her side, written in a letter I received on 25 October 2001 on pages torn from a cheap notebook. I guessed it stood as her farewell epistle as she, at last, had returned to her full raging self as I knew her when I was a boy.

Her letter began, 'Des, you are good at giving information to other people but now listen to me. You make me out as a bad mother but I could tell you a lot about your father Olav Magnus Nilsen who is your father in spite of what you say. I know because I was never with anyone else at that time.' She said that Olav Magnus Nilsen was paying her 10 shillings a week for me and Olav junior and reasoned, 'Do you think he would have paid that for you if you were not his?' She told me that after she'd married Adam Scott and had her other four children, Olav senior had sent letters to her mother asking to meet her with the hope of getting back together, adding, 'but I never took any notice of this'. Eventually, her tirade ended, 'From now on, Des, you won't be hearing from me or [the letter writer]. You will not hurt me any more than you have done already. Betty. PS I don't seem to be good enough to be called "mum".'

My whole life had been clouded in maternal deception and everything that I now knew about my immediate family circumstances came mainly from external sources many years later. I didn't set myself up as a judge over my mother's past life, I just wanted to be told the truth, whatever that was. Whoever my father was, he was worthy of the validity of an identity and, whatever his past, worthy of the respect of his recognising son. Who was Sylvia's father? She didn't say. Neither would she reply to, nor acknowledge, my assertion that my grandfather, Andrew Whyte, wasn't the saint he was made out to be.

On the morning of Tuesday, 27 November 2001, after I'd collected my breakfast, I was suddenly taken off and asked to pack up my property. In the space of a few minutes, I'd managed to stuff a few things into a plastic bag and, by 9 a.m., I was shackled into a category A security van on the road to Full Sutton Prison. It was my first glimpse of the rolling fields of England in years and the journey took a couple of hours or so.

12

HMP Full Sutton | 2001

Upon my arrival, I was transferred to the Punishment Block where I'd spent the most part of a year between 1990 and 1991. It was now called G wing Induction but was, basically, still a Segregation Unit with twenty-three-hour bang-up and, more or less, a Punishment Block regime (I was told that I was being kept there until an empty cell was available over in one of the Vulnerable Prisoner Unit wings). So there I was, banged up in a Segregation Unit with no privileges, no job, no earning capacity, with my only approved category A visitor, Mark Austin, 170 miles away in Bedfordshire.

The prison was managed by the number 1 governor, D Roberts and his team – information I'd obtained from all the notices that had been stapled to the picture board in my cell, overlain with the commandment in vivid red marker pen: DO NOT REMOVE. All my cell furnishings were fixed, according to the model plan of the official standard layout, and the bedstead was firmly bolted to the floor as befitting any punishment Segregation Unit.

My small, modern cell was almost half the size of Victorian cells, meaning I could only stretch my legs three paces forward and three paces back. There was a metal sink, a toilet, a small locker, a cupboard (with one of its drawers missing) and a table with a metal surface supporting a small Matsui TV, intended to keep us amused for the duration of our solitary confinement. In this sparse venue, I spent twenty-three hours a day finding the confinement both crowded and empty.

Respite came from an hour's exercise in a tall, concrete box open to the sky and covered in a thick, wire mesh, frilled with razor wire. This dank, damp enclosure allowed no orientation with things and vistas beyond it and with no overcoats available, we (four prisoners at a time) shuffled around in a tight, anticlockwise circle, regaining the art of human conversation for a spell – while freezing our bollocks off. A camera surveyed us from its high vantage point near the corner of the concrete wall and a screw watched us from a warm cubicle attached to the Unit.

In the first couple of days there, I was ordered to give a urine sample for mandatory drugs testing and had a brief routine visit to the medical centre where the doctor complained that he was overworked, unable to cope and needed another two doctors to share the load. Our exchanges amounted to little more than a quick check on the details on his form: name, age, etc. He knew nothing about me and hadn't seen my file but, because I was alive and breathing, he marked me down as A1 fit.

We joined the flow of the other prisoners going to the workshops and, in a bedraggled stream, we descended into the sunless tunnelling and the subterranean depths of some architectural underworld, where we were to receive an education department 'induction' session.

This was a depressing place with pale-faced, hollow-eyed prisoners standing about in groups waiting for their classrooms or workshops to commence. They seemed to be slightly disorientated and there was an air of indecisiveness about the whole place; a wan, desperate, rootless drift. I could see many faces that I recognised from my prison past and the men I'd remembered behind the faces seemed to have shrunk in human stature, dwarfed by the sheer size and immovability of the mechanism in which they had become trapped; their spirits sapped of vitality. We sat in an empty classroom for some minutes before being told that it was cancelled, at which point we were moved back to the Induction Segregation Unit.

Midway through December I was, at last, moved to B wing on the VPU where I was ushered to a cell on the ground floor. The smell in there was so overpowering that I spent the first ten minutes vomiting into the sink. The odour was a mixture of sweat, urine, shit and general body odours but, like most things, I resolved that I'd just have to get used to it. In a few days, I wouldn't even notice it, as it became part of the atmospheric landscape. There was no plug in my sink and the small plastic mirror was glued to the wall above with toothpaste! The toilet bowl was encrusted with ten years of hard-caked, black gunge, reminding me of the infamous toilet bowl scene in the movie *Trainspotting*. There was no electric kettle there, like we'd had at Whitemoor, and if I wanted a hot drink I'd have to go to one of the boilers set slightly apart in the corridors in wall recesses. During long periods of bang-up those were the only means by which I could fill my thermos flask.

The view from my window was almost entirely obliterated because the plastic Perspex with which it was 'glazed' had, over the years, perished to the extent that it was practically 'frosted'. I kept the window wide open, in any case, because it helped dissipate the smell. There was nothing much in the tiny cell which contained the same sort of furnishings and layout as in the Induction Segregation Unit but I'd be able to explore my wing surroundings in greater detail when I would be unlocked at teatime.

I still hadn't had my property forwarded from Whitemoor; my legal and private papers, letters and addresses, music system, photos, magazines, clothing, files and personal mementos. I missed listening to my cassettes, CDs and BBC Radio 3 and Classic FM and the original manuscript of my autobiography was still wrapped up in a clear plastic bag in a box under my bed in my cell in Whitemoor.

The prison landings were about six feet wide comprising narrow corridors with a conglomeration of cells close together, face-to-face and side-by-side. They were, largely, screw-free and what dominated was the inner-city rule of the 'gangster'; it was a free-for-all for bullying and intimidation. The exercise yard was enclosed within the square of the wings that made up the building. Exploring the labyrinth, on my first evening, I could see a pattern developing. Most of the prisoners that I knew and encountered on the landings were men who had long since been rejected by the prison system; the mentally ill, those who had learning difficulties or a lack of social skills, those lacking communication skills, notorious child killers and those considered to be not amenable to treatment courses. In short, those who the system had 'given up on' and had to be hidden away and forgotten. B wing was little more than a dumping ground for unmentionable personas. I hadn't been able to check out the shower room on my landing because it had been locked with an 'out of order' notice on the door. Christmas Eve had just dawned and, to compound my developing sense of despondency, I noticed blood in my faeces and my scalp had broken out in small sores. What did it all mean?

A week later, my property finally arrived from Whitemoor and I was escorted to reception to pick it up. I then had to sift through a mountain of personal papers and letters, etc., to decide what to keep 'in possession' and what to store for handing out to Mark when he next visited me. The reception screws took my tracksuit bottoms off me stating that garments containing a substantial amount of black material were regarded as a security risk and were, therefore, not allowed. None of my previously confiscated gay literature was returned to me and the few pictures of naked men I was allowed at Whitemoor had now completely disappeared. Neither would they let me have my Panasonic radio/CD/tape system before it could be security checked and resealed. Clearly, they didn't trust the Whitemoor security seals.

Over the early months of 2002, I settled into my new surroundings but, in the March, I was saddened to read about a prison officer I'd known from Whitemoor. The report in the *Sun* was headlined, 'Jail Guard is Sacked for Boob Grabbing'.

The story claimed that Terry Ford* had, effectively, sexually assaulted a female security officer. 'There was a discussion about uniform shirts and he put his fingers on the outside of the female officer's shirt between her breasts.' Terry Ford had been at Whitemoor as long as I had. He was a tall, awkward, big-boned carthorse of a man with unruly black hair. He was a solitary loner in the crew peer group and didn't really fit in. I wasn't slow to sense his loneliness and I often felt sorry for him and wondered about the quality of his home life. He seemed to move between a conversational jokey 'high' to periods of depressed silence. I liked Terry because he seemed to have an endless store of jokes, which he'd impart to me, though I could always sense his sadness beneath the veneer of humour. I never saw him as capable of a malicious act of violence or aggression and, I suspected, the Whitemoor 'gang' had found a reason to dig him out and expel him from the fold into which he'd never really fitted. I found him to be one of the nicer officers at Whitemoor and, perhaps, I should have known that, in time, something had to give. One could hear Terry coming a mile off because he wore metal studs in his boots. Sitting there in the quiet of my cell, I could still hear his feet clacking along the landing and his 'oop north' accent and high-pitched infectious laughter. Leaving the prison service might well have been the best career move he ever made.

By the end of April, I was starting my first day at learning how to translate written books into braille for the RNIB. I was hoping this would be a worthwhile career, in terms of a good cause, and one that would give me access to a great number of books. Six months later, I had taken the RNIB examination for the proficiency certificate and failed! To pass, one was allowed to make a maximum of three mistakes and I'd made four. However, I took the examination a second time and, in January 2003, I was handed a letter from the RNIB training officer in Peterborough: 'Please would you convey my

---

* *Not his real name.*

congratulations to Mr Nilsen as he has passed his braille proficiency examination with a perfect paper. A certificate will be sent to Mr Nilsen shortly.' So, eight months of hard work had produced a positive result, although I also owed my success to instructors Mick and Kevin who hammered into me the need to check and double-check the accuracy of all my transcriptions. That exercised a bit of the pragmatist in me and I was, by then, a good way through transcribing my first paperback novel into braille for printing.

• • •

Earlier in the year, I had opened a letter that had been forwarded on from Whitemoor Prison where I was introduced to Mikkel Haugerud, a twenty-year-old Norwegian ballet dancer. This one-pager, on unlined paper, stirred my sense of curiosity, companion and psychological libido. Here was human interest unparalleled. For me, there was something sexually exciting about having communion and emotional empathy with a lithe, young, male ballet dancer, a species of human I had not previously encountered. I immediately wrote off in reply and received a letter within a few days. I could sense his isolation and loneliness in his text and, feeling akin to his situation, I decided to continue the correspondence. In all my replies to Mikkel, I strove to project a positive, optimistic demeanour, charged with interest for the subjects which seemed to interest him. The correspondence continued and, as he was young, I guessed that he had a beautiful body, though I was able to suppress any libidinous feelings towards him. Neither of our written exchanges radiated warmth as we tentatively explored one another around the fringes of our cores and I wondered how he expressed himself sexually (he revealed nothing in this area).

I pondered on what might have prevailed had I met him personally in the early 1980s. Had he been twenty then, and a visiting tourist, we might have met in a Central London bar. In the booze-filled haze of my longings, his balletic proportions would have fully engaged my attention to the point of invitation. I might have prevailed upon him to come back to my place for some music and for some refreshment that could have been 'flavoured' with a quantity of crushed sleeping pills. There, we would have chatted away into the long night on the sofa as my heartbeat would have increased in direct proportion to his drowsiness. It would have been, very much, a one-sided seduction; a marriage of some permanence; the antithesis of the wedding vow, 'till death us do part' – or more 'till death us do join'. What would the headlines have shouted afterwards? 'Norwegian National Ballet Dancer Missing in London'. He wouldn't have died because I hated him or was angry with him or anything in the scale of 'normal' motivation. Mikkel's body would have to be ritually cleansed of its past identity so as to make it pure to receive the imagined spirit. His athletically naked balletic body would have lain limp in my arms as I carried it to be cleansed in the bath. It would have been a thing of beauty, weight and movable substance. His entire body would now have become mine; all mine.

This was my potency in bygone days; long since vanished; faded by time and bored through repetition, to be replaced by the older, more mature drives of the paternal instinct where, perhaps, I felt for Mikkel Haugerud as a father would for a son. I was probably not much of a role model for the average young man. However, Mikkel was not your average young man.

In one of his letters, he commented on the television documentary, *The Trial of Jack the Ripper*, and I was slightly taken aback by his seeming inordinate interest in the crimes of serial killers and horror movies. I'd hoped to encourage him to concentrate on dance and music and not his morbid fascinations, which brought focus to depressing effects. In one letter, I had mentioned *Tubular Bells* and he'd responded with, 'Isn't that the music used for the film, *The Exorcist?*'

Then I received a startling, handwritten letter. He had, apparently, woken up with a dead woman beside him in bed. He had no memory from that night and had called the police and ambulance but was arrested and charged with her murder. I suspected there was something else going on; perhaps an ingrained and evolving core of personal emotional and social alienation had crept up on Mikkel and overwhelmed him and, perhaps, all his morally inhibiting factors of clear cognition.

In March 2003, five judges found him guilty of murder and he was sentenced to fifteen years. The *News of the World* reported it under the headline, 'Beast Pal "is killer"'. The story began, 'A male ballet dancer obsessed with serial killer Dennis Nilsen strangled a prostitute in his honour, a court heard. Mikkel Haugerud, 21, became a pen pal of Nilsen and described him as "my best friend in the world".'

Mikkel had been one of the few people who had connected, emotionally, with my musical compositions. Perhaps Paul Hartnett was another, to a finite degree. Mark Austin liked my lively bits but I guessed the rest didn't quite reach him. Mark was an Elvis enthusiast. I was left buzzing, however, from the compliments paid to my musical efforts from my friend Judith, in a letter I received in August 2002: '…the tape with your music on it… Thank you so very much. It's the greatest present… It's as if a piece of you managed to get outside of there…'

That same month, I received a letter from someone I usually defined as 'a true-crime enthusiast groupie'. He'd read a lot of serial killer books and said that he had a healthy interest in the subject; a kind of obsession with several jailed killers. He wasn't connected with any kind of formal study into offences but what set the inner alarm bells ringing, was his comment that, 'However much someone enjoys what he or she does in life, be it work, play or serial murder, there must come a time when the person thinks about calling it a day.'

In September, Brian Masters, who would deny me autobiographical rights, announced the publication of his own autobiography, entitled, *Getting Personal.* The month before, he had given an interview published in the *Observer* in which I was removed in one, short paragraph, 'He no longer sends Christmas cards to Dennis Nilsen (the one who boiled human heads on his stove and shoved limbs down the drains) because Nilsen got bored with him a few years ago and stopped writing. He wanted fans. He's now got lots of people who write to him because they think it's thrilling to be in touch with a murderer.'

• • •

Myra Hindley was pronounced dead in November 2002 and her corpse was put under police guard in Suffolk Hospital mortuary lest cyphers for the mob should defile it. They burned the witch's body in a prison, after her inquest, and hid the ashes. That was her State funeral, which said more about us than it ever could have said about her, and 'this good Christian woman' (as Lord Longford called her) vanished into the ether, leaving our smell behind.

Earlier, signals of equal outrage emanated from the local TV news with the revelation that a prisoner was in York Hospital awaiting a triple heart bypass operation, having been seen by some to have 'jumped the queue' ahead of decent, law-abiding folk. Well, the prisoner in question was Russell Bishop, my neighbour four doors down. I also knew him fairly well when he was with me (same wing and workshop) in Whitemoor Prison. He had been inside for about twelve years after having been convicted of the abduction of two girls and of an attempted murder. He was previously cleared at trial of the murder of another two small girls, a case known at the time as the 'Babes in the Wood Murders' in Brighton*. A few days later, I

---

* *Russell Bishop was subsequently found guilty of these murders at a second trial in 2018, six months after Dennis Nilsen's death.*

was surprised to bump into Russell, filling up his flask from the hot water boiler outside my cell. 'I thought you were in hospital having a heart operation?' I asked. He gave me the passionless reply, 'I was, but the Home Office blocked it.' So the tabloid outcry seemed to have had some effect. Perhaps the Home Office and the hospital authorities didn't want the lynch mobs congregating around the hospital or the prison.

Another B wing prisoner at Full Sutton, John Cannan, was aggrieved, around the same time, that the media was full of accusations that he was the killer of Suzie Lamplugh. She was a pretty, young estate agent who had gone missing many years ago when she went to show a property to a potential buyer called 'Mr Kipper'. The police wanted to charge John with her murder but the Crown Prosecution Service judged that there was insufficient evidence against him to have hope of a conviction. The victim's body has never been found.

Christmas morning 2002 arrived and I treated myself to a full English breakfast; one of the few such occasions in the year. Strange that I never heard the words 'Happy Christmas' mentioned once. In prison, it was just like any other weekend day. Once the routine Christmas cell searches had been completed, there was a flurry of activity among the cons with their sudden demand for empty two litre cola bottles. I also had a visitor to my cell looking for pure orange juice and another was on the scrounge for coffee – and so the hooch-brewing season began. In spite of all this, the prison culture remained relatively orderly and stable.

I smoked too much and, over that Christmas period, I sometimes had dizzy spells, which affected my eyesight. I also had a shortness of breath as my lungs slowly deteriorated in their efficiency to deliver oxygen to the blood and vital parts. I gained some sustaining moral and emotional sustenance by watching the film, *The Caine Mutiny*, in which I was able to identify with all of the movie's main characters including the paranoid Captain Queeg, who was driven to the point of breakdown under the unremitting pressure of his life (Bogart performed convincingly in the role).

A few days later, Mark Austin visited me, having spent four hours in blinding rain to drive up from Bedfordshire. It was always good to see a friendly face from the outside world and, during the visit, one of the 'gangsters" offspring walked up to the table and 'shot' Mark in the back of the head with the triangular, clear plastic container of a canteen sandwich. I guessed he was only about five years old and might have followed his dad's footsteps into violent crime and the resulting imprisonment.

Earlier in December, the 'H' on my old faithful Olivetti Lettena 25 typewriter snapped off but Russell Bishop stepped in and lent me his own machine. Unfortunately, he needed it back for five days over Christmas so, during that period, I caught up with my correspondence in longhand in my cell. I also used the time to catch up with some housework. Apart from sheets and pillowcases, I did the laundering of all my own clothing in my cell and hung the items out to dry on my metal bedrail and, in the case of socks, underwear and towels, on the twin pipes of the 'radiator', making my cell look very cramped and crowded.

To end the year, a letter with a US postmark arrived with the sender including his full name and address. Let it never be said that the Americans are a shy people.

'Dear Mr Nilsen,

I hope this letter finds you in good health and spirits…

I've read about your case over the past few years and was quite impressed by the descriptions of your activities with the deceased. You see, Mr Nilsen, I am a necrophiliac. As such, I have visited an estimated 54 funeral wakes (not counting friends and family) over the years and have actually managed to touch the 'guest of honor' (briefly, when no one was watching) several times. I will gladly tell you more if you write me back…

Other hobbies and interests include heavy metal music, travel, reading/writing and computer work. I hope you will write me back as I would love to have you as a pen pal.

Take care and best wishes to you.

Sincerely... [his name]'

We welcomed in the year of 2003 just as I was getting used to Russell Bishop's typewriter again when, suddenly, he was 'snatched off' on a category A move. As he hurriedly packed his kit to leave, I had to remind him that I still had his typewriter and went to fetch it. I followed him wheeling all his stuff on a trolley down towards reception when, to my horror, his typewriter fell off the top and landed on the corridor floor with a mighty crash. 'So long, Russell,' I thought, 'and definitely so long, typewriter!' Imagine then, my surprise, when, after work at the end of the day, his cell card had been reposted on his door. He had miraculously returned – like Arnold Schwarzenegger. He explained that he'd arrived at Whitemoor, had been rejected by the prison and had had to be driven all the way back. So, by chance of the prison service's routine incompetence, I had regained access to his typewriter, which, though battered and bruised, still worked. They don't make 'em like that any more.

I knew I couldn't carry on like this for too long and I resolved to get myself a new typewriter from funds in my private cash account but was told that I'd only be allowed to buy one from my current spending account (wages). So, in order to accrue the required £70.98, I'd have to save up, bit-by-bit, and wait. In the meantime, I handed back my TV (for a saving of £1 a week) and cancelled my subscription to the *Observer* (another £1.30 a week saved). Eventually, with the required amount in the correct account, I submitted an order through ARAMARK (the private prison canteen supplier) for Argos to supply me with a Brother AX 100, which was both a typewriter and word processor.

A week later, I was told that the permitted model wasn't

obtainable through ARAMARK or Argos. The only model that was available to prisoners at most other dispersal prisons was not allowed at Full Sutton where it was objected to on 'security' grounds (it could hold about eight pages of text, in its memory). I talked to the duty B wing senior officer about the problem and he said he'd 'look into it'. Eventually, following reams of paperwork and countless discussions, I picked up my new typewriter/word processor from reception on 25 May – almost six months after I'd initially ordered it. The instruction book ran to ninety-four pages so, until I came to understand the computer language associated with the word processor side of the technology, it would remain in typewriter mode.

On 9 February 2003, I was moved to consider the events of exactly twenty years previously, when I stepped forward to write on that blank page the story of my life. Thereafter, the hype started, the myths began and the folklore of the legend increased. The pundits wrote a lot and condemned a lot but never knew the truth. They were wheeled out to cloud the truth with their 'expertise' and their theories with tales of cannibalism and boiled heads on the stove and quips about blocked drains that blocked their understanding. Since 1983, I had been making one kind of official representation or another. What had I learned from this experience? Well, the main thing was that nobody had been listening to me.

As I matured with age, I'd kept away from the discordant bustle of the noisy cliques and their 'gang' culture where folk just shouted at one another without the pretence of social etiquette. I was openly sociable and pleasant to everyone in our routine, social interactions but I largely kept myself to myself. I knew a few fellow prisoners by name and was satisfied by the personal security of distance as prisoners tended to 'do each other's heads in' with continual and unremitting intrusions into each other's small lives and private space.

One of Yorkshire's most colourful prisoners happened to be my next-door neighbour who went by the nickname, 'Spanner'. He had become totally institutionalised over a period of twenty-eight years in prison where his only remaining ambition had been to eat, shit, read the *News of the World*, play with his toys, wank and sleep. There was an overwhelming childishness in his general demeanour where he had achieved a kind of secure 'happiness'. He would eat anything that passed his eyes and, despite him being Jewish, this included pork. If he didn't have a good store of fodder in his cell before bang-up, he felt insecure. His favourite plate had a long crack in it from which the tomato sauce from his baked beans would dribble out on to the table and, at night, he would retire to his cell with lots of grub and a saucepan full of leftovers that he'd scavenged off the hotplate from the evening meal.

I attended his sixty-fifth birthday 'party' one afternoon in a room on the ground floor on the far side of the wing. There were about nine of us crowded into that small room; the cramped space made worse by a six-foot table in the middle, absolutely covered with plates piled high with various food; cakes, sandwiches, sausage rolls and a birthday cake. I stayed for about ten minutes while cracking a few jokes and wishing Spanner well while everyone seemed to radiate an awkwardness devoid of conversation and high on eating. In any case, my departure created the space for others to attend and it was nice to have been invited.

When Spanner wasn't eating, he was cooking and would frequently pop his head around my door, unannounced, with the offer of a chicken leg, a small wedge of custard tart or one of his cooked breakfasts. Another time he gave me a strange curry with spinach. It was edible but needed a squirt of my Encona Original Hot Pepper Sauce to jazz it up a bit. One warm, May evening just before tea, he approached me on the landing to announce that 'we' were having spaghetti bolognese the following week despite having told him often enough that I wasn't fond of pasta. He looked crestfallen until I suggested that, by way of a compromise, I'd bring a packet of Smash instant mashed potatoes and that if he supplied the minced beef side of the bolognese I'd have that and mashed potatoes. Another morning as I was doing my washing in the sink, he popped his head in, carrying a saucepan under his arm containing the remnants of a stew. 'Get your bowl!' he said but, not being ready for another bout of food-poisoning (usually associated with one of Spanner's dinners), I declined.

Later, I could hear the incessant rattle of gunfire and explosions coming from next door. Upon investigating, I found Spanner locked, obsessively, into his Playstation game with finger on his firing buttons and eyes, fixed, staring at the screen. He didn't look up but intoned, gleefully, 'I'm killing Germans. Loads of Germans.' A man who had few communication or social skills could feel personally potent for a while. However, there was a chink of understanding from Spanner's behaviour: being Jewish, he, perhaps, didn't realise that by objectifying the 'Germans' in his game, he'd relegated them into fearful and subhuman symbols for casual destruction. Were lessons ever learned? I say this with no malice, as that was just how he was.

My other neighbours were equally unique in different ways. Mr Hussain made 'dib-dib-dib' noises in his cell – over and over – for long periods of time, but 80 per cent of the dib-dib-dibs, during the day, came from other prisoners taking the piss out of his condition. There was a word for this: bullying. He gave me the most delicious foods including kebabs and curries and, although he may not have been all right in the head, there was nothing wrong with his ability to cook. Another neighbour, Mr Addis, was a constant visitor to the Block after smashing up whichever cell he was housed in. I wondered if he might have been on a quest to destroy Full Sutton one cell at a time. Mr Miller, a few doors down, came to my cell one morning asking me how I obtained my 'hard-core pornography'. I told him that I didn't have any but he countered that he'd read in the *Sun* that I'd taken the Home Office to court and had won my case. I made him aware of the true facts surrounding the aborted court case to gain access to ordinary gay (non-hard-core) pinup magazines and told him that a couple of years ago I did have a copy of *Razzle* and *Escort* – two soft-porn heterosexual magazines – but these had been loaned to Mr Morley, who had suddenly been posted off to a secure hospital.

During the nights, there was frequent banging on doors as some felt inclined to throw their rattles out of their prams. One evening, there was the noise of a sharp clatter on the concrete out in the yard. Taking a look, I saw that one of the 'gangsters' upstairs had thrown his TV remote control out of the window. This would probably result in some innocent prisoner having his remote control stolen to replace it – as was the way with 'gangster' thinking. Grunts, yelps, cackles and shouted, fractured phrases would come from limited vocabularies. Nobody had asked them to come to prison and many of these young men had wasted their lives outside and seemed intent in also wasting them in here. On Friday nights, there was usually a hard core of hooch-brewers who couldn't hold their drink and they upset a lot of prisoners with their wild, drunken rantings out of their cell windows. These guys were never that moderate of tone and volume when they were sober so one could imagine their blind drunk profile as they performed their street-dog antics.

Mr Searle, one night, told me that he was seriously thinking of killing himself because he didn't see any kind of positive future, being well into middle age, having done 'all the courses' and then having been sent to 'this shithole'. I tried the casual, humorous touch, comparing his situation (of a ten-year tariff) with my own (whole-life tariff) while reminding him that I had already been 'in shitholes like Full Sutton' for twenty-four years. It seemed to cheer him up and he was up and about the following morning to face a new, sunny day. I reminded him of the millions of people all over the world who might like to come and live in Full Sutton, which would have been a vast improvement on their present condition of starvation, material poverty, fear, violence, etc. I didn't think prison was a pleasant place, only that we should adapt, positively, to our environment as best we could. Where there was life there could be hope but not otherwise.

Around the wing, I was still getting unfriendly snarls of contempt from Mr Adile (a young 'gangster') with occasional, physical digs in the meal queues. He was a true example of an uncultured, feral, street dog and I tried to keep well away from him and his dangerously dysfunctional ilk. In the corridor going to work, Adile would spit out, in his broken English, the words, 'batty boy' in my direction.

On another occasion, I was passing the meal queue when a chap quipped what he thought was a jokey reference to the 'boiled head' of one of my victims. I didn't have either the time or the inclination to reply to him there and then but, later, I went up to him, tweaked his cheek and said, 'Who's been a cheeky boy then?' This completely floored him and there was real fear in his eyes in the first second of my sudden approach in that tea queue.

In the exercise yard, I was taking a turn (walk) with a guy and we were talking about prison and politics, which turned to Islam. As the conversation progressed, I happened to mention 'bacon sandwiches' at which point he interjected with a most inappropriately impertinent question, 'I've wanted to know…how does it taste?' I asked, 'What, bacon?' He rejoined, 'No, I mean…you know…human flesh?'

I was even once asked: 'How many did you kill?' by a prisoner I didn't know from a bag of beans. Taking no expressed offence, I replied with, 'Nobody, so far this week.' What I missed the most in prison was good conversation.

· · ·

Sometimes, moments overtook me when I least expected it. After lock-up one morning, I was playing a Buddy Holly tape, which I'd borrowed from another prisoner. 'Peggy Sue' transported me back to 1958 as reams of emotion flowed in a single shot image of myself in Burnett's Café in Strichen High Road, aged twelve, listening to the record for the first time on the jukebox. Such power of remembrance on the mind of a new boy. The song has remained there ever since, still as fresh and strong.

On the prison video channel one evening, I watched much of the film *Brokeback Mountain* but the pain of its emotional content scared me off and I couldn't sustain my viewing of it; far too personally painful…it was unbearable. I had travelled that wound-strewn road and it hurt, hurt, hurt. I was actually scared to watch it in all its interpersonal intimacy – enough to break a heart and a mind – through recollections of personal experience. I kept flipping channels (to watch the *Book Awards* on Channel 4) while taking in the movie one traumatic moment at a time as if to avoid some building measure of personal implosion. It depicted me and a great part of me and my emotional struggling past.

Similarly, I had pinned up a colour photo cut from the sports section of one Sunday's *Observer* that brought a sharp potency to my feelings and to my memory. The picture seemed to have been taken in the 1980s and was of a boy in his early teens, dressed in a Wolves football shirt. Tears were streaming down his face at the news of his team's defeat and relegation, as he was being supported by a man I assumed was his father. My frisson of memory seemed to come from an amalgamation of factors. The first was from the reality that he had a father figure for support in his life. The second was that the boy reminded me of that boy I'd fancied all these years ago in the yard at Fraserburgh Central School. And the third core of attention came from the fact that he was crying copious tears…unashamedly and uncontrollably. I envied him because I was never able to do that. Somewhere in my infancy, I had lost the basic, emotional ability to weep. Juxtaposed on the image was the alternative notion that the man in the picture was an abuser, 'grooming' the boy. In that image there came a focus on the two possible roles. That's the mess I was in.

I'd been feeling run down during those early months of 2003 but had begun to feel a lot better with a daily portion of pure orange juice (vitamin C), a daily cod liver oil capsule (omega 3) and a zinc tablet, all purchased from the canteen.

Lying quietly in bed one night, I watched a late documentary about Robert Maudsley, whom I'd met a few times when I was in the Punishment Block in Wakefield in the 1980s. Back then, I'd spoken with him through the wire of our respective cages during the exercise period and Bob had managed to slip me some tobacco, papers and matches for which I was eternally grateful. No serious effort had been sustained to understand him nor to offer remedial counselling with the aim of returning him to the greater prison community. They just gave up on him and locked him away in a darkly obscure corner of the prison where he'd been in virtual solitary confinement for about twenty-five years. In the documentary, he was described as the 'most dangerous prisoner' in the system. Most of the Maudsley material came from another documentary made in 1982, filmed in F wing. Memories came flooding back as the camera panned around that odious Punishment Block at Wakefield where I'd spent so many unhappy hours, and I wondered if the thugs and bullies who ran it then were still in place in the prison service. They'd kept Bob there for many years, like their pet alligator, to show off and exhibit to visiting VIPs, but I certainly found him easy to talk to and he struck me as being a warm, orderly person.

The following morning, I awoke just before 6 a.m., had a piss, made a mug of black coffee from the hot water in my flask, put on BBC Radio 4, sank the coffee and lay dozing in bed. I must have gone back to sleep because I then had the strangest dream: I was transported back to my boyhood and found myself in bed with my 'brother', Olav, who was lying next to me, masturbating under the covers. When he was finished, I propped myself up, leaned over and, gazing for a moment into his beautiful, young face, I slowly and deliberately kissed him full on the lips. There was no reaction from him whatsoever as I woke up in my present, cellular location. Strange!

In June, Jeremy Bamber joined us from Whitemoor on a category A transfer and came to work in the braille shop. He was located on D wing and he told me that his appeal against his conviction and sentence would go on, as he was seeking new evidence to place before the courts. He said he'd even set up his own website. A couple of years later, his latest appeal had hit the headlines where the *Sun* told us, 'His lawyers have found pictures of ex-model Ms Caffell, taken the morning the bodies were found, showing her covered in fresh blood… They say she could only have been dead for two hours – and Bamber had been in police custody from 3am after reporting a row at the house in Tolleshunt D'Arcy, Essex. Bamber has lost two appeals and now wants a third.' Well, I later saw Jeremy in the workshop and it wasn't his case he was gushing about but his new stereo; proudly telling all within hearing range of its features, price and how superior it was to all others. He was one hell of a materialist with outward bluster and charm to conceal a gross absence of empathy.

He had a girlfriend who visited him and sent him money to keep him in the style he became accustomed to in his privileged life. In prison, this was restricted to gadgets and material things. I think he did kill his entire adopted family in order to inherit the estate so that he could spend the rest of his life impressing folk with the power of his acquired toys.

One morning in the braille shop, he came and sat at the scanner next to me. Unsolicited, he began to ask me about the Atefah Sahaaleh documentary, the previous night, adding that what had happened to the girl was terrible (this Iranian girl had been executed, after having been charged with adultery and crimes against chastity). I, of course, agreed and added the observation that these public executions seemed to have no limits as, a couple of years earlier, they had hanged two young men for being gay. Bamber interjected saying that *that* was understandable because homosexuality was, after all, an abomination against humanity. I asked him if he was serious and he repeated that, in his view, it was. I said. 'Well, I'm not surprised to learn you're a homophobe', which he immediately denied. A heated row ensued and got very personal as Bamber added his distorted malice and accused me of having no friends on B wing, except for Spanner. I countered that I had *no* friends on the wing – not even Spanner – and neither did he have any close friends in prison. I finished with: 'Jeremy, you represent everything that I despise in a prisoner. You're a denier, a "boss" boy, a manipulator, a shit stirrer and a friend of the prison service.'

Some months later, I was passing the 'Halal Ramadan Holy Month' food service hatch, where the food of 'true-believers' must be handled by one of their own and not an infidel. I noticed that a few of B wing's immoral and bigoted 'rag, tag, and bobtails' had become 'good Muslims', including…wait for it…Mr Bamber… which might have explained his remark about homosexuality. Well, Mullah Bamber would maintain his faith so long as the fad lasted and he could get some material and psychological advantage from it.

In April 2007, he'd been telling everyone in the braille shop about his 'victory' in passing a recent polygraph (lie-detector) test, which, he said, had cleared him of the murder of his adopted family. I concluded that evidence was not to be garnered from a volatile machine but from the hard facts and, in his case, the hard facts of evidence were against him and his fantasy innocence. Later, while passing him on the landing, I quipped, 'Jeremy, you were quite right about the polygraph test. It works. I took one this morning and it said I'm innocent!' So, it was no surprise that he solicited engagement on the subject in the shop later that morning, as my quip had probably been doing the rounds by then. He was adamant that the polygraph principles were sound science and, during the discussion, his little coterie of 'gangsters' were supporting and geeing him up while I remained unmoved in my view. Jeremy didn't like to back down or concede an argument on which his entire prison fantasy life was based, especially in front of his 'gang'. As the tempo increased, he suddenly lost it. His eyes glazed over and he thrust his head forward as if to head-butt me, pulling away at the last moment. I had confronted him with unremitting reality and he, momentarily, had broken his cover, revealing his true, unguarded self. The young screw in the shop panicked a bit before telling us to keep away from one another. A couple of minutes later, Jeremy came over and apologised, which I accepted. What was clear, was that Jeremy's affected front had broken under the stark pressure of reasoned opposition, which wouldn't bend to his manipulative will. And this had brought, to him, the crisis of hard truths and a loss of face in front of his 'followers'. I guessed that what I had seen in his eyes was the same, staring look his family saw the moment he killed them.

He attended the High Court in April 2009 to have his whole life tariff set aside and replaced by a lower, fixed sentence. But this – and his later appeal against the decision – was rejected. I doubted very much that that judgement would have tempered the arrogance of 'Pope Jeremy the Innocent', as he continued in denial of shooting all five members of his adoptive family, as he cunningly devised a new strategy in the sole material interest of 'me, me, me'.

• • •

Over the years, I had been continuing to document my life and write more autobiographical material and, in June 2003, I had a letter from a journalist, Russ Coffey, who had been to visit Mark Austin. I had asked Mark to let him read some of this material – which I'd passed out to Mark quite openly through the normal channels – and I thought it would be journalistically important to Russ, who was proposing to write an article about me and my autobiography. Two months later, I was handed the *Sunday Times Magazine* where it had made the front-page feature as Russ Coffey finally delivered his article. In it, I took issue that Mr Coffey said, about me, 'he wants to exercise what he sees as his right to be heard.' There was no right to be heard. What I was trying to establish was a right to *express*. Whether anyone listened would be another matter entirely. When I related my positive achievements in prison, he described this as 'bragging' and he seemed unable to give me the slightest praise where some rehabilitative praise might have been due, just as he was 'mystified' that Mark – or anyone – could possibly be my friend.

Russ Coffey himself was clearly determined to hold his prejudice intact (à la Masters) as shown by this admission: 'I never felt particularly uncomfortable writing to Nilsen, because it was in a professional capacity, but I was aware that in having any empathy for his arguments, I was in danger of being manipulated, as were other correspondents.' So the truth, sincerely expressed by me, came down, not to honesty, but to 'manipulation'. This came when one had already formed a prejudiced view of the man one was writing to. As for 'manipulation', it was Russ Coffey who contacted me 'offering a degree of empathy', addressing his letters to me, 'Dear Des', something he completely abandoned in the text of his article, in favour of the cold, impersonal 'Nilsen'. The very profession that he followed (journalism) was precisely all about the manipulation of facts and often their misrepresentation. He didn't offer any evidence about how I strived to manipulate him; he asked questions and I answered them. If he wanted to criticise my answers, then he was free to do so.

Russ Coffey never told me which paper his article was to appear in, nor on what date, and he never bothered to send me a copy of what he proposed to write, nor a copy of the article itself. He did read it in its entirety over the telephone to Mark, the day before it was to be published, giving Mark no time to relay its content to me beforehand. The rules of journalism seemed to include cultivating one's primary source and then dropping them. Everyone had an 'angle' and his was a story to sell.

A few days later, a screw passed me a copy of the *Daily Mail,* which allowed full latitude for Brian Masters to berate me for my attitude and for my autobiography. His piece was delicately headlined 'The Monster Who Must Be Silenced' with the article opening with, 'Here, the man who knows him best, says he must be stopped.'

He would have been pleased on 20 December 2003, when the *Daily Mirror* had a 'jubilant' piece saying that I had failed to win Mr Justice Kay's heart and legal mind in his decision to 'throw out' my Judicial Review (in being allowed to have my autobiography published). I wondered how long I'd have to wait to read his judgement after just about everybody would have had access to it. The *Daily Mirror* piece slanted its reporting with untruths about the content of *History of a Drowning Boy* being about killing and cutting up bodies and, of course, I expected nothing else from the tabloid. The report had been written by one, Kate O'Hanlon (barrister), with the judgement being handed down by Lord Phillips of Worth Matravers, master of the rolls, on 17 November. O'Hanlon, of course, writing for the press, added a bit of flourish to her report, misinformingly describing *History of a Drowning Boy* as, 'The details of the murders [which she described as being those of 'homosexual partners'] and what the claimant had done with the bodies were horrifying. The claimant wished to publish those details.' This was, of course, untrue, though to find those details you'd have to read Masters' version – hammered out in graphic fashion – which had been in the public domain for almost twenty years by then. The community was now stuck with Masters' and the tabloid view of my past and the sham of British justice was looking flimsier by the hour.

The television media were no better. Earlier in the year, Granada TV had requested a copy of *History of a Drowning Boy* from my solicitor, which I'd denied them. They would, of course, have just taken what sensation they could have found useful in their programme and discarded the rest. Well, fortified with a sleep-retarding cup of black coffee, I stayed up to watch their documentary on me and my case in a series entitled *Real Crime: Murder in Mind*.

For as much as it hadn't moved on in either information or insight, it could well have been made in 1983. Its main material came from a garbled confession I'd made to the police on my arrest; the spillings of a calmly desperate man trying to parry exposure of his inner thoughts and motives. At the time, I just wanted to confess to my actions and diffuse the addressing of my motives, which weren't clear to me at that time. Granada TV's production values were poor and cheap with tepid reconstructions being injected. They even used a non-lookalike actor to parrot small segments of my police confession text. All the old favourites were interviewed and the only new witness was an ex-colleague from the Met Police, now interviewed like the rest of them, in their advanced age, twenty years after the events described. For a series called *Real Crime*, I thought the programme was not so much 'real' as a mixture of short, tabloid-selected 'facts', speculation and fiction. The finale of the programme compounded its errors, stating that the Home Office could not stop me in my autobiographical efforts – something which they had plainly done; a fact known to most informed people, especially in the media.

The programme did bring back a rush of painful memories: images from the house at 195 Melrose Avenue, the flat at 23 Cranley Gardens, David Gallichan and my dog, Bleep. The most strikingly traumatic image was a colour photo of Martyn Duffey, one of my victims. His face had faded from my memory until it was thrust back into my mind, which brought back a total recall of him and the stark fact of how I'd robbed him of life and caused so much loss to his parents. His father gave testimony of his great pain and lasting sense of loss, caused by me and my actions. He said that he would not approach any measure of contentment until he heard of my death. Completely understandable.

Elsewhere on TV, I revisited an importantly traumatic part of my childhood when I watched the 1952 movie, *Hans Christian Andersen* with Danny Kaye in the title role. I'd seen it in the Saturday afternoon matinee at the Fraserburgh Picture House when I must have been seven or eight. Even at that age I was enthralled and mesmerised by the character of Peter (played by Joey Walsh) the orphan boy who had been taken in by cobbler, Hans Andersen. Wow, I was smitten, and the boy in the playground at Fraserburgh Central School reminded me of him, hence my frisson of excitement at the very sight of him. I'd never felt such a rush of passion. Seeing the film again had left the feeling undiminished over the passage of time. Peter was beautiful... *is* beautiful and, with hindsight, he was part 'self-reflection'; that first image of myself that I had loved.

In the summer of 2004, I was feeling worn down. I'd had frequent dizzy spells and impaired vision, which had remained for some minutes. Then a bruise appeared on my left wrist with an adjoining artery or vein becoming sore and slightly swollen. Parts of my head felt 'bunged-up' and I thought my sinuses were blocked. A tinia infection had returned to my scalp and I thought I'd inherited my grandfather's low blood pressure, poor circulation and heart condition (well, that's the way the cookie crumbles). I submitted the usual written application to see the doctor and later, for the tinia infection, I was given a prescription for a product called Nizoral shampoo. First thing on the Saturday morning, I attended the treatments hatch on B wing to pick up my prescription. A simple procedure? You decide:

Nurse: 'Haven't you got it already?'

Me: 'Obviously not.'

Nurse: 'Well, when I go back to Healthcare, I'll try to find where it is. It could have been put in the wrong box.'

Me: 'When will I get it?'

Nurse: 'If not today then we'll put it in for tomorrow.'

It seemed that the simple act of taking a bottle of Nizoral from off the shelf in the dispensary had many complications to it, quite beyond staff thinking skills. The following day (Sunday), I attended the treatments hatch again, giving my name.

Nurse: 'Is anything due to be collected?'

Me: 'No, I always attend the prescription hatch when I am not due a prescription.'

Nurse: 'Did you see me yesterday about it?' [The missing Nizoral.]

Me: 'You were not on here, yesterday, were you?'

Nurse: 'No, I wasn't.'

Me: 'Well, that answers your question.'

Nurse: 'Calm down.' [Always a good official back-up favourite when lost for any sensible answer.]

Later that morning, I got to the B wing office to enquire about the missing Nizoral and, coincidentally, found the original nurse there. He informed me that he'd checked the file and found that I had 'not been prescribed' Nizoral, but that Nizoral was 'on my file'. He added, 'We haven't got the keys to the dispensary so we'll have to wait until Tuesday to check the matter out.'

The following Tuesday, the Healthcare treatments hatch on B wing still had no Nizoral as the authorities were still 'looking into' the problem but on the Wednesday, the sky was blue and the sun was shining. I attended the treatments hatch, yet again, and the nurse registered surprise, 'Know nothing about it, luv', and like all the others, she promised to 'look into' the matter and report back. The treatment of patients was entirely at the administrative convenience of Healthcare, fitted entirely to their needs. In the end, Ketoconazole was substituted for Nizoral.

• • •

Early in 2005, a duty senior officer told me that the Metropolitan Police were coming to see me and a letter from my solicitor, Nick

Wells, provided more details. He'd spoken to a detective inspector (DI) from the Met who wanted to interview me about an unresolved missing person from 1978. The interview would be under caution and related to a missing fourteen-year-old from that period. The DI had informed Nick that the main purpose was to see if that missing person case could be closed and to give an answer to the family as to the fate of the individual. The interview would take place on 16 March at 9.30 a.m.

That Irish youth couldn't have been as young as fourteen, could he? Well, unless he had been well advanced for his age. If he was a boy, he could have been described as a 'well-developed' boy, not tall of stature but well proportioned. I remembered his chest was hairless with a fine down on his legs and thighs with a hardly discernible finer down on his arms. He had some fine pubic hair but no line of hair to his belly button. The hair on his head was short, light brown and slightly curly. His face was slightly roundish and it didn't look like he was yet quite of shaving age. If he'd grown to his late teens or early twenties, I guessed he might have had the body of a builder or, perhaps, a rugby player. A significant point was that if he was just fourteen years old, would he have been drinking in the Cricklewood Arms? And would the barman have served him if he'd looked that young. To me, and the assembled, he could have passed for eighteen. Well, come the event on 16 March, I waited and waited for the police visit until, at 11.30 a.m., I was told by the wing office that the visit had been cancelled – with no explanation.

Over six months would pass before I would hear any more about it and then it happened quite unexpectedly. On the last day of September 2005, as I headed off to work, I passed Officer Caldwell who was ticking off the role board as we left the wing. He surprised me by announcing that I had a legal visit in the afternoon, which was news to me. I carried on at work in the braille shop until just after 10 a.m. when a screw suddenly announced that I was to have the legal visit 'Now!' There and then, straight from the workshop and unprepared, I attended the visit in a small room next to the main visitors' hall.

The two Metropolitan Police murder squad officers, led by a detective chief inspector, began by apologising for the previous meeting they'd cancelled. They then told me the reason for the visit was to establish the identity of my first victim. I told them that Met Police officers had already visited me on the subject in 1990, here at Full Sutton, and the detectives replied that they were slightly aware of that (handled by Camden Police Station) but that the file on that event had been lost in a flood of the station basement or something. They told me that they had a strong idea concerning the identity of the young Irish man and they passed me a photograph. It was in grainy monochrome and depicted a boy who was a few weeks from his fifteenth birthday. The police told me that their subject was named Stephen Dean Holmes who had been born, lived with his family and had been educated in Kilburn, North London. He liked to sport an Irish accent and was into Republican politics and the cause of Irish Republicanism. He also liked Rockabilly music and dressed older than his age.

On the night of 29 December 1978, he'd been out at a club in Willesden Green or Cricklewood with his sister, where he'd last been seen waiting for a bus in Cricklewood Broadway near the Cricklewood Arms public house. This was where I'd gone that night after having had a good drink at home alone a few minutes' walking distance from the pub. After the bus stop sighting, he had never been seen again and was reported missing.

I was formally cautioned for the interview, which was also tape recorded. The police asked me if I might have met my victim at a bus stop outside the pub and I said it was possible. I told them that my usual modus operandi was that I'd establish rapports with men in the pub standing at the bar. I reminded them that, on a busy night, Irish working men's pubs like the Cricklewood Arms were usually jam-packed with hundreds of drinkers at that time of night, perhaps more so because of the festive time of the year. Looking at the photo, I could only say I was eighty per cent sure that the person was, indeed, the youth I had killed. For a fully positive ID, eighty per cent was not enough to be conclusive to be able to bring closure to the family. I'd need a clearer photo.

Then I turned to something which struck me as being more important in establishing a one hundred per cent positive ID. I reminded them that I'd pointed out the exact spot in the garden where I'd burned the first victim's body on a fire on its own and bone fragments and teeth might have been found on the spot when it was excavated and sifted. I reminded them that, with DNA from his sister and DNA from a tooth or bone fragment, a perfect match could be made – or not. But the detective told me that everything had been subsequently destroyed after my trial. I asked, with some questioning amazement, 'All destroyed? Even while it was known that some victims had not been identified?' He reminded me that things were different then, in both method and scientific knowledge. The interview finished and the tape was switched off at around 11.30 a.m. I shook hands with the two senior policemen and left the room.

Back on the wing, the first effect from the police interview – hitting me almost immediately – came from the fact that with each piece of human, individual information: a name, a history, personal details, etc., the 'prop' I had used in the ritual had been humanised more and more. I immediately experienced a fresh – and more severe – feeling of guilt about the *real* boy that I had destroyed and the real pain I had brought to his family. I felt bad, bad. There was the added dimension that the youth I had killed might have been a fourteen-year-old boy. Images bounced around my mind and there was a kind of 'click' in which everything snapped into place.

It is the early hours of that December morning and I am lying naked in bed with the naked, brother-like boy. The feeling is sublime but then

305

the notion strikes me that 'Olav' might wake up and discover and
scorn me for my homosexual inadequacy and the feminine filth of my
unacceptable perversion – a power Olav has to belittle me; to denigrate
the 'love' or 'lust' I have for his body. It is as if I want to perpetuate the
perfection of the scenario: Olav asleep, naked and seemingly unaware
of my passion for him; a perfection to be destroyed by his awakening.

I had a desperate need to prolong this frisson; to keep things as they were – for ever – with the totally passive and naked 'Olav' in my arms, there to be fondly explored. But I had a fear, too, of the Irish youth waking up; the same fear I had of Olav waking up.

The two Met Police detectives turned up again, a week before my sixtieth birthday; however, there was no solicitor in evidence due to some administrative error. They'd brought a couple of original photos of Stephen Dean Holmes for me to look at. One was a group shot where I homed in, immediately, to a laughing – almost elfin-featured – youth. It unnerved me, as did the second photo, which was the original version of the photocopy I'd been shown before. My eighty per cent certainty now rocketed to ninety-five per cent plus. I was sure it was him! In the black and white photos, his hair was longer but just as wavy as I'd remembered in his shorter haircut, and the realisation made me as numb as a dead log. The police decided to tell the family without waiting for a formal statement from me and I returned to the wing.

• • •

In February 2006, I finished transcribing my last book into braille using the 'MegaDots' system as we awaited training in the 'Duxbury' system. However, none of the new screw instructors knew anything about it, leaving us prisoners to muddle through the best we could (with the help of some of the 'computer geek' prisoners). Suffice to say, my productivity ground to a stop for a time. Disaster struck a week later when I lost about three-quarters of a book scan, which I'd saved on the Public file and had then been deleted by someone else. I was so disheartened that I seriously considered a job change. In the endless treadmill of the braille shop and its unsatisfying transcriptions, I still felt despondent at just copying out other people's creative work while having my own writing constantly under official attack. Life in the braille shop was becoming annoyingly tedious and very frustrating but I persevered, and by July 2007, I'd been given my hundreth book project, *Back Home* by Michelle Magorian.

My mood was temporarily lifted when the 2006 football World Cup games began. I went all extravagant in that week's canteen order, having put down for a packet of five Hamlet cigars (£3.39), and I'd be smoking the first when the match kicked off on the Saturday afternoon between England and Paraguay in Frankfurt. There was a large part of England that was an integral part of me now, having been attached to it since 1961. I had had both laughter and tears in England; in Scotland, only tears. On 1 July, I settled back to watch England play Portugal in the quarter finals. At half-time, it was 0–0, then the whistle blew for the start of the second half. It was 0–0 at full time then Ronaldo succeeded in securing Portugal's place in the semi-finals by scoring the winning penalty. Upstairs, I could hear Mr Walker smashing up some furniture!

The following day, the scousers in the braille shop defended the conduct of their hero, Rooney (who had been sent off during the match), with the excuses that football was a contact sport, 'shoulder charges' were all part of the sport and that stopping such behaviour would reduce it to ballet. This was as distorted a view of football as you would get but a view shared by many of the macho ilk who sought any excuse for violence. Andy Murray was later knocked out of the Wimbledon Tennis Tournament ending British hopes of getting a title this year again.

In idle moments of inactive creativity, I would lose myself in a good film and, on one such afternoon, I chanced up the 1944 movie

The Way Ahead; a storyline which followed a platoon of British army recruits through their training and on to the battlefields of North Africa in 1943. Looking at the film brought a lump to my throat; first, for the scenario depicted; second, for the knowledge that all the actors were now dead; and third, for the memories it brought from my early life. I looked back, almost in tears, at a lost world and with the knowledge that there were millions of *real* casualties in the *real* backdrop of the ongoing Iraq war; millions of dead and, for me, the realisation of those who had died around me and those that I had caused to die. All that past crowded in on me that day in my cell as I sat like a hidden shadow of yesterday in the new and changing world of 2006.

Watching the film, I had a momentary recollection of my family, all sitting down together for a meal in the 1950s. How optimistic things seemed back then, full of joyous hopes and expectations within the feel and colours of the time. I saw them all now, in living technicolour; those real images in the years before I became something else.

In the movie I recognised the .303 Bren gun and .303 Short Lee Enfield rifle that I'd shot in my time in the Gordon Highlanders Army Cadet Force as a boy in Aberdeenshire. A million reels of memory were there, all to be lost when I'm gone; memories of an age vanished with its people and their actions. The movie sprang forward to my boy soldier days at Aldershot from 1961–4; those days of certainty in A Company comprising Gale, Owen, Venning, Scarisbrick and Byford. Yes, our lives were, indeed, spent living and dying at the same time and we'd wondered if all our ancestors had felt like that when they had faced their own mortality and their dawns of change.

Later, I was embarrassed by old memories as I watched a news item on the homeless young, a high percentage having been dumped from care homes or foster parents when they had 'come of age'. I was not forgetful or in any kind of denial when I recalled that, twenty-five years ago, I might have picked up such a young man who was living on the street, taken him back to my flat and killed him for use in my fantasy ritual. A vision rushed through me of that high bed platform in the middle of the night in Melrose Avenue, astride that Scottish boy, with my back pressed securely against the ceiling, with hardly a tremble, as I tightened the ligature and held the situation secure until the trembling stopped. I didn't remember undressing him of vest and pants but just standing on a chair and sliding his warm, naked body into my arms and standing there for a long moment, savouring the vision of him – as me – held in my arms. It was a vision only, with everything else numb.

In a trawl through the TV channels I came across another ITV *Real Crime* programme, subtitled, *The Truth About the Babes in the Wood*. The murders of two children had remained unsolved for many years, with a man called Ronald Jebson being a main suspect. In 1999 he came forward (in prison for another, similar offence) and confessed to the crimes, going to the site and pointing out things, as well as describing the details of the crime which only the killer would have known. I recognised Mr Jebson straight away as he had been at Whitemoor while I was there – living under a different name. When I talked to him at Whitemoor, I found him a fast talker who showed a reluctance to meet my eyes; a fevered kind of talker with something deep on his mind. I guessed, at the time, that he was probably in for some offence regarding children and other prisoners had said that he was a controversial suspect connected with the 'Babes in the Wood' murders.

A few weeks later I had tried (unsuccessfully) to stay up and watch another *Real Crime* programme, this one entitled *Mr Nice Guy*, about Brian Field with whom I worked in the braille shop. He had been convicted of killing a fourteen-year-old schoolboy and was suspected of killing many more. The following day, I noticed he was his quiet, old self; a paragon of gentle and polite self-control. Coincidentally, in that day's newspaper were pictures of bulldozers taking the topsoil off areas of ground where Brian was known to have worked and dumped rubbish in his days as a gardener. The police were looking for the remains of two boys missing since 1996.

I also watched the *Real Crime* programme about Donald Neilson ('the Black Panther'). The documentary touched on the three sub-postmasters he'd shot dead, while robbing their premises, but mainly concentrated on the Leslie Whittle kidnapping and murder when the ransom money was not paid. I was surprised to learn that Mr Neilson had served as a soldier in Cyprus and Aden. Well, he'd been inside since 1976 and he, too, was on a whole life tariff. I heard his thick Yorkie accent for the first time in a taped police interview, unofficially recorded, and he didn't strike me as being among the most articulate of men. He did, however, seem to have a touch of pride in his 'military orientated' offences, carried out in army combat fatigues with black head mask and guns. A screw later told me he was in the early stages of Motor Neurone Disease.

I often received Donald Neilson's mail in error and, I presumed, he received mine. Due diligence was never a high priority inside this dysfunctional apparatus. They even mixed us up for real when Mark Austin was seated at a table in the visitors' hall with Donald Neilson. Neither had a clue who the other was until, on further investigation with a duty screw, the blunder was revealed!

In November, news of the recent identification of my first victim had been released to the press and Staz (a neighbour) brought me in a cutting from the *Daily Mirror* headlined, 'Nilsen IDs first victim 27yrs on By Jeff Edwards, Chief Crime Correspondent'. 'Serial killer Dennis Nilsen has finally identified his first victim, 27 years after the murder... Nilsen, jailed for life for 15 killings in 1983, confessed to a 16th murder but was never charged with it as there was no ID... His victims were incinerated on bonfires or cut up and flushed down drains at homes he rented in North London.' Edwards managed to cram so many inaccuracies into his short piece that I won't labour on them as they are abundantly self-evident to anyone informed about my past.

Later, the Home Office passed on to me an enquiry from *Independent on Sunday*:

'I am seeking to confirm that Dennis Nilsen, the serial killer, is currently being held at Full Sutton prison near York. This is for a small "where are they now" piece in *The Independent on Sunday* this week.' Of course, it was 'Dennis Nilsen, the serial killer' they were interested in and not Dennis Nilsen, the writer, composer or long-term prisoner in order to resurrect the story and its attending frisson of sensation as a black mark in history.

On another occasion, I was called up to the wing office to sign a consent form to have my whereabouts disclosed to a reporter from the *Muswell Hill Journal* who also identified me as 'Dennis Nilsen, the serial killer'. Had I agreed, I would have dismissed him with, 'I am Dennis Nilsen, the ex-serial killer.' To own his label, I would have had to have spent the past twenty-five years going around the prison landings killing people.

I was getting tired of journalists and media people writing to me for titbits of information in order to construct a slanted and editorially partisan story. The me they sought to relate to was not the me of now but the perceived image of me a long time ago, bound to the core of my facts as interpreted in that period from 1978–83. Nothing more than that! As in showbusiness, I was only as interesting as my last public sensation and it was the easiest thing in the world to be a public critic of one who had done such dark, past deeds and who had been labelled 'serial killer' and of whom nothing remotely positive could ever be said.

• • •

In the latter part of 2006, I decided to grow a moustache but as I passed Mr Miller on the landing, just before bang-up one evening, he commented that I looked like a porn star! In the end I shaved it off; it was becoming far too bushy and out of control, leaving half the coffee I was drinking absorbed into its dense forest of visual humour. Someone asked me: 'Where's the moustache?' I replied, 'I got a good price for it on D wing!' Ask a silly question.

Then in another change, the week before Christmas, I moved from cell number 5 to cell number 2. The condition of the new cell was ten times better than the one I'd been in since December 2001; in the new cell, the windows and sill were not rusted up and the walls were clean. Most of the furniture was fairly new, the lighting was so much brighter that I could actually see what I was typing. And so I was locked up for the rest of that afternoon having time to rearrange my new cell, putting pictures up on the picture board and putting all my stuff on to the shelves, in the cupboard or stored away in the two blue volumetric control boxes under my bed. As a bonus, this new cell was further away from Spanner's cell, so I was expecting to be pestered less by him, which couldn't have been a bad thing. His existence was still focused on his PlayStation and eating and hoarding food. Speak of the devil… Spanner just came to my cell to remind me that 'lunch is up' so that I could go and tell the serving screw to give mine to Spanner! He was only ever moved off his arse in the concentrated interests of his big, fat belly.

The new year of 2007 opened with a steady stream of letters from abroad and I was not at a loss to guess why folks should want to write to me. Later, I was called up to the office and informed that the prison had confiscated a menu from the Golden Lion pub in Dean Street, London, sent in by someone for me to sign. I was told it had been sent to my stored property to prevent it from being sold. Well, I suppose collectors would buy anything connected with celebrity infamy, denoting ghastly historical crimes.

In March, I got a letter from Mark Austin, my oldest friend, who still retained contact with me. Correspondents came and went but Mark remained and I valued his friendship above all others.

In the letter was a picture of an item for sale on eBay; a copy of 'Aftermath', a poem written by me on 28 March 1999 and published that year on the front page of the prison magazine, *Inside Time*. The one being auctioned was a copy typed out on my electric Brother typewriter a couple of years earlier and it was signed. The seller was unknown to either of us.

A few days later, I had a most pleasant morning talking with Mark in the visitors' hall although the vending machines were unserviceable and we couldn't get a hot drink. A screw came to our table and asked Mark to remove his coat from the back of his chair, enforcing some sort of obscure regulation or another. Mark was telling me that he was up in court soon, after he had pleaded not guilty to an alleged motoring offence of jumping a red light. He was not to be legally represented and said he would be stating his own case, which I advised him was, perhaps, unwise. Mark had this instinct not to be browbeaten or dominated by authority in any of its bullying forms and he never seemed to lose his combative vigour when it came to questions of injustice and individuality against the oppression of large institutions and organisations. A black Labrador drugs dog was sniffing around inside the visitors' hall, although I thought that the whole object of having them was to stop drugs from getting into the prison at the gate. And there seemed to be just as many staff members in and around the visitors' hall as there were prisoners. Jeremy Bamber and Mr Smith were also seeing visitors. The morning ended all too soon and I took my reluctant leave of a very dear friend.

Back on the wing, two works screws came to stick strange labels over the water taps in each cell. A red one was stuck on the wall above the hot water tap inscribed, 'Not Drinking Water' and a green sticker was applied to the wall above the cold water tap inscribed, 'Drinking Water'. When I enquired, they told me that they were carrying out a requirement being made by Yorkshire Water. I informed them that the patch of wall immediately above the taps had to be wiped and washed frequently and that the labels would eventually wash off, but they had little regard for this intelligence. I asked them if they were going to put a label on the waste-paper bin saying, 'Not Shitting' with another above the toilet bowl saying, 'Shitting'. He said, 'Don't be ridiculous.' I replied, 'Well, you started it.' After they'd gone, Spanner gave me (for some unexplained reason) a photocopy of a black and white picture of the Hanging Gardens of Babylon while gaping at me for a reaction. I quipped: 'They'll hang anything in Iraq these days!'

Over the previous few years, I'd been aware of the decline in my general health. I could sometimes sleep for eleven hours and still feel tired despite being engaged in no physical exertion. Was this old age or a more serious problem? Meanwhile, my sole remaining front tooth clung to the rock of my upper jaw like a mollusc. On the way back from work while going through the body rubdown search, by the security X-ray machine, the screw searching me asked, 'Have you anything on you that you shouldn't have?' All I could think of by way of reply was, 'How about erectile dysfunction?' In the braille shop, one morning, my eyes went fuzzy in front of the computer screen. I took a break and had a cup of coffee and the condition cleared up after half an hour but this seemed to happen from time to time and I was starting to think that it may have been oxygen starvation to my brain or optic nerve, possibly aggravated through smoking, etc. Could it be something to do with a heart condition?

As we bade farewell to 2008, an item in the *Sunday Sport* was brought to my attention: 'New Year's Kiss…of Death… Sex-starved Gay Serial Killer Nilsen Writes Hogmanay Snog Hit List…a wish list of coldhearted lags he wants to snog… The gay butcher…' blah, blah, blah… The non-existent, and entirely imaginary, list gave the names of my intended 'snogging' victims as Kenneth Noye, Michael Stone and Jeremy Bamber. The first two of these prisoners I had neither met nor seen and was not ever likely to in our separate wing locations. The nonsense continued, 'This list is one of the sickest things we've ever seen... It's like a who's who of some of the most horrific murders to have taken place – and Dennis can't wait to get his filthy hands on them...' I suppose things could have been worse had they depicted me lusting after Spanner! I later passed Jeremy on the B wing landing and he commented with reference to the piece: 'Remember, no kissing!'

It occurred to me that about ninety-five per cent of the wing didn't talk to me at all – as evidenced by the sullenly aggressive stares as I passed them in the narrow corridors – and I wondered if I was the only person so alone? Going to work every day, I'd noticed a tall, older man (whom I had also seen in Whitemoor some years ago) shuffling along this prison's long corridors from his location on C wing to the workshops. I'd recognised him but didn't know his name, though I knew that he was Scottish by his accent. I guessed that his painfully slow shuffling gait had probably been due to his having had a previous heart attack or something and, like most Scotsmen I have known, in or out of prison, work remained a source of esteeming pride. I hadn't seen him of late and the news came in that his name was Mr Peat and that he'd died one weekend of a terminal illness in York Hospital. In the prison context – even when he did exist – he never really existed and now that he was gone, as an item and a person, he seemed to exist even less. So now I make this brief record of him and his lonely, anonymous death.

I was warmed by some welcome news in the braille shop at the end of September 2009 when we were visited by the High Sheriff of East Yorkshire together with a governor and, what I took to be, a posse of similarly antiquated, suited citizens. None of them came anywhere near me but Jeremy Bamber latched on to them the moment they entered the shop, as was his fashion. At its peak, there were approaching twenty of them in there for an official presentation of certificates to us workers, for being the national winners of the Elton Trophy for the best prison workshop in the land, amongst hundreds of others. Everyone in the shop had also been awarded a

£5 bonus in that week's pay statement, for winning the trophy, and I was photographed receiving my Elton Trophy certificate from the hand of the director of prison industries. I was, however, informed that my copy of the photo would be lodged in my property box in reception because the regulations required that I held no self-images in my possession.

That same month, the Metropolitan Police were back on the trail of missing persons and, during a legal visit, Nick Wells, my solicitor, showed me three A4 sheets of photos of a number of young men (who looked more like boys), some of whom he said had gone missing around the time I'd lived at Melrose Avenue. Two police detectives had driven up to Liverpool (my solicitor's office) all the way from London just to deliver these three A4 sheets. Nick asked if the pictures might arouse some recognition in my memory, concerning some of my victims there, who had remained unidentified. I slowly looked over them – time and time again – but no recognition was forthcoming. Of course, some of the images reminded me of people I had known in my life before and since my offences but none of them in an offence-related capacity.

I was also interviewed by a prison service management psychologist, where I engaged combatively with her fixed mindset that followed its usual negative trajectory. Her view of me was basically the same as that which had been religiously written by my jailers over the past twenty-seven years, with whatever additional negative refinements they could add from their records. She didn't like my 'attitude' because I had completely failed to be a 'good dog' in the narrow eyes of my jailers. To me, however, resisting the unrelenting pressure to be trained and conditioned by the system was a real achievement.

Sometimes my infamy appeared suddenly when I least expected it. One night, after a bath, a cup of coffee and a smoke, I sat down with my Friday fish and chips then, later, watched the fourth part of *Psychoville**. I was mentioned by name in the homicidally fussy narrative between the grotesque David and his equally mad mum, Maureen. Mum had got mixed up in her descriptive modus operandi of 'Donald Neilson' when she attributed him as having cut up his victims in the bath. But she was corrected by the avid 'true crime-reading' David who interjected, 'no that's Dennis Nilsen'.

• • •

In March 2010, I had the rumour confirmed that my mother had died the previous November, after apparently leaving instructions not to inform me to prevent the family embarrassment at the possibility of me turning up at her funeral and ruining the dignity of the occasion. She needn't have worried because I didn't do funerals, fundamental Christian or otherwise. I guessed she'd rejected me emotionally on the day I was born and one cannot lose what one never had.

Later, the news came to me (again, well after the event) that the key tactics and legal arguments being deployed by my lawyers had been ruled inadmissible by a panel of judges in the European Court of Human Rights in Strasbourg. So the legal challenge on the State ban on my literary work (namely, my autobiography) had to be renewed, this time through a different lawyer who might be more amenable to accepting my instructions.

On 23 November, I officially retired, as I had reached the age of sixty-five, but I resolved to continue working as there was no proper pension for old lags after twenty-eight years in penal bondage. In any case, I wasn't the retiring sort. I worked on in the braille shop and, in 2011, I was starting my hundred and fiftieth book transcription: *Ian Botham: The Power and the Glory*, by Simon Wilde. But I was tiring. In the braille shop, we had a visit from the chairperson of the Independent Monitoring Board who introduced herself but refused

* *A British psychological horror-thriller black comedy mystery television series.*

to shake my hand. So, naturally, I asked her to go away as I didn't appreciate prejudice where the chairperson had no difficulty shaking hands with the jailers but did not with the prisoners. That was a first for me because nobody had ever refused to shake my hand after they had first approached me with an introduction. I, on the other hand, would have shaken hands with the devil, if he'd taken the effort to turn up.

The remainder of the year – and much of 2012 – passed slowly and insignificantly until the media and nation were in the grip of Olympic fever in 2012, a scenario enhanced by the opening ceremony, which I watched from start to finish. What prompted my curiosity – that kept me up until a quarter to one in the morning – was the knowledge that the ceremony had been directed by a film director, Danny Boyle, and not a tiresome committee. In this, he had hit all the emotional buttons, which is what good movie directors do well. The scene that tortured me most was the one of the 'Letting Go/Death Dance' with the juxtapositioning of the singing of 'Abide with Me' by a solo female voice. That reduced me to tears as I thought of the great wounds of loss that my past actions had caused to so many. Our moments of truth are always there to bring traumatic reminders.

In the bleak, opening weeks of 2013, I read again Brian Masters' *Killing for Company*, which had lain festering in my blue box since 1985. Back in 1983, I'd had a need to eject thoughts, feelings and instincts that had lain dormant for years and I produced instinctive outpourings on paper without proper, reasoned construction. Reading some of my notes, almost thirty years after I had written them, showed me the unreasonable rubbish much of it was; gut searches for 'answers' inside the tormented heat of the moment and my closed circumstances. Also, there was the 'drive to completion', as Masters was virtually my only visitor and I felt I owed him a murder story for his book.

In late September, I had a letter from Russ Coffey to tell me that he was publishing a book entitled (he said) *Dennis Nilsen*, and he thanked me for my candour and help over the years. Russ hadn't been entirely truthful as the full title of the book was, in fact, *Dennis Nilsen: Conversations with Britain's Most Evil Serial Killer*. In his letter, he said he had tried to be fair and balanced but there didn't seem to be anything fair or balanced in the title, which, perhaps, betokened what was still to come in the text. It was clear that it was the working scratch-marks of a pay-writing journalist, supplying a cheap but sensational product for John Blake, the publisher, to peddle to his 'true crime' clientele. It was terrible! He even resorted to repeating confected stories taken from the tabloids as if they were true. I still remembered that quote from John Blake back in the nineties, that he would never give a platform to 'scum like Brady and Nilsen', and that was the clear indication of the terms of reference for the book and its 'line'. I guessed that, with products of that sort, there would be another along in a minute to feed the hunger in the populist maw.

Maybe Coffey's book had reawakened interest in the Nilsen myth because the Metropolitan Police, again, requested an interview with me concerning a missing person, this time, from 1981. Attached to the letter from my solicitor, for my forewarning, was a five page 'interview strategy' for 'Operation Black Snow'. Here was the gist:

'In 2013, Ms Sheila McCabe* reported her brother, Paul McCabe*, as a missing person. He was last seen alive in 1981, when he was 21 years of age. At the time Paul went missing, he was living in Walm Lane, Cricklewood, some 100 yards from 195 Melrose Avenue, the home of Nilsen at the time. Paul was a keen pool player and played for a team from The Castle Public House in Cricklewood. The pool team played in the local league.'

* *Not their real names.*

319

The only local pub near my home back then was the Cricklewood Arms where I'd met Stephen Dean Holmes. Afterwards, I'd waited to be arrested because I knew it was a local pub where both victim and perpetrator might have been recognised. So that was me finished with local pubs (and I'd never heard of The Castle nor been there). I didn't play pool and I confined my social activities to generic gay pubs in Central London. I had not heard the name 'Paul McCabe' and found it strange that the police were making the assumption that he was dead. People did change their names and sometimes assumed new identities, as may have been the case for 'Paul McCabe'.

I found the misinformation coming from a team of so-called, expert homicide investigators quite alarming. Their report said that 'only 3 of the 12 victims found at the Melrose Avenue address have been formally identified'. The facts were that there were nine victims at Melrose Avenue (not twelve), consistent with the forensic examination of bones and teeth from the pyres in and around the garden. Five of these people had been identified. They were Stephen Dean Holmes, Ken Ockendon, Martyn Duffey, Billy Sutherland and Malcom Barlow. At my Cranley Gardens address, all three homicide victims had been identified: John Howlett, Graham Allan and Stephen Sinclair.

The discrepancy in the Melrose Avenue numbers had been explained by me years ago and written down in, amongst other things, letters out of prison. To comply with the number fifteen that I gave the police officers at my arrest, I invented three victims: the punk rocker with the words 'cut here' on his neck; the long-haired hippy; and the 'anonymous Irishman'. So, today, four remained unidentified. Of those, I remembered an emaciated young man, a fair-haired Scot with a blue and white striped football scarf and a 'gypsy-looking foreigner'. I kept no written record at the time and what material evidence there was had been mostly destroyed in three bonfires. It was always a possibility that 'Paul McCabe' might have been a victim but only if he was the young, fair-haired Scot with the football scarf. Otherwise, he seemed to be highly improbable as a victim.

By this time, I'd been in a kind of social, cultural and emotional isolation pushing thirty-four years, longer than many of the prisoners at Full Sutton had been alive. This started at a time in history when Margaret Thatcher was running the country and TV sets had knobs on. In the great pantomime world of legend, myth and dreadful fantasy, it seemed that the villains who were still remembered in the populist mind – the Krays, Fred West, Harold Shipman, Ian Brady, Myra Hindley, Donald Nielson, Archibald Hall, Michael Ryan – were now all dead and gone, with only myself and Peter Sutcliffe left from that era. It was, perhaps, a good thing that few people recognised me in the visitors' hall, as the murder-pundits were still firmly attached to that thirty-seven-year old man of the early 1980s when my interest was stuck, like death itself, in that distant past.

On a recent visit from Mark, I looked longer than could be normally expected at his Bank of England note on the table. That was because I hadn't actually seen one for years. I had also never seen a real mobile phone, let alone ever used one. What was a metal knife or fork or a china mug where reality, for me, was little better than that plastic baby's beaker?

I felt sorry for many of my fellow prisoners as I witnessed their slow collapse into vacuous despair over the years; their minds, bodies and hopes crumbled after too much conditioned exposure to the numbing, inhuman routines of prison life and its controlling mentality. In all my years in the maximum prison estate, I have lived with many prisoners, some well-known, others not so, but all convicted of serious offences. In all these men, I divined substantial human degrees of conscience, guilt-feelings, caring, warmth, humour, resilience, morality, and all such factors within the human condition; an amalgamation of human strengths and weaknesses as in any cross-section of society. I found no 'monsters', 'beasts', 'evil demons' or 'psychopaths'. However, each of us had, in our lives and interactions, developed slowly in key, maladaptive ways in our own separate funnels of circumstances, channelling slowly to the point of our offences.

Since the political assignation of a 'whole life tariff' prison sentence, there had been an officially static view of the containing quality of my prison life; of endless incarceration in a high security prison with its terminally inhuman regime of active restrictions, right across the board. I was just a piece of merchandise to be processed within the self-justifying needs and self-interested aspirations of the owner. I was housed, fed, watered, worked and contained under a mountain of routine rules and restraints. However, at the same time, I was being asked to indulge in the official 'rehabilitative fantasy' by being an active participant in the insane bureaucracy of the pretence of 'progressing through the system' while no such progress was officially envisaged. This might well have conspired to make the institution look good but, apart from being wasteful of resources, it did nothing to inspire confidence in the system, nor did it advance the emotional or psychological well-being of the dehumanised prisoner. So, for many of us, the hard and prejudiced bureaucratic and meaningless rituals of form (sentence plans, category reviews, etc.) rang hollow against the reality that had long been set in its predictably negative posture. The mechanism could see no difference between the Dennis Nilsen of 1978–83 and the Dennis Nilsen thereafter.

There was a fixed, mechanical pattern to my life where inspiration had to be imagined and generated inside my own head, for want of official stimulation or understanding pertaining to human needs. I never lost my freedom of mind and the pleasing release of dreams continued to arrest me again and again under the dull knife of reason:

I sink into a placid ocean and, as I awake on the shore, I am met by myself as a boy. He looks at me with a lost expression and I know I am home. I hold out my arms to him and he comes to me. It has been a long absence but the tears are in my eyes, not his.

I take his hand and go about the past. He follows like a lamb and we skirt the old wilderness, drifting in and out of scenes. When I relax my grip on his hand, he tightens his and refuses to let go. I tell him who and what he is and what he will become, and he slowly nods in acknowledgement. I kneel to his level, look him in the eyes and ask him, 'Do you know who I am?'

'Yes, you are a man returned from the sea just like my grandad.'

'How long has your grandad been away?' I ask. 'He has just this minute gone, as always,' says the boy to me, as if I were the child.

'Do you think he'll be back soon?' I ask.

'Of course,' says the boy, 'He is always coming back soon. I must stay here on the beach in case he gets me. He's a bad man and wants to take me away.'

'Maybe I'm that bad man. What do you think of that then?' I ask and he laughs, 'No you're not. You came out of the sea just like grandad. The bad man is out there,' he says, pointing towards the town.

We walk, hand-in-hand, along the sandy shore, along the sea front and on to the piers of the harbour and, suddenly, we are confronted by a solid, concrete World War II pillbox with its ugly slit windows. The boy stops and, saying nothing, just points to it. I want to see inside but he stands rooted to the spot. He will not let go of my hand and he will not move forward with me. I pull him towards the mysteriously small structure and he is resisting me with all his strength. I am winning and he is now screaming. As we reach the slim entrance, he breaks free and runs down to the sea. I halt and watch, to judge the pursuit. Which way will he turn, right or left? He goes straight on, right into the foam.

I am bemused by his foolishness because, out there, there is no place to go; no escape, so he will have to turn back. He plunges in further and deeper and disappears into the body of a wave. I frantically abandon my clothing and take to his direction. I swim against the force of the *incoming tide with periodic gulps under the surface to try to find him in the noiseless, green calm of the undercurrents.*

Then I see him, suspended in the liquid green, half-standing, half-leaning forward with arms outstretched like in a grotesque dance, slow and rhythmically waving. His eyes are fully open and staring and his hair is floating and turning with the ocean's movement. He is hanging there in the sea and I seek to save the young me from drowning.

I take him up to the roaring surface where we bob in the forward swell, and I strike out for the land, finding my feet on sand after a half a dozen strong strokes. I stride from the frothy tide with the me-boy in my arms and mount the upwards incline of the sandy shore towards the wet dunes. He is gently laid down on the soft, warm sand and I am undressing the wet clothing from myself as I am aged about five years old.

Somewhere else, I have laid 'him' down on the warm carpeted floor of my room in Melrose Avenue. I fetch two disposable razors from the drawer and pull down his wet underpants. He looks not like I wanted him to look. I want him smooth; dead smooth and clean enough to eat a chicken salad off his belly.

Compulsion, compulsion, compulsion. I shave off all his bodily hair but for a small triangular tuft of pubic hair and the hair on his head and his eyebrows. 'What am I doing, what am I doing, what am I doing?' I ask myself but continue to do it just the same. The feel of him, the touch of him and the smell of him all lock together in a searching vision of I know not what. There he lies, allowing all my manhandling blandishments, giving negative 'consent' in that great contradiction of negative love.

I am kneeling by the side of the boy lying on the beach. I spread his clothing out on the sand to dry and sit with him in my arms.

I am rocking him in my arms on the couch at home; the bigger version; the boy-man.

A shimmering camel pads towards us from the distance on the beach. I am mesmerised by its slow, menacing approach. It nears to just a dozen feet, and my grandfather dismounts. He walks closer. 'Yours or mine?' he enquires, indicating the sleeping boy in my arms. 'Yours, I think.'

He takes the boy-me from my arms and heads towards the concrete pillbox adding, 'You can have him when I'm finished with him, if you like.' I stand there extruding all the potency of an abject coward. I keep my unshifting gaze on the pillbox. After ten minutes, I'm surprised to see the boy-me walk out. He comes over and looks pleasingly up at me.

'Where's grandad?' I ask him.

'I don't know. He's gone. Says he'll be back soon,' says the boy-me, slowly and deliberately. He starts to pick up his dry clothes from off the hot sand and he dresses. 'Mam will kill me when she finds out,' he says. 'She's had dreams of me drowning in the sea and only being able to identify my body by its underwear. Underwear hugs secrets. Underwear tantalises. Underwear accentuates.'

'Wait here a minute while I check something,' I tell him, and cautiously enter the dark recesses of the pillbox. It has a sandy floor strewn with a few old John Player fag packets, an old lemonade bottle with the neck broken off and, on the far side, there is a freshly laid little boy's turd. What was so relevant in this irrelevant concrete enclosure? What had happened in there to so traumatically fix the imagination? Too many dreams to subvert the shaming power of my reality.

I walk out of the dungeon of my past but I can never escape from it. There, on the dunes, is my past in the shape of a small, confused boy.

'Did it hurt?' I ask him.

'Sometimes,' he replies.

'But you liked the ice cream, the sweets, the toys and the attention, didn't you?'

'It was OK,' says the boy-me. 'He liked to play with me. Said I should be a big, brave boy when it hurts.'

The small boy is now wistfully looking towards the horizon.

'Come,' I say. 'Let me take you home.'

I lead him by the hand, along the beach and up the grasslands towards the great overhang of Fitful Head. We look out over the arc of the world as I put my hand on his shoulder. I kneel down on one leg and look him straight in the face. Our eyes fix and melt into mutual smiles as I say, 'Dennis, I am you and you are me. We are one and the same,' and we embrace, both with tears in our eyes.

I stand up and I am hugging this slight boy's body in my arms. As the red orb of the sun sinks to her destination, I thrust him out in front of me and he is thrown, in creeping slow time, out over the cliff where he vanishes into the crimson air.

I am alone and he is gone. A blizzard of sea birds engulfs the point, wheeling and circling around the lone man. At last he turns from the natural wonders in his eyes and walks away. His eyes are old; his hair is grey, just like his grandfather's.

13

Leaving Life | 2018

At 3 a.m. on Thursday, 10 May 2018, Dennis Nilsen awoke with abdominal pain and was unable to get back to sleep. At 6.40 a.m., prison officer (PO) Birch was checking each cell on B wing for the morning roll-call when she looked into Mr Nilsen's cell and saw him sitting on the edge of his bed, rubbing his face. He was usually an early riser so this observation didn't unduly worry her and, as nothing seemed amiss, she continued on her rounds before returning to the wing office a few doors away from Mr Nilsen's cell.

Forty minutes later, Mr Nilsen's cell bell sounded in the wing office and PO Birch commented that he'd never used his bell in all the time she'd been working at the prison. She went on to the wing and looked through his cell door hatch. He was sitting on his bed and she asked him what was wrong. As he stood up to walk towards the hatch, she could see he was struggling; he was hunched over and looked pale and clammy. He told her that he was in excruciating pain around his stomach and that it had worsened in the last half an hour.

She phoned Healthcare (the medical centre within the prison, operated and staffed by a private company) and was told that someone would attend Mr Nilsen's cell as soon as possible.

Nurse Fletcher arrived at the wing office and, together with PO Birch and another PO, they walked down to Mr Nilsen's cell. As he was a category A prisoner and the cell door was being opened outside the normal cell-opening time, a dog handler had to be called to attend. Once inside, the nurse took Mr Nilsen's general, physical observations, which appeared to be within normal ranges, and advised him to take plenty of fluids, adding that she'd book him into the clinic later that morning.

At 9.20 a.m. Mr Nilsen attended Healthcare, pushed there in a wheelchair by another prisoner, and was seen by Matron Dennett. He described the constant, sharp pain as being across all of his abdomen and round to his lower back. Then Dr Chidlow examined Mr Nilsen's abdomen by palpation and identified a slight tenderness in his right groin area as well as deeper in his bladder. She also heard normal bowel sounds through her stethoscope. Eventually, she considered that Mr Nilsen might have been suffering from a renal infection, so she suggested he provide a urine sample. Unfortunately, he wasn't able to 'go' so she gave him a sample pot to take back with him, as well as some paracetamol for the pain.

Mid-morning, two prisoners called at wing office and reported seeing Mr Nilsen 'asleep' on his toilet. This was highly unusual so prison officer (PO) Tomaszewski and his colleague, PO Cousins, attended the cell. PO Tomaszewski said he could see Mr Nilsen sitting on the toilet leaning on the privacy screen and asked him if he was OK. He responded but PO Cousins knew something wasn't right and the two officers discussed whether or not the event met the criteria for them to call an emergency response: either a 'code blue' or a 'code red'.

A 'code blue' was predominantly called where the patient was experiencing breathing difficulties, for example either through an illness or possibly a suicide attempt, whereas a 'code red' was called when someone was experiencing severe blood loss. Mr Nilsen's symptoms didn't really fit either of these; nonetheless, the officers knew he needed medical attention and decided that PO Cousins would monitor Mr Nilsen while PO Tomaszewski went back to the office to call for help. PO Tomaszewski spoke to senior officer (SO) Bottomer who advised him to call Healthcare but, when he did so, he was told that Mr Nilsen had been seen earlier and he needed to provide a urine sample. PO Tomaszewski wasn't aware of this so accepted what he'd been told.

At 12.50 p.m., POs Tomaszewski and Cousins carefully lifted Mr Nilsen off the toilet and moved him over to his bed. Mr Nilsen seemed 'absent', as though he was drunk, and his underwear was soaked in urine. PO Cousins also noted that one of Mr Nilsen's arms was much hotter than the other. They were seriously worried about his condition and, over the next four hours, a series of telephone calls and visits to Healthcare were made by various prison officers amid great confusion. Often, those speaking with Healthcare hadn't actually attended Mr Nilsen's cell and couldn't, therefore, confirm the condition of his health. In addition, some staff in Healthcare knew that Mr Nilsen had been seen earlier and assumed that prison officers were aware of this. Healthcare staff asked Mr Nilsen to be brought to the medical centre and prison staff asked Healthcare to visit Mr Nilsen on the wing but neither seemed able to make a conclusive decision one way or the other. Throughout those four hours, Mr Nilsen's health deteriorated so much that he became incontinent of faeces.

By 4.50 p.m., custody manager Cormack called Healthcare and demanded they attend Mr Nilsen's cell as an emergency. Dr Chidlow arrived and saw a marked deterioration in Mr Nilsen's health, since that morning, and she quickly suspected and diagnosed an abdominal aortic aneurism (AAA).

An ambulance was called and it arrived at the front gate just after 6 p.m. The two-person crew attended to Mr Nilsen in his cell fifteen minutes later. The paramedic lowered Mr Nilsen's blanket and immediately saw a large, pulsating mass in his abdomen; a clear sign of an aortic aneurysm, a critical condition. The different blood pressure readings in each arm corroborated the diagnosis.

The ambulance left the prison at 6.52 p.m., with Mr Nilsen and five prison officers on board, and arrived at York Teaching Hospital half an hour later. PO Tomaszewski noted that, at one point, Mr Nilsen removed his oxygen mask to vomit. After an assessment in the Accident & Emergency department, Mr Nilsen underwent an urgent CT scan, which confirmed the diagnosis of a ruptured abdominal aortic aneurysm measuring 6.7cm.

At 9.30 p.m., vascular surgeon Mr Kordowicz, examined Mr Nilsen along with Dr Jonathan Redman, consultant for Intensive Care, and told Mr Nilsen that he had a life-threatening problem and that, without surgery, he would almost certainly die. Mr Nilsen opted for open surgery and was immediately transferred to the operating theatre.

At 10.15 p.m., Mr Kordowicz performed a surgical procedure to repair the ruptured AAA with a prison officer present throughout the four-and-a-half-hour operation. Afterwards, Mr Nilsen was admitted to the Intensive Care Unit (ICU).

The following morning, Friday, Mr Kordowicz handed over Mr Nilsen's care to consultant vascular surgeon, Mr Cavanagh, who was later called to the ICU and was alerted to Mr Nilsen's cold left foot, indicating an impaired blood supply. He suspected a deep vein thrombosis must have occurred after Mr Nilsen's earlier surgery and, half an hour later, he performed a laparotomy to re-explore his left groin and then performed fasciotomies on the left calf. Afterwards, Mr Nilsen was, again, returned to the ICU.

At 11.30 a.m., Mark Austin, Mr Nilsen's next of kin, was telephoned by a prison officer and informed of the recent events. Together with his wife, they began the four-hour journey to the hospital. Meanwhile, Mr Cavanagh reviewed Mr Nilsen and was not optimistic that he would ever regain consciousness. He had a very low blood pressure and both his feet and hands were mottled. He was also systemically shutting down. Mr Austin and his wife attended Mr Nilsen in the ICU at around 4 p.m. and Mr Cavanagh explained to them that Mr Nilsen's chances of survival were extremely small.

The following morning, Dr Paw, consultant intensive care doctor, and Mr Cavanagh, saw that Mr Nilsen was rapidly deteriorating, despite the best efforts of the Intensive Care staff, and agreed to withdraw treatment.

Dennis Nilsen's time of death was recorded at 9.19 a.m. on 12 May 2018. He was seventy-two years old.

Epilogue

By Dennis Nilsen

And so it is that my crimes live on in a kind of immortality, forever fixed and independent of me and any irrelevancies I articulate now or tomorrow. In my obituary, it will be my killing of twelve men that will be remembered. I became an artefact at the moment of my arrest and there seems to be no opinion of me outside of my past offences.

In spite of the wreckage caused by my crimes, I have always, naturally, been well intentioned. It can be said with a degree of confidence that my brisk acts of violent strangulation were totally out of character and never the norm of my personality. I was not prone to expressing myself in violent anger, as so many men are; in fact, I always found it difficult to express anger at all. Nor was I ever motivated by feelings of hate or anger against any of my victims.

I never lost sight of my victims. They had lost – been deprived of – everything and the relatives of the lost will have no remission. I owe everything to my victims and it will be a great day when the natural cycle obliges me to join them.

The inadequate is a victim, too, and the primary inadequacy is an inability to accept that one even has an inadequacy. There are no hopeless cases, just hopeless solutions fostered by hopeless institutions that believe they can cure by punishment.

Will most people find this work full of expedient, observed

inventions or will it enlighten them with things more deeply human? What was my motive? What was my ambition in writing this book? It was to be recognised as 'human' and to lay the guts of my psyche before you. Well, those who read this will have the knowledge that the man they are reading about is long dead. I write for the future where judgements can have no effect on us; the past having conclusively happened. Let this be the concluding chapter of my testimony; the vain spoutings of a weak man searching for humanity.

I apologise to all those I have grievously offended and this is as sincere as the fact that millions of stars twinkle brightly in that great crystal void of the universe. I am sorry for all the things I have lost and caused to be lost. I was capable of killing my fellows, not because I was a monster but because I was human. And therein lies the true horror. There is no suffering like the truth of seeing one's own face in life's mirror and I am not sorry that I looked.

What is so extraordinary about my life is that I did not implode earlier. I have so much guilt that a great peace will come only at my own death. I cling to the slippery wreckage of lost lives only because of the instinct to survive. There are two opposing factions: the drive to cling and that secret whispering in my head, repeating softly, 'Let go, let go.'

I do not fear my mortality because when the darkness approaches for the last time I can, finally, 'let go'. If I could go back now to my childhood and, as an observer, see again the small boy, I think I would like to hammer a stake through the heart of his misery.

I think back on the misery I have wrought and I drift back to the beginning. There is always the sea and the rocks and the sky. Green grass, the hills and the trees. And the sands, rivers and dunes. Always back to the sea. To the drowning boy, me.

Appendix

Complete autobiographical documents

Power in the Blood
Gone
Looking at the Sky
Time and Tides
Faded Outlet
Terror at Sunset

The Human Institution - Part 3
   – written between April 2004 and May 2005

Whatever Next?
Gathering Nuts in May
Green of the Flowers
The Summer of Discontent
A Lethargy of Purpose
Days of Mood and Sad, Sad Movies
Looking In
A Turn of Weather
Extended Holiday
Creeping Cold and Halloween 1
Creeping Cold and Halloween 2
All Things Bright and Beautiful
Rulings
England, the only country...
Time
Over the False Rainbow
Cracks in the Ice
Another Long-Lost Boy
The Light of Darkness Inside the Right of Reason
The Murder of Crows

The Human Institution – Part 4
   – written between June 2005 and August 2005

Sex and Sin and the Whole Damn Thing
Day by Day

All People That on Earth Do Well
In Character of Sorts
Time
The Lay of the Law

The Human Institution – Part 5
– written between September 2005 and January 2006

Acquiring, Possessing and Expelling
Sterile Harvests
Messages from the Fall
Third Bagpipe at the Drag-Arse's Secret Ball
Winding Up and Winding Down
Senior Citizen
Soon it Dies
Eye of the Leech
Story

The Rule of Fantasy: Commentator from Prison
– written between January and July 2006

Continuation Shots
– written between August and December 2006

Chronicles
– written between January 2007 and May 2010

APPENDIX

Complete musical compositions and recordings

1	Suite No. 1	Masters
2	Suite No. 2	Autobiographical I
3	Suite No. 3	Autobiographical II
4	Suite No. 4	Descent into Madness and Old Age
5	Suite No. 5	The Life & Death of Adam Scott
6	Suite No. 6	Spirit of a Man in a Strip Cell
7	Suite No. 7	David Martin (1947–84)
8	Suite No. 8	Breaking Up
9	Suite No. 9	One Night Stands on the Gay Scene
10	Suite No. 10	Summary of Evidence
11	Suite No. 11	A Lull in the Fighting
12	Suite No. 12	School Days
13	Suite No. 13	London
14	Suite No. 14	The Desert
15	Suite No. 15	Aspiration
16	Suite No. 16	Untitled I
17	Suite No. 17	Untitled II
18	Suite No. 18	Mark Austin
19	Suite No. 19	Lily Whyte (1895–1990)
20	Suite No. 20	The Ruined Kirk: Andrew Whyte 1889–1951
21	Suite No. 21	Prisoners at Newgate
22	Suite No. 22	Interlinks
23	Suite No. 23	Jimmy
24	Suite No. 24	Sennelager
25	Suite No. 25	The Coming of the Herring Fleet
26	Suite No. 26	Culloden
27	Suite No. 27	Scapegoats
28	Suite No. 28	Homeless Under City Lights (plus 'Pop' version)
29	Suite No. 29	Betrayal
30	Suite No. 30	Iron John
31	Suite No. 31	Full Circle
32		SYMPHONIETTA OF SUITES NO. 1
33	Suite No. 32	The Performer's Fear / Hamish
34	Suite No. 33	The Festive Season
35	Suite No. 34	The Ritual
36	Suite No. 35	Discord in Natural Life

71	Suite No. 61	Warrior/Peacemaker
72		SYMPHONIETTA OF SUITES NO. 4 (IN 4 MOVEMENTS)
73	Suite No. 62	The Broch
74	Suite No. 63	Year Fading
75	Suite No. 64	Midnight
76		SYMPHONIETTA OF SUITES NO. 5 (IN 4 MOVEMENTS)

Find out more about RedDoor Press and sign up to our newsletter to hear about our **latest releases, author events,** exciting **competitions** and more at

reddoorpress.co.uk

YOU CAN ALSO FOLLOW US:

  @RedDoorBooks

  Facebook.com/RedDoorPress

  @RedDoorBooks